I0793249

IMAGES of Rail

Yreka Western Railroad

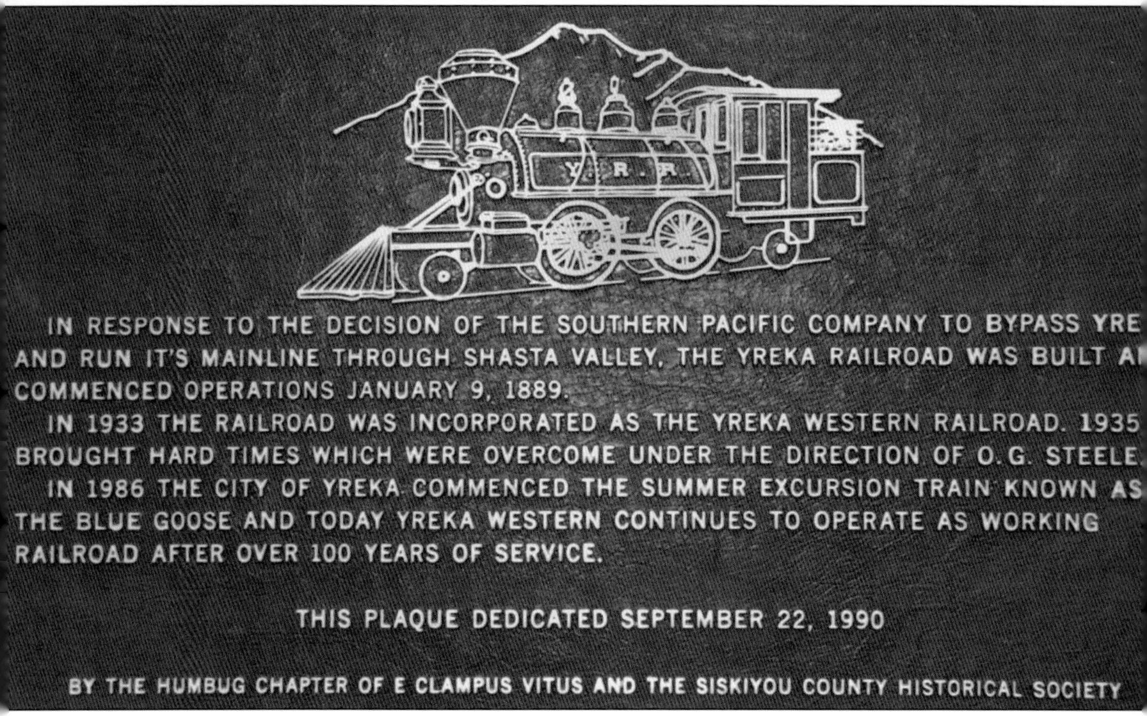

This plaque sits in front of the depot at Yreka dedicating the building of the railroad to keep Yreka connected to the rest of the country and its ability it continue operating after over 100 years of service. (Courtesy Yreka Western Archives.)

On the Cover: Nos. 19 and 18 lead a railfan excursion train through the Shasta Valley on May 31, 1964.

IMAGES
of Rail

YREKA WESTERN RAILROAD

Matt Starman and Tim Stricker

ARCADIA
PUBLISHING

ISBN 978-0-7385-7430-1

Published by Arcadia Publishing
Charleston, South Carolina

Printed in the United States of America

Library of Congress Control Number: 2010935476

For all general information, please contact Arcadia Publishing:
Telephone 843-853-2070
Fax 843-853-0044
E-mail sales@arcadiapublishing.com
For customer service and orders:
Toll-Free 1-888-313-2665

Visit us on the Internet at www.arcadiapublishing.com

This book is dedicated to all past and present Yreka railroaders who have managed to keep the railroad running even through the darkest of times.

Contents

ACKNOWLEDGMENTS

This book could not have been accomplished without the help and support of a great many people. We would first like to thank the Siskiyou County Historical Society for bringing to light and sharing their collection of rare photographs with us. Additionally, we would like to thank those who have shared their image collections with us, including Bob Morris, Jeff Moore, and Don Hansen.

Furthermore, we would like to thank Claudia and Don East for their tremendous amount of help and encouragement throughout this process, as well as our editors Sabrina Heise and Laura Chaney for all of their help and answering all our questions.

We also would like to thank a group of present and past Yreka Western railroaders, including Bill Killion, Dennis Woodruff, and Bill Ainsworth for the willingness to share their knowledge and stories with us. Thanks also goes to Yreka Western's general manager, Court Hammond, for allowing us to dig through the YW's archives and for giving us the opportunity to volunteer and work on a truly wonderful shortline railroad.

Finally, both of the authors would like to extend a huge thanks to our friends and family and for all of their support and encouragement throughout the making of this book.

All photographs, unless otherwise noted, appear courtesy of the Yreka Western Railroad Archives.

Introduction

In 1848, James Marshall discovered gold at Sutter's Mill near Coloma, California. Maj. Pierson B. Reading visited the gold discovery area that same year. He returned to his rancho in Northern California and washed out the first gold on Clear Creek in Shasta County. He then went up the Trinity River to continue prospecting there. Shortly thereafter, in 1849, prospectors began moving north, making one discovery after another. One day in March 1851, a party from Oregon on their way to a mine at a location known as Greenhorn stopped to camp in the area known as Yreka Flats, which was a common place for prospectors to stop on their way to other diggings. Before breaking camp that morning, a member of the party, Abraham Thompson, decided to do a little prospecting before leaving through a ravine later known as Black Gulch. It did not take him long to realize the richness of the area.

The party would later organize a mining district and name it Thompson's Dry Diggings. Soon after, other miners and prospectors began flocking to the area in droves, all arriving at Thompson's Dry Diggings. Within six months, the name of the town was changed to Shasta Butte City and boasted a population of just over 5,000. By 1852, the town was renamed Yreka, which is derived from a local Native American tribe word *Wyekah*, meaning "White Mountain," which refers to nearby 14,162-foot Mount Shasta.

Early transportation into the area was by pack train, horseback, or on foot. Pack trains soon gave way to freight wagons and stagecoaches as the trails improved. The first stage between Yreka and the Scott Valley was in 1854. Within a few years, roads began to develop. Soon, the agriculture industry began to grow in the area. By the 1860s, roads had developed between the gold camps in Siskiyou County to a connection with the steamboats on the Sacramento River at Red Bluff. In May 1869, the transcontinental railroad was completed, linking California with the rest of the union. Not long after, the Central Pacific Railroad began building north from Sacramento to Oregon under the name of the California and Oregon Railroad.

In 1872, the railhead reached an area known as Poverty Flats, and the railroad established the town of Redding, named after B. B. Redding, Central Pacific's first land agent. Construction halted here for the next decade because of the financial panic of 1873. By 1885, construction had resumed, and the Central Pacific purchased the Oregon and California Railroad, whose railhead was at Ashland, Oregon. By January 1, 1887, the railhead reached the southern end of the Shasta Valley at Edgewood station. On December 17, 1888, the two railroads met at Ashland, completing the railroad over the Siskiyou Mountains between Sacramento, California, and Portland, Oregon.

During construction, the original survey of the railroad made by Central Pacific's chief engineer, Samuel S. Montague, had placed the railroad running through Yreka. When he died in 1883, William Hood succeeded him as chief engineer for the railroad. However, when Hood took over, he opted for a less expensive and more level route through the Shasta Valley, bypassing Yreka all together. In November 1886, a Yreka delegation consisting of James Vance, H. B. Gillis, and Dr. D. Ream met with directors of the railroad in San Francisco to discuss the advantages of building through Yreka. At the same time, another citizen from Yreka, Fred Autenrieth, met with William Hood at Edson's, which was near Mount Shasta. The delegations returned to Yreka with high hopes after receiving positive feedback from the railroad directors and the chief engineer. However, a letter from Timothy Hopkins, railroad treasurer, ruined the hopes of the citizens of Yreka when it was determined that the route through Yreka would add 5.5 miles to the proposed route and was more costly to build.

Without a rail connection to the outside world, the citizens of Yreka feared that the city would lose its prestige as a money center in Siskiyou County and eventually die. In December 1886, the citizens of Yreka decided to attempt to build a railroad of their own. Yreka then formed a committee to try and build the railroad. In March 1887, Fred Autenrieth, a committee member, acquired surveyors to find the best possible route to a connection with the Central Pacific. The first proposal called for a 10-mile route from Yreka to Julians, which was 9 miles south of Montague near the present town of Grenada. However, this would require building a depot on the Central Pacific, which would increase the total cost of the railroad.

On August 27, 1887, an election was held to bond Yreka for $85,000 to build a shorter route over Butcher Hill to Montague, a town site laid out by Central Pacific and named after the late Samuel Montague. There was opposition to the railroad by four men running the stagecoaches between Yreka and Montague. The bonds were passed, with a vote of 241 for the bonds and only 4 against. It is rumored that the four votes against it were from the stage drivers who ran between Yreka and Montague. However, the bonds would not sell due to a boom in Southern California, making money scarce.

Finally, a third attempt was made, and unlike the first two, this one succeeded. On April 24, 1888, the Yreka Railroad was organized. Five local citizens were elected as directors. They were H. B. Gillis, Charles Iunker, Jerome Churchill, J. W. Walbridge, and Fred W. Autenrieth. A month later, on May 28, 1888, Jerome Churchill was named president of the new railroad when it became incorporated. The railroad sold $100,000 worth of stock that was divided into 4,000 shares at $25 per share. An additional $40,000 was borrowed by the railroad, with some of the directors signing the note.

A contract was signed with A. J. Gillis to build the railroad, and construction began in mid-August. An order was made with a supplier on the East Coast for rails and other supplies totaling 520 tons. The supplies were shipped via Cape Horn and arrived in Montague by mid-October. A contract was also signed with a sawmill in Igerna to cut 20,000 ties. By mid-September, grading had been completed between the Shasta River and Montague. Later that month, construction began on the terminal in Yreka, which was located in the center of the triangle block created by the intersection of Main and Second Streets (now Broadway). By early October, grading was completed to the Shasta River, and the piles were being driven for a bridge. Also at this time, crews were blasting rock on the east side of Butcher Hill. The first rails were laid in Montague on November 26, and one week later they reached the Shasta River Bridge. On December 19, the rails had reached the Yreka depot, with the construction work on the depot being completed at the same time. The same day, the railroad's first locomotive had arrived from Baldwin Locomotive Works, which had been ordered at the same time as the rails. The railroad officially opened for business on January 9, 1889.

One

The Yreka Railroad Company

Traffic on the Yreka Railroad was slow to develop over the first few years. On top of this, the railroad was plagued with the frequent flooding of Yreka Creek. By the turn of the 20th century, the persistence of the directors and an increase in business finally got the railroad to make a profit, however it was marginal at best. In May 1904, meetings were held in Scott Valley (to the west of Yreka) for the purpose of building the Yreka and Pacific Railroad to bring rails into the towns of Fort Jones and Etna, but the citizens of the valley were unable to raise the money for the railroad. In April 1906, the railroad was purchased by the San Francisco firm of Scott and VanArsdale, who were also the owners and founders of the nearby McCloud River Railroad. They renewed interest in the Scott Valley extension. Surveys were made for a route, and construction was set to begin on April 18, 1906, however, that was the same day of the San Francisco earthquake and fire. Scott and VanArsdale were hit hard by financial losses due to the quake, and the funds available for the extension were no longer available, so the project was cancelled.

In 1910, a decision was made to relocate the depot and yards in Yreka to the opposite side of Yreka Creek to avoid further flooding issues. On March 14, 1910, land for a new depot and yard was purchased on the east side of Yreka Creek in what was Yreka's Chinatown. The land was purchased from the Chinese firm of Gee Duck Tong, whose members were Kee Hong, Quong Wah Lung, and Wong On Kee. The old line across Yreka Creek was then abandoned and the engine house and depot sold off. A larger depot and a four-stall roundhouse were built on the new site.

In early 1920, Scott and VanArsdale deemed the railroad too expensive to operate and put the line up for sale for $25,000. The firm announced that if the line was not purchased in three months they would file for abandonment and scrap the line. A local campaign was held to buy the railroad, and on April 1, 1906, the railroad changed ownership and was once again owned by the city of Yreka.

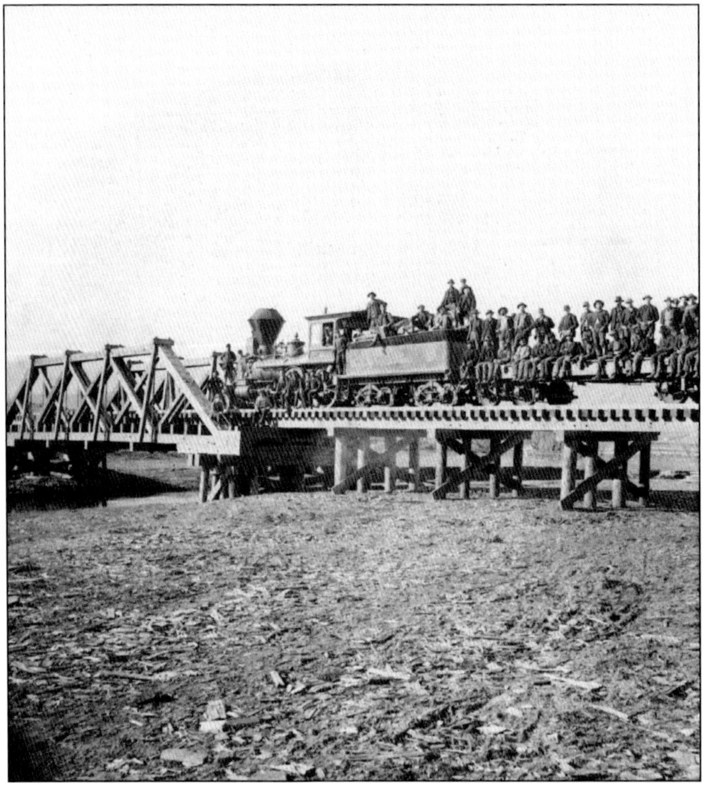

The Yreka Railroad leased California Pacific Railroad No. 2, the *Marysville*, for use in construction of the railroad. The engine was a 4-4-0 American-type built by Mason Machine Works in Taunton, Massachusetts, in February 1867 with builder No. 246. The engine is pictured with a construction crew here at the recently completed Shasta River Bridge in late 1888. (Courtesy Siskiyou County Museum.)

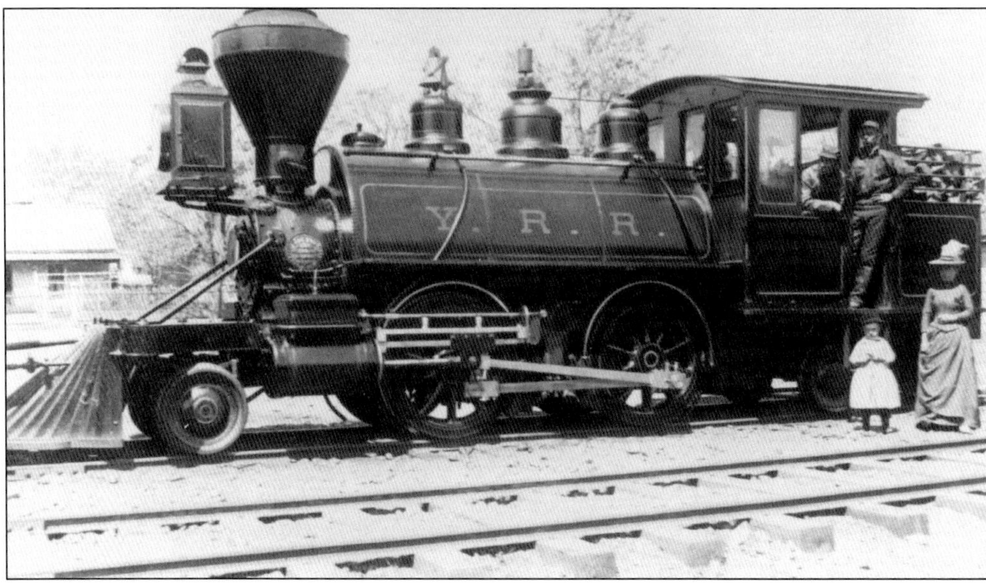

Yreka Railroad No. 1 was a Baldwin Locomotive Works 2-4-2T built brand-new for the railroad in 1888. The locomotive was quickly nicknamed by the crews as *Ol' Betsy*. She sported 46-inch drivers, 12-by-18-inch cylinders, weighed 52,000 pounds, and had a tractive effort of 6,300 pounds. She is seen here in her first years of service in Yreka. The man hanging out the window is most likely Archie De La Montania, and the fellow on the gangway is Jim Garvey. The woman and child are unidentified.

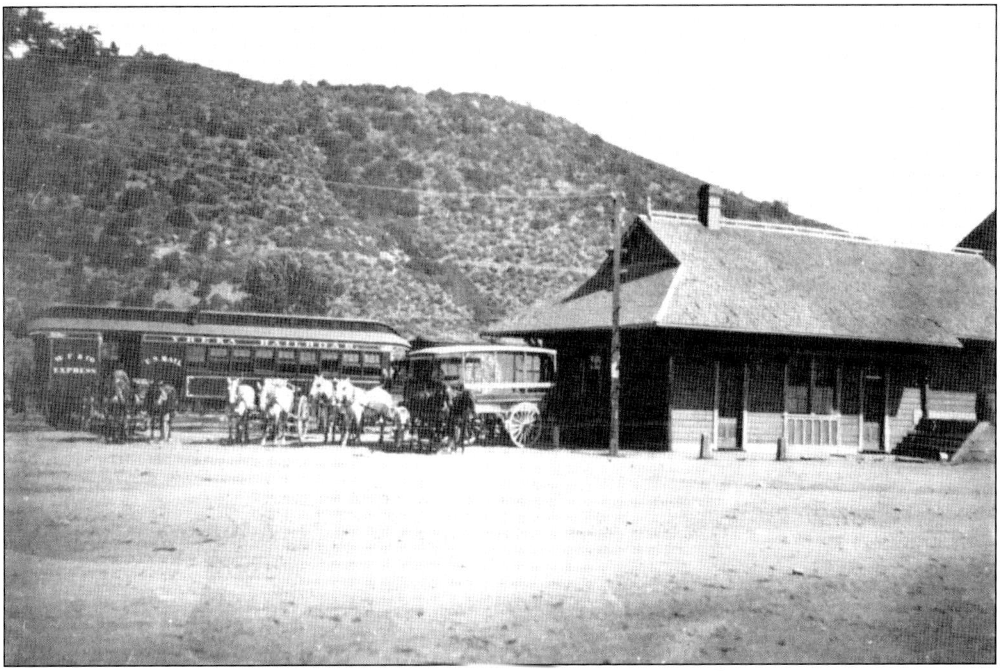

Much of the railroad's early business was passenger traffic. The stages from Scott Valley and other points west would meet the train in Yreka, where passengers, mail, and other express shipments were transferred.

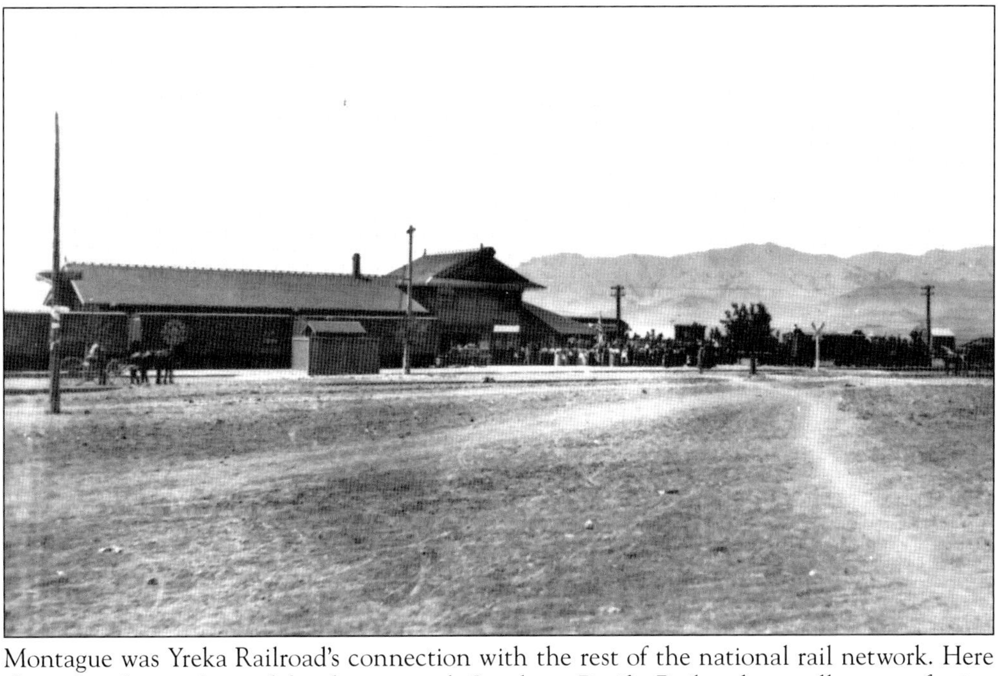

Montague was Yreka Railroad's connection with the rest of the national rail network. Here the railroad interchanged freight cars with Southern Pacific Railroad, as well as transferring passengers and less than carload freight. Montague was named for the late Samuel S. Montague, original chief engineer of the Central Pacific and Southern Pacific Railroads. (Courtesy Siskiyou County Museum.)

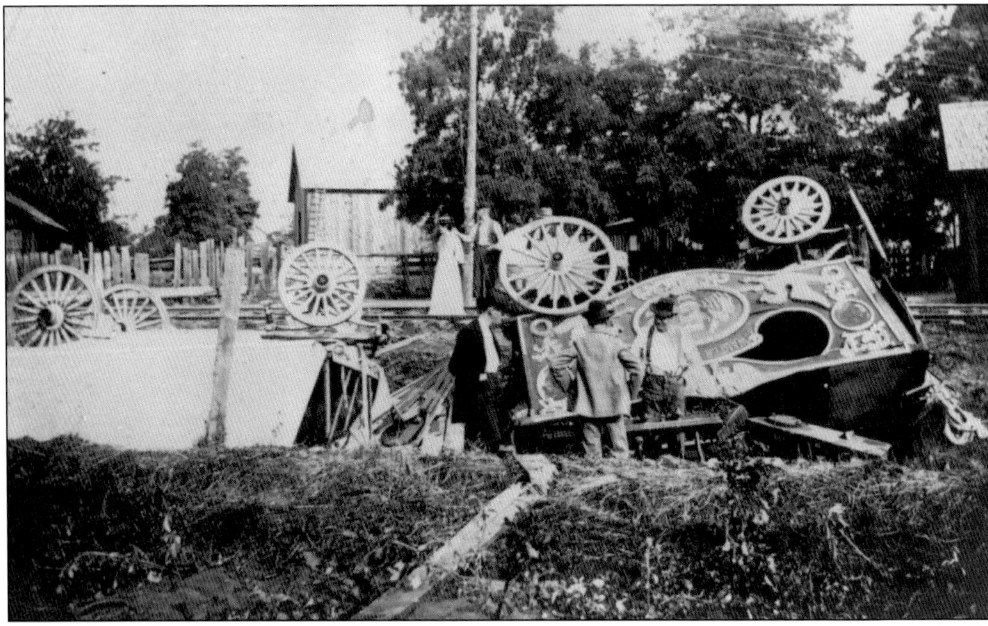

On August 3, 1897, the Walter L. Main circus came to Yreka. After putting on a show for the town, the circus was packed up and loaded onto an outbound train. However, after pulling out of the depot, a rail broke and the train derailed. It is said that elephants ran free through the streets of Yreka that night.

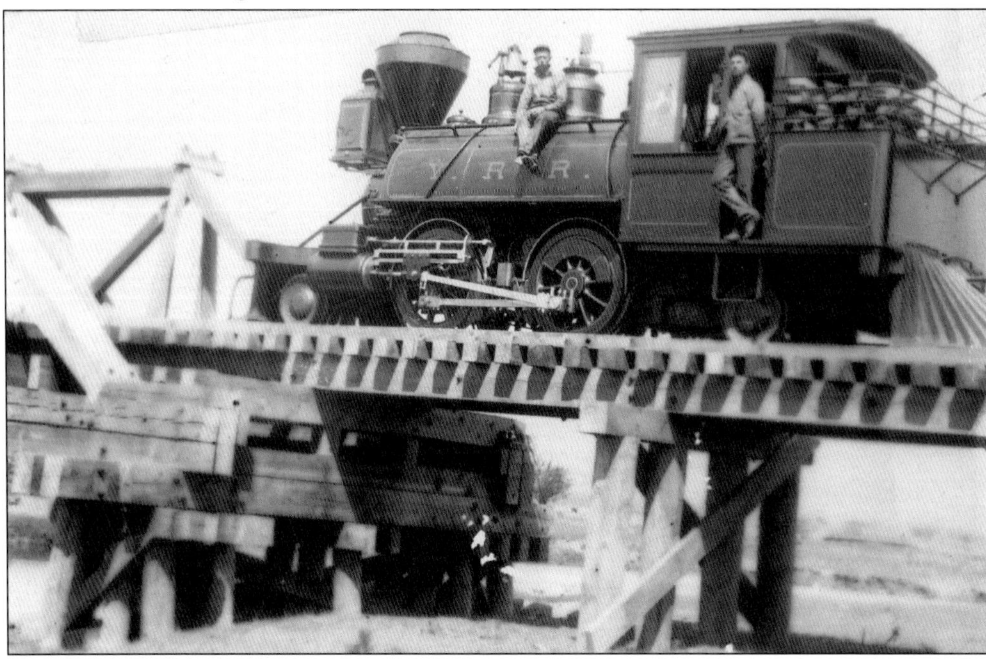

The two bridges of any real significant size on the railroad where at the crossings of Yreka Creek and the Shasta River, with the Shasta River Bridge being the biggest on the line. The two views here show the bridge as it originally appeared. Several modifications were made over the years to cope with the growing size of railroad equipment. The two men in the photograph above with engine No. 1 are Jim Garvey (sitting on the boiler) and Archie De La Montania (in the gangway).

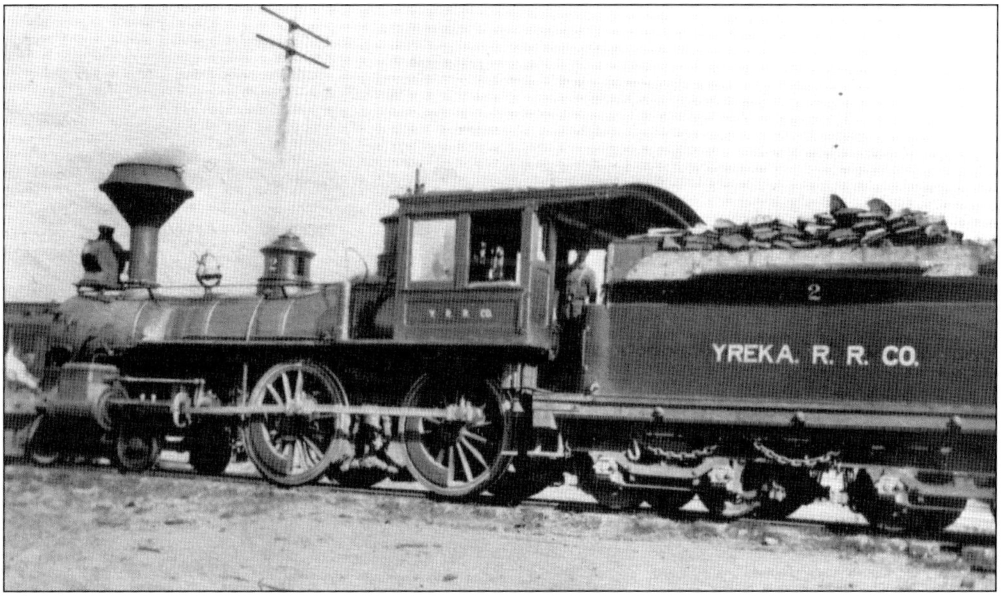

In 1896, the railroad purchased a second locomotive. The locomotive was purchased secondhand from the Corvallis and Eastern Railroad and was originally their No. 6. The engine—a 4-4-0 built by Cooke in May 1886—carried construction No. 1719 and became No. 2 on Yreka's roster. She sported 54-inch drivers and weighed 64,000 pounds. No. 2 was scrapped in 1918. In this photograph, she is seen in Montague around 1908.

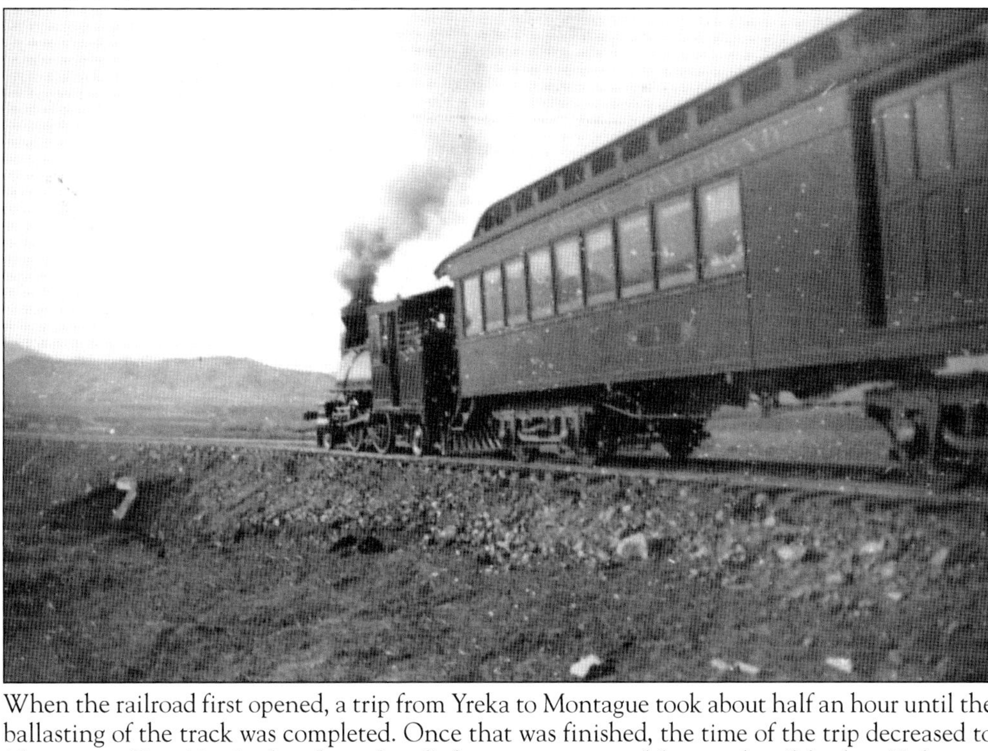

When the railroad first opened, a trip from Yreka to Montague took about half an hour until the ballasting of the track was completed. Once that was finished, the time of the trip decreased to 15 minutes. Here No. 1 takes the railroad's first passenger car (also number 1) back to Yreka as it rolls across a fill somewhere west of Montague.

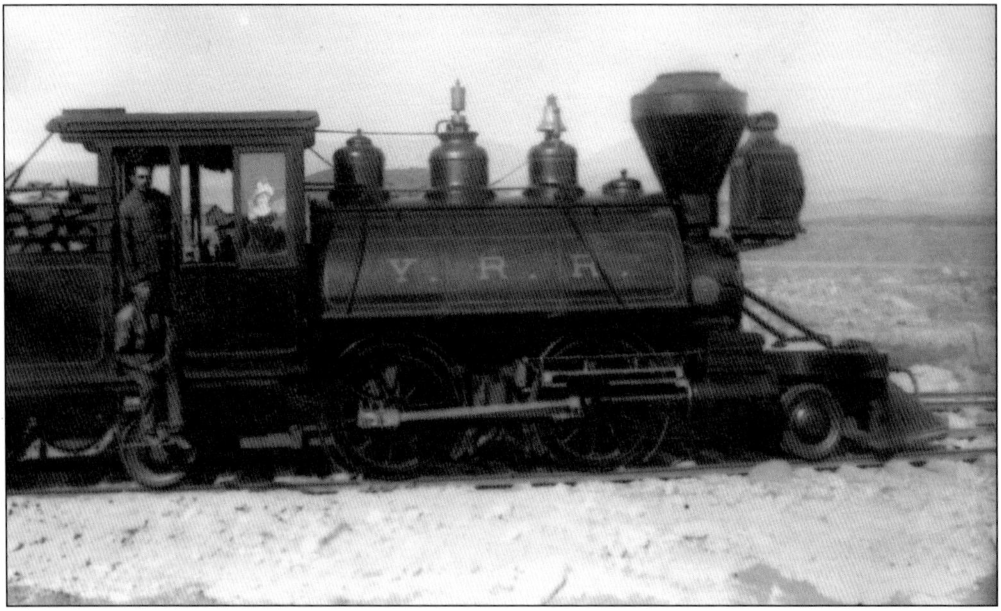

When the Yreka Railroad was opened, the cost to build the railroad had reached $110,000. The line was 7.32 miles long and was laid with 40-pound rail. It was soon realized that the rail would be too light but was decided that it would work for initial needs. The lightness of the rail is evident in this photograph of No. 1 somewhere out in the Shasta Valley.

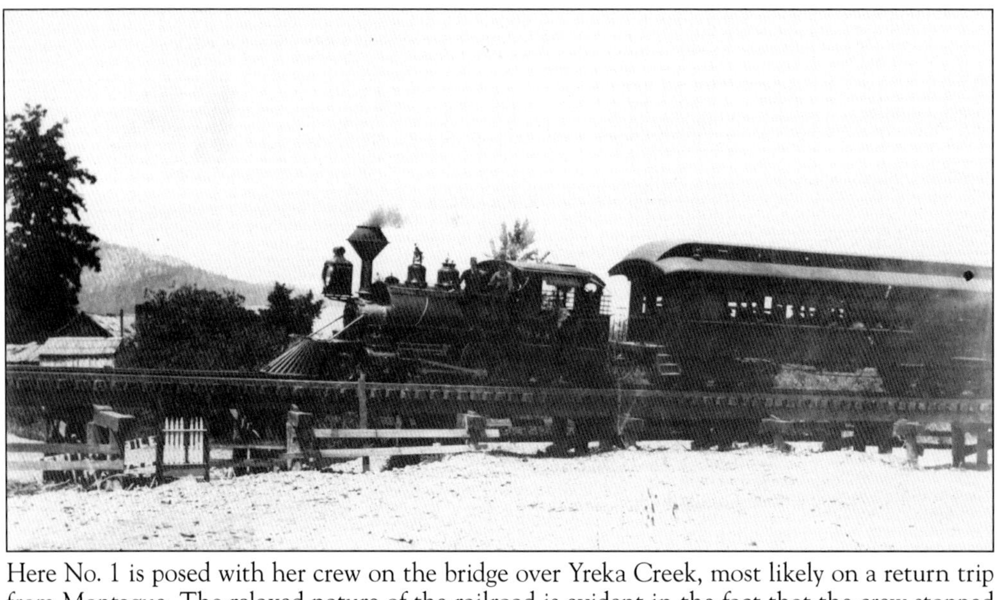

Here No. 1 is posed with her crew on the bridge over Yreka Creek, most likely on a return trip from Montague. The relaxed nature of the railroad is evident in the fact that the crew stopped a full train for the sake of the photographer. Passenger fares at this time were 50¢ one way and 75¢ roundtrip. (Courtesy Siskiyou County Museum.)

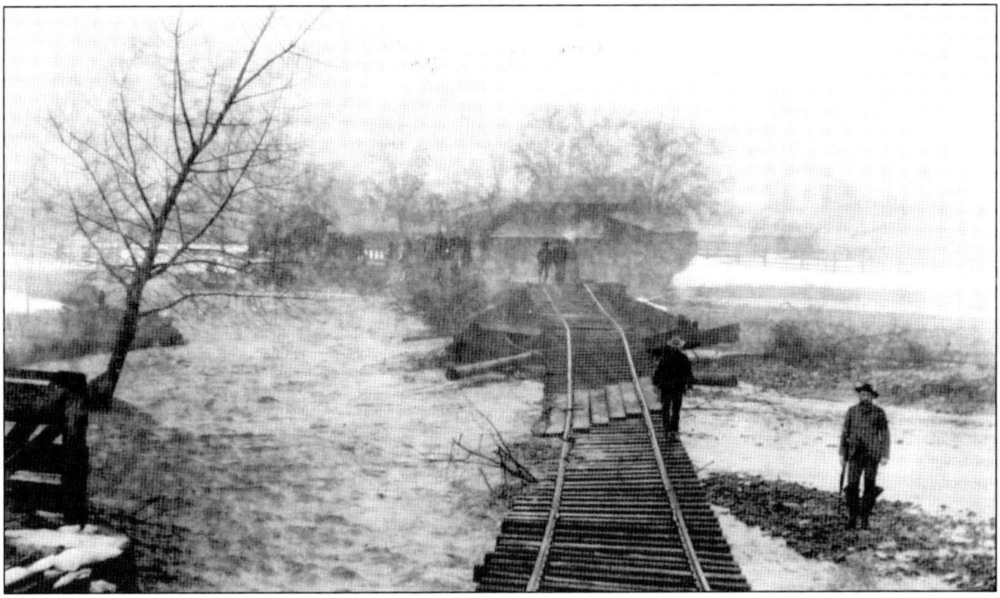

The winter of 1889–1890 proved to be a bad one, with high levels of snowfall in the higher elevations and runoff from the melting snow that caused the Yreka Creek to flood and damage the railroad bridge. Flooding of the bridge proved to be a problem for the next 20 years, with the entire bridge being taken out on numerous occasions. The photograph above was taken February 5, 1890. (Both photographs courtesy Siskiyou County Museum.)

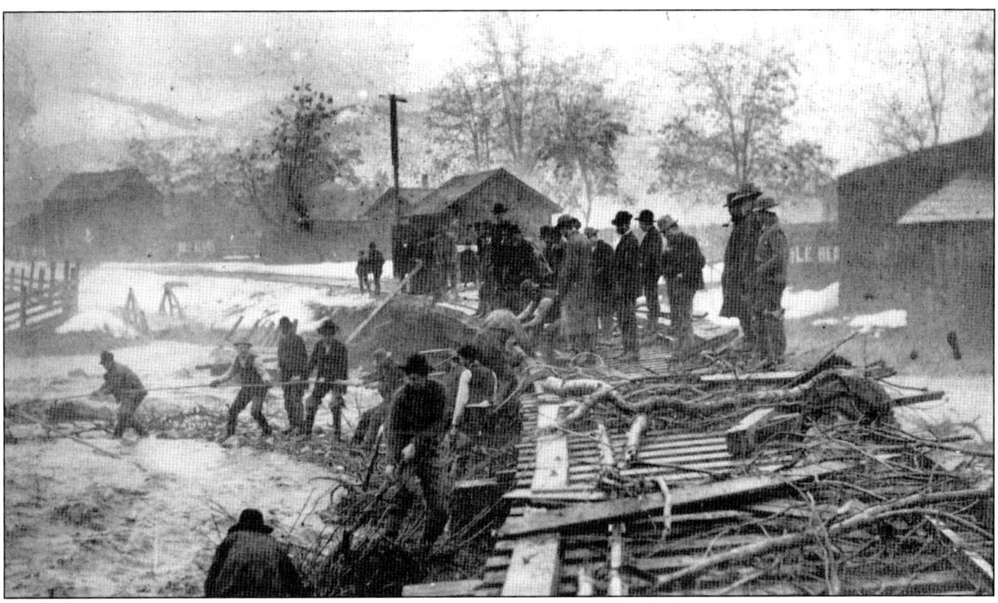

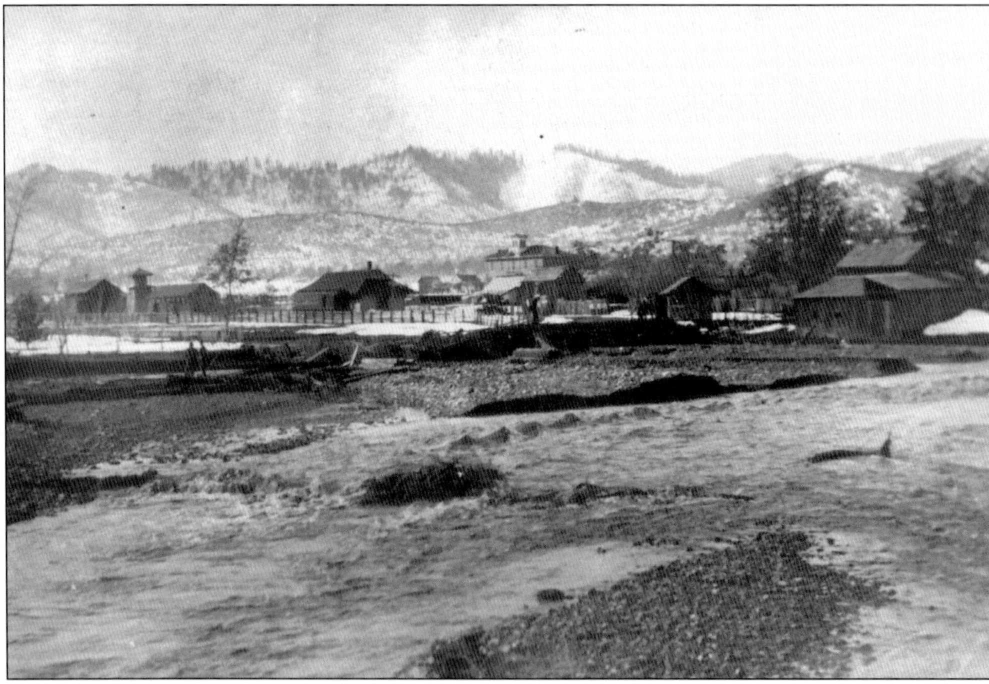

Here's another shot looking towards the town of Yreka after floodwaters in the creek have subsided. The railroad's bridge has been completely destroyed. The bridge would have run from the left of the photograph to about the middle as it curved back around towards town. The depot, engine house, water tower, and wood shed, are all to the left above the location of the bridge. The two-story brick building in the center was Yreka's first permanent grammar school, which was built in 1856.

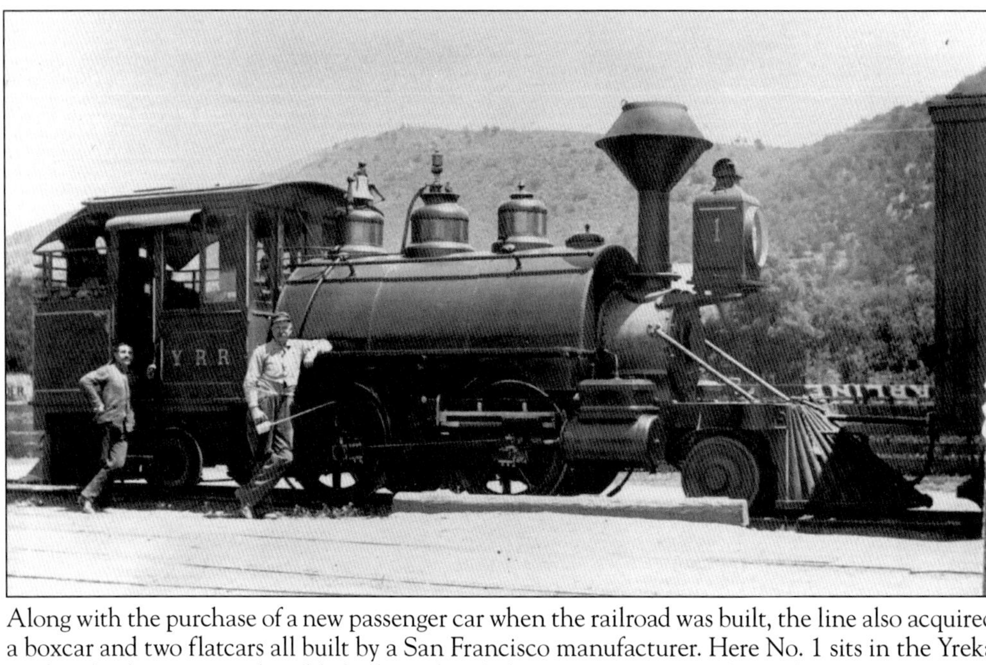

Along with the purchase of a new passenger car when the railroad was built, the line also acquired a boxcar and two flatcars all built by a San Francisco manufacturer. Here No. 1 sits in the Yreka yard with what is more than likely the railroad's boxcar sometime in the mid-1890s.

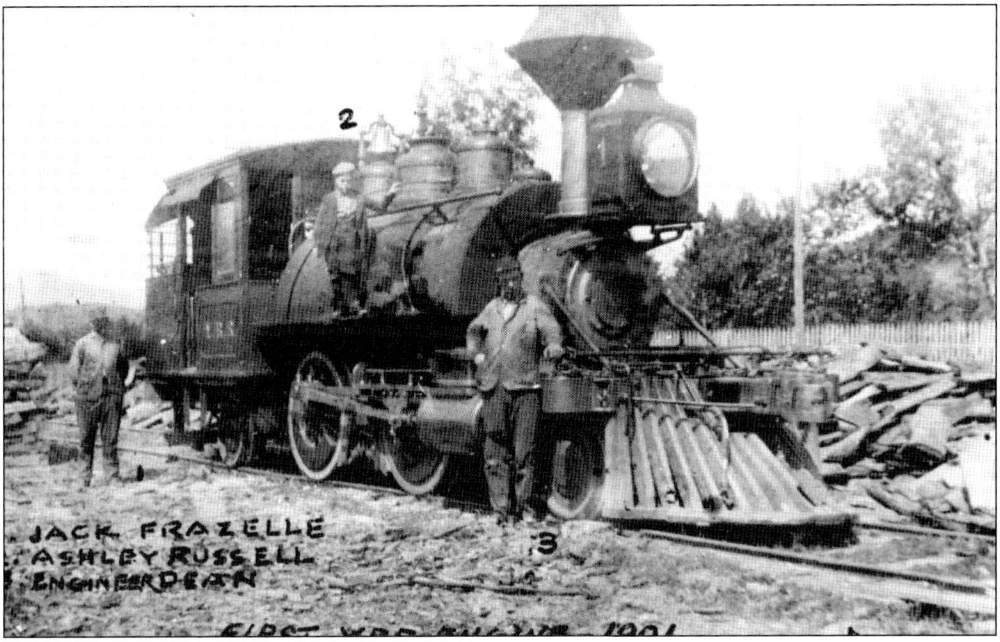

Around the start of the 20th century, No. 1 had a few modifications made. The original stack with the Radley Hunter spark arrestor was replaced with a smaller stack and a simpler diamond-type spark arrester. Also replaced were the old link and pin couplers for the recently invented and safer automatic knuckle coupler. (Courtesy Siskiyou County Museum.)

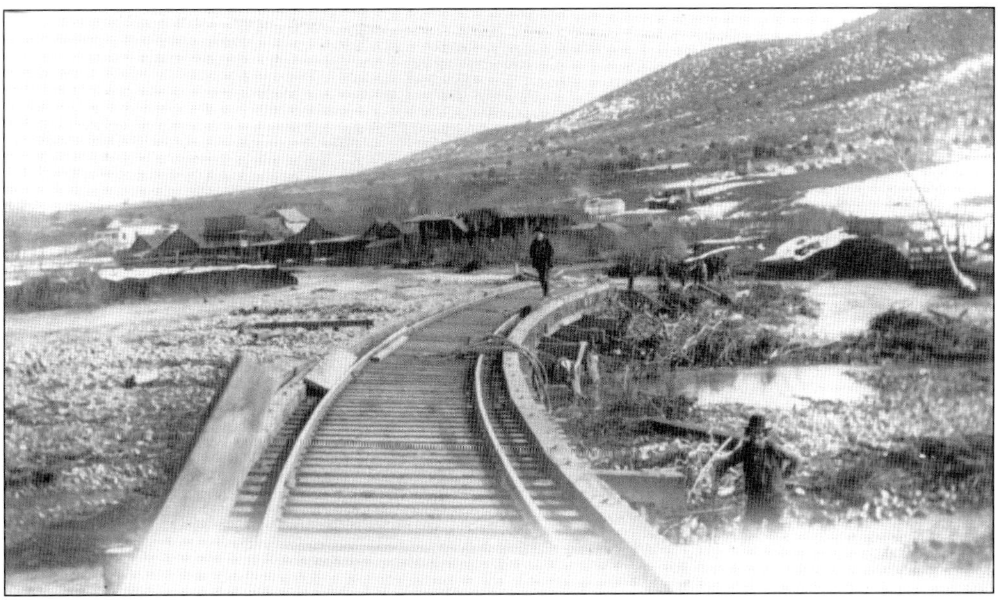

Here is another view of the aftermath of a flooded Yreka Creek from 1890. This shot is looking east towards Montague. The hill on the right is Butcher Hill; also seen is a portion of Yreka's Chinatown, which is towards the center of the photograph. This location would later become the new site for the depot and yards when they were moved in 1910.

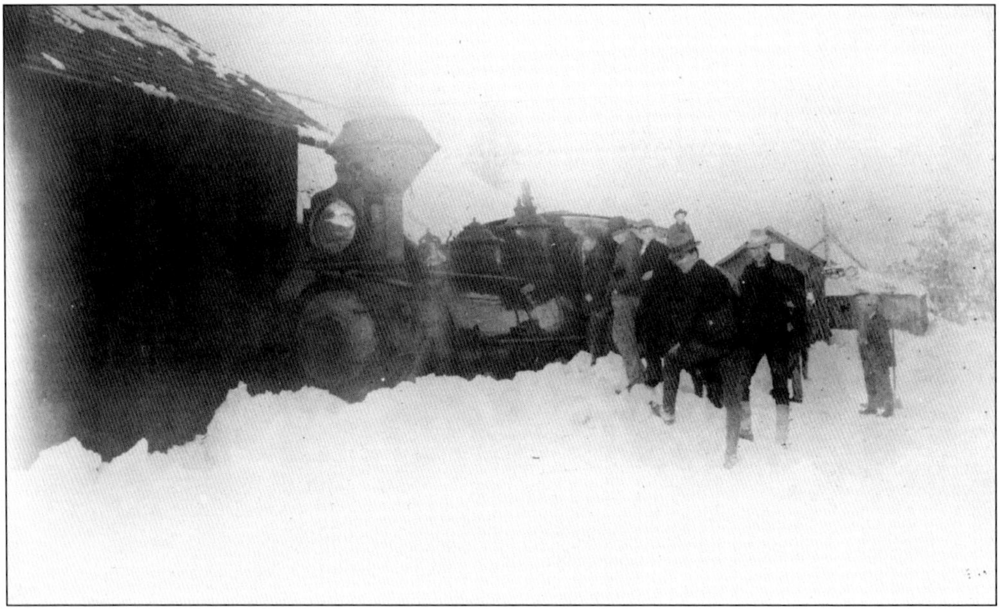

In the winter of 1901, Yreka experienced an unusually heavy amount of snowfall. The amount is evident in these two photographs of No. 2 as crews try to clear out the railroad and keep trains moving. (Both photographs courtesy Siskiyou County Museum.)

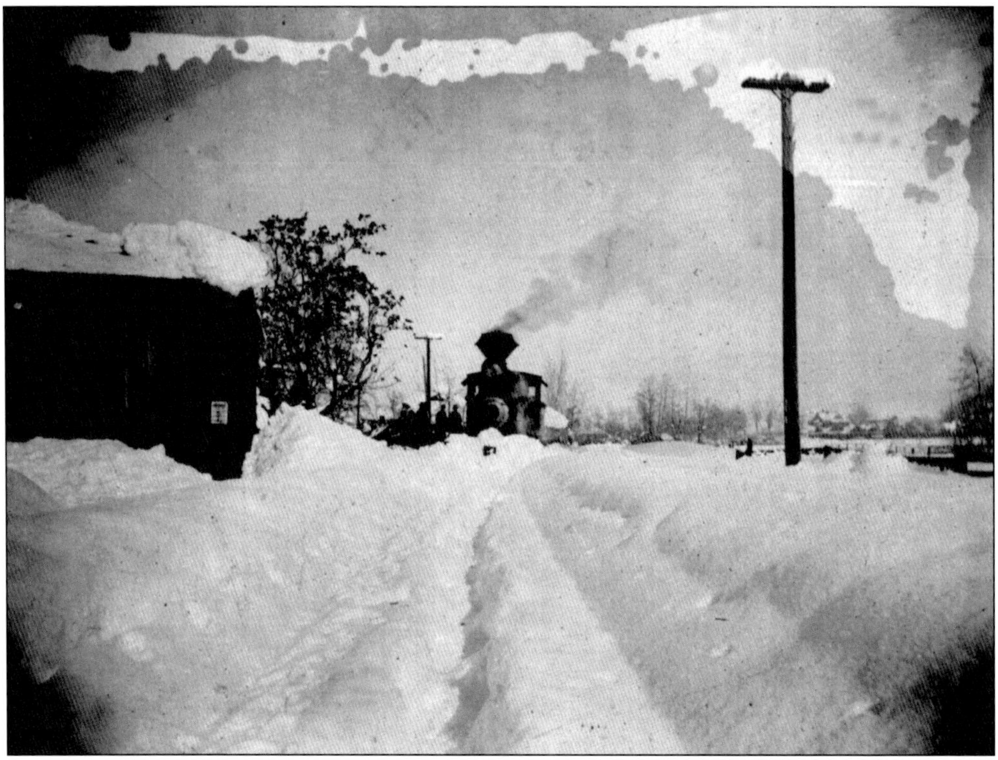

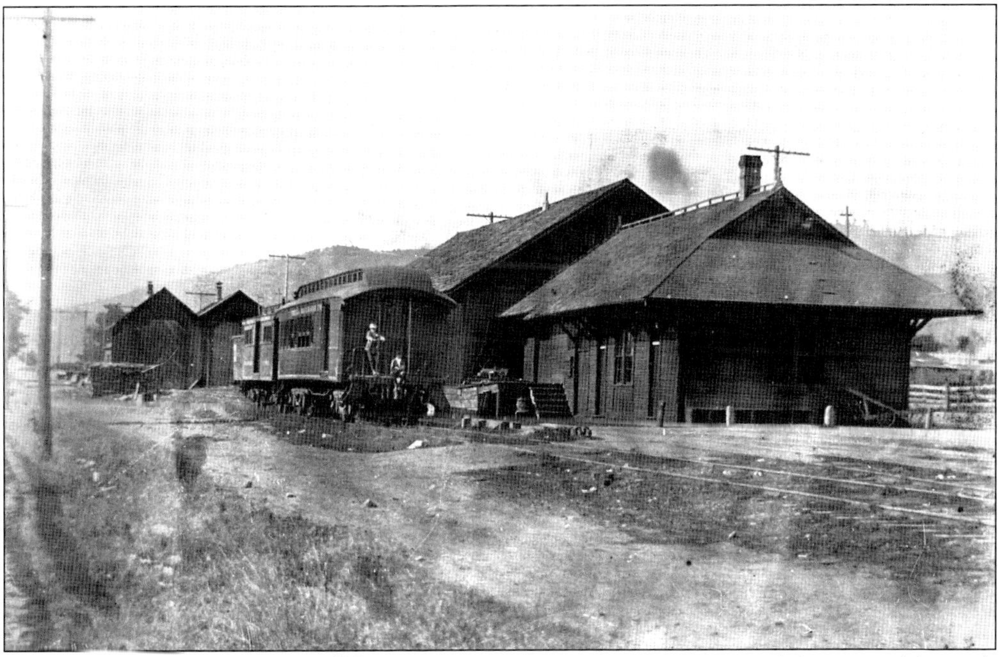

These two shots show the overall feeling of the Yreka Railroad from around the turn of the 20th century. These pictures were most likely taken on a Sunday afternoon, judging by the lack of activity around the depot and yard and the nice clothes worn by the two boys on the end of the combine. (Both photographs courtesy Siskiyou County Museum.)

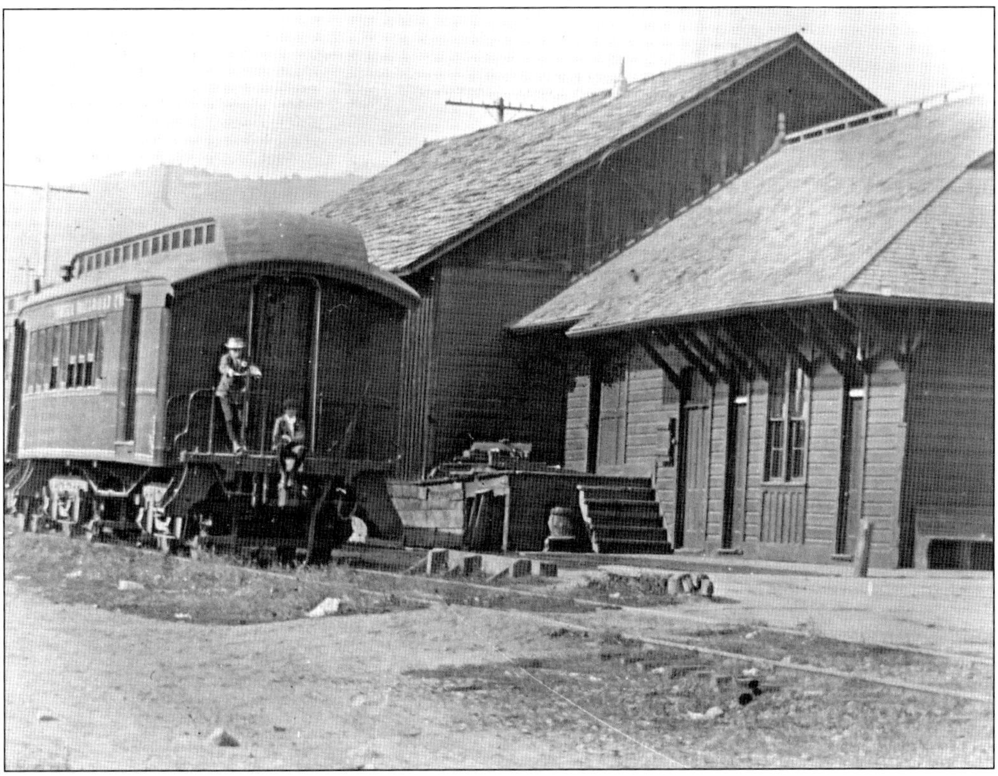

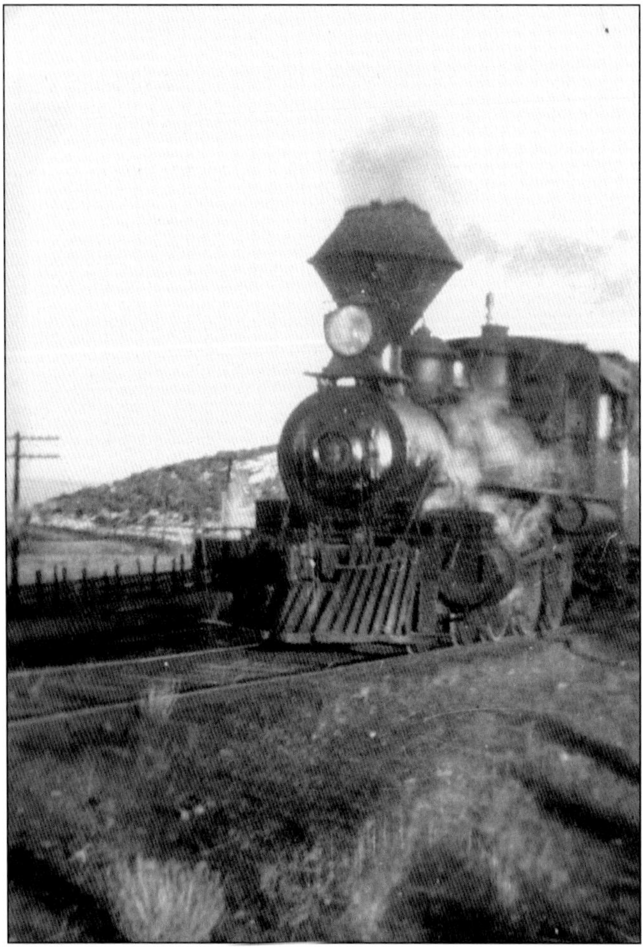

In September 1906, a third steam locomotive was added to the roster, this time a 4-6-0 10-wheeler, which was also purchased secondhand from Southern Pacific. The original number was 2093. The engine was built by Schenectady in December 1882 and featured 57-inch drivers and weighed 89,100 pounds with a tractive effort of 16,230 pounds. Here No. 3 is climbing up the east side of Butcher Hill on her way back to Yreka as she is about to cross the old Yreka-Ager Road.

Here No. 3 waits with the daily passenger train in Yreka. In the early years of the railroad, a majority of the revenue came from the passenger business. The high point of this was in 1912 when the railroad hauled 30,801 passengers, bringing in 67 percent of the total revenue at one time. However, after 1912, the passenger business started to decline as people started using automobiles for transportation.

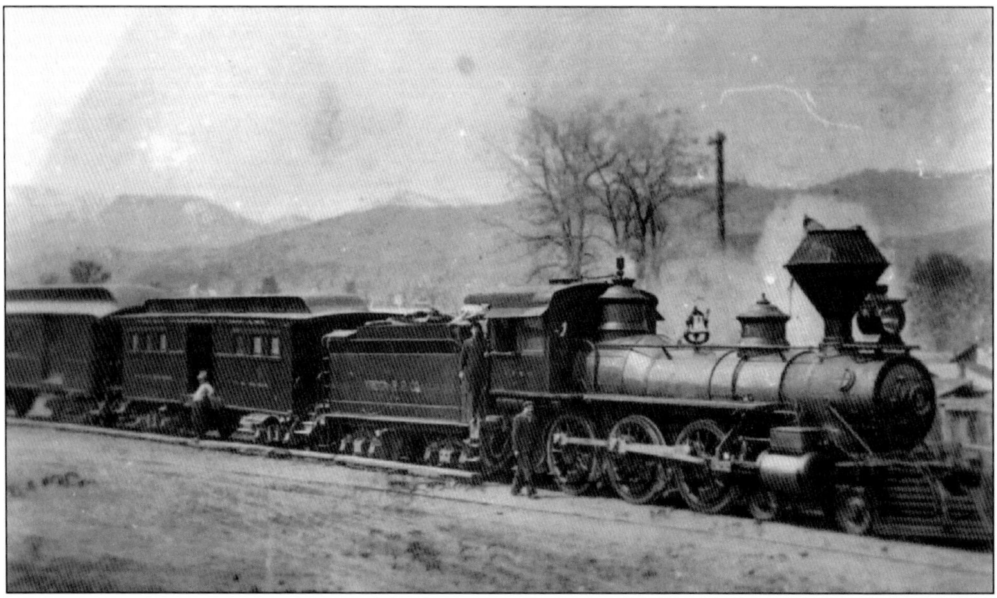

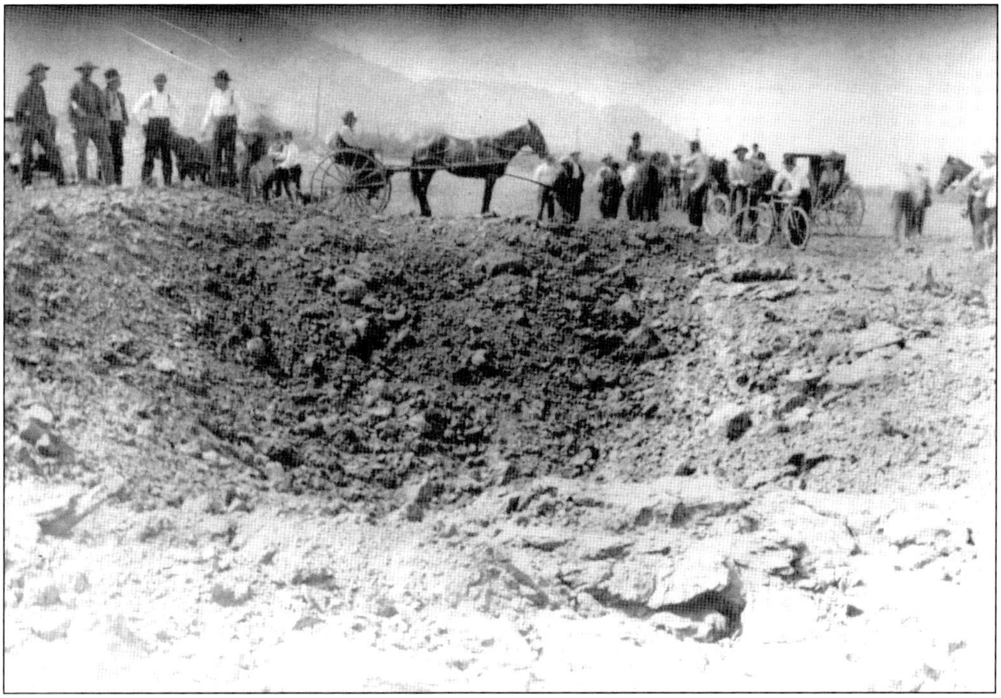

On August 19, 1906, a large explosion from a nearby powder house disrupted the peaceful morning in Yreka. At one time, there were three powder houses on the east side of Butcher Hill along the railroad tracks. Each house was spaced a couple hundred yards from each other and each had a dimension of 10 by 10 feet. Three local children who were carelessly shooting at the powder house closest to town caused the explosion, resulting in the aftermath shown above. Below is the picture of the other the powder houses that were left standing. Note the misaligned roof on the closer powder house due to the force of the explosion. (Below, courtesy Siskiyou County Museum.)

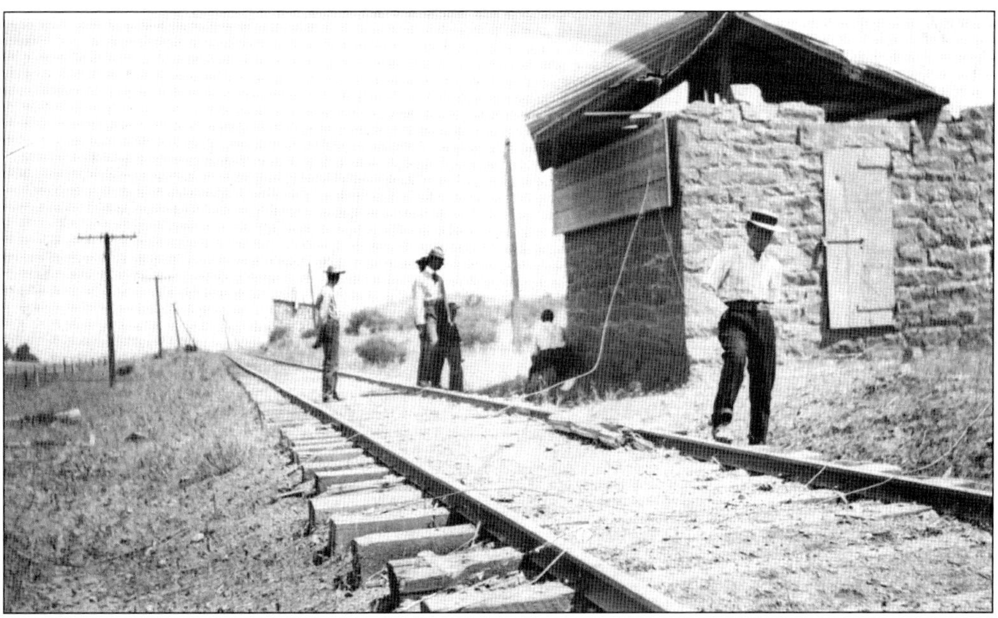

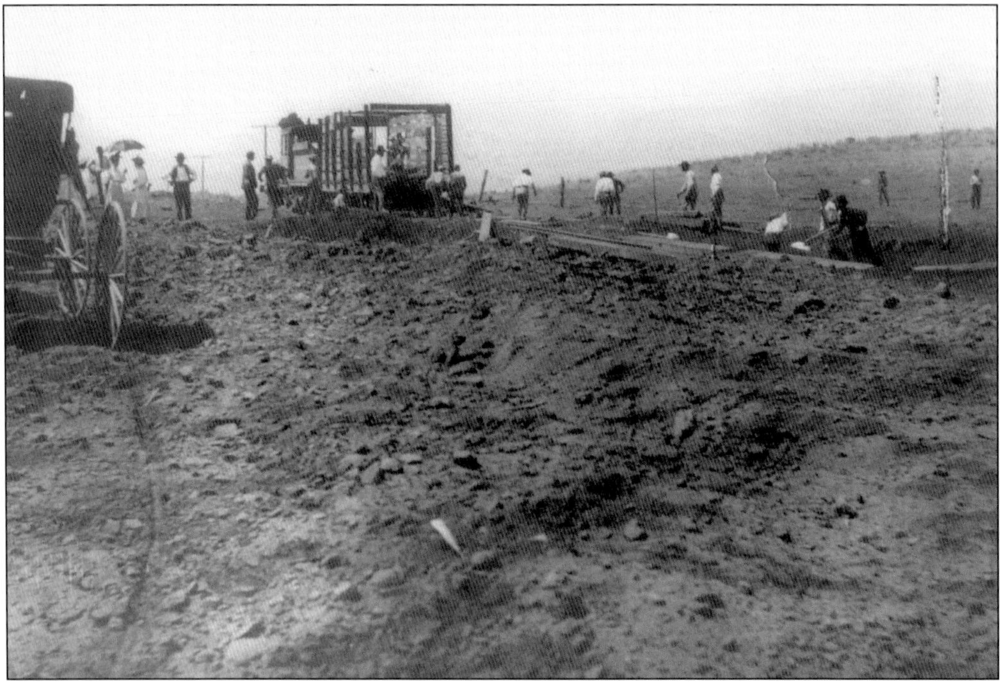

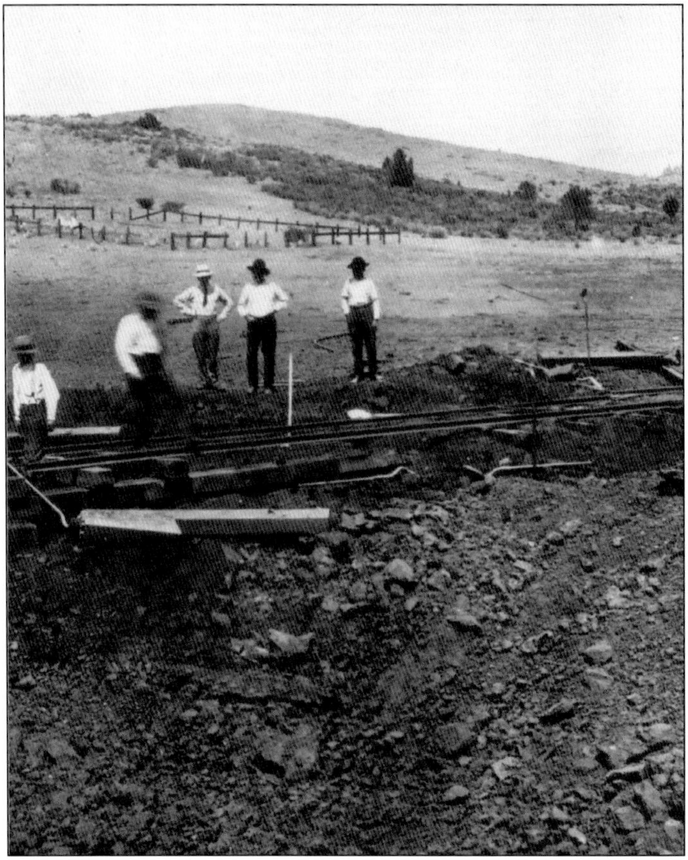

The explosion also destroyed the Yreka Railroad by creating a 10-foot crater where the rails once were. Here crews are attempting to rebuild the railroad and bridge the gap over the crater with a small temporary bridge to get the trains moving again until the hole could be filled. The old Yreka Chinese Cemetery is in the left background of the photograph below.

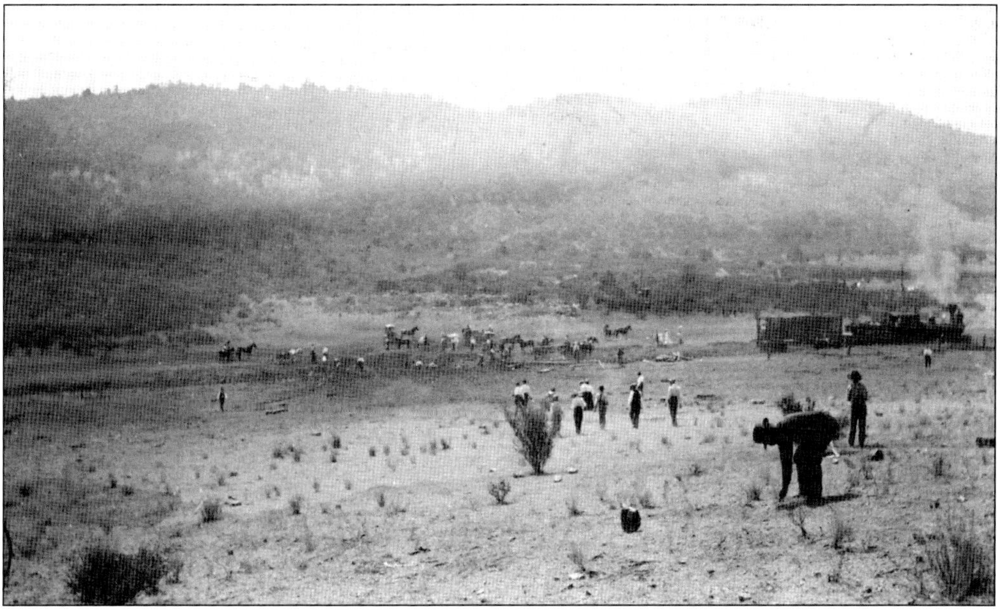

Of the three boys, one survived, but with serious injuries that disabled him for the rest of his life. The other two were next to the powder house when it went off and were literally blown to pieces. The photograph above is an overview of the scene of the explosion, with townsfolk combing the hillsides for the body parts of the two boys. In the end, enough body parts were found to fill a small washbasin. The photograph below shows engine No. 2 with new rails and ties as crews work to rebuild the damaged portion of the railroad. (Both photographs courtesy Siskiyou County Museum.)

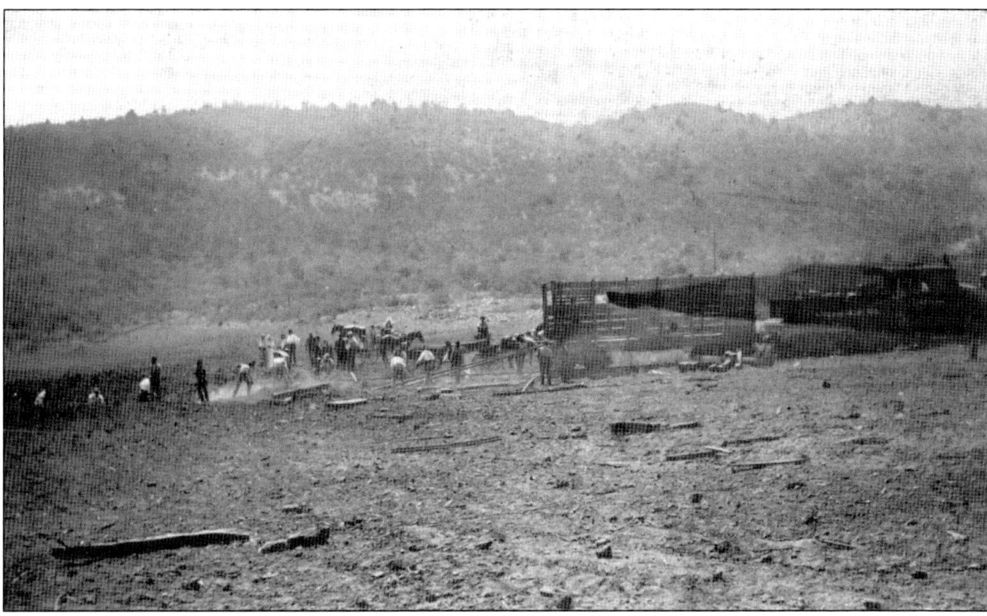

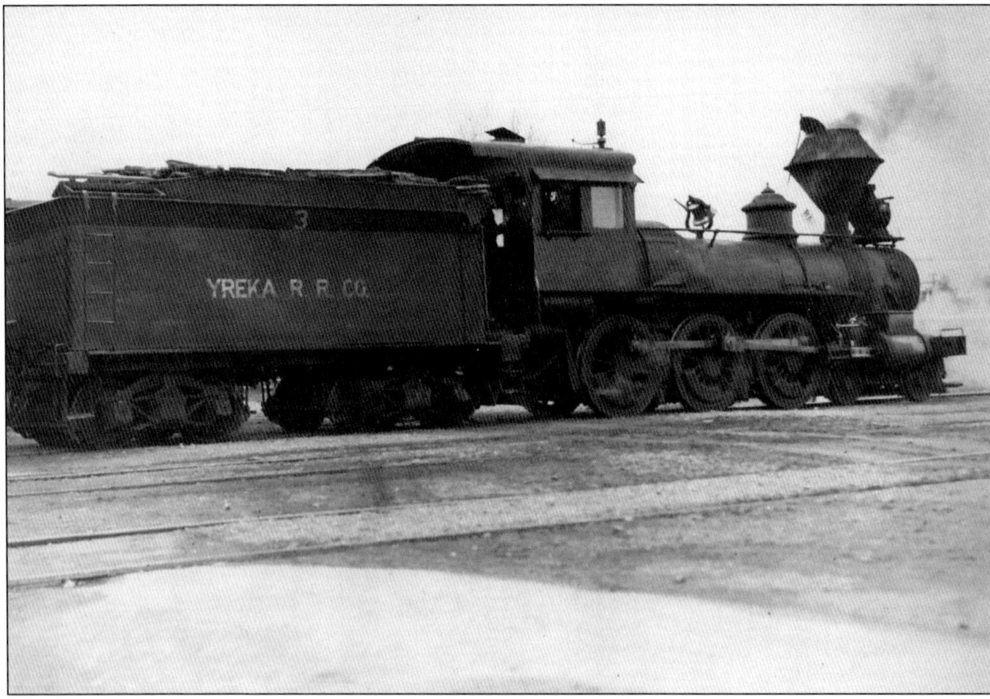

Here No. 3 rolls over a crossing in Montague on a cold day around 1910. (Courtesy Siskiyou County Museum.)

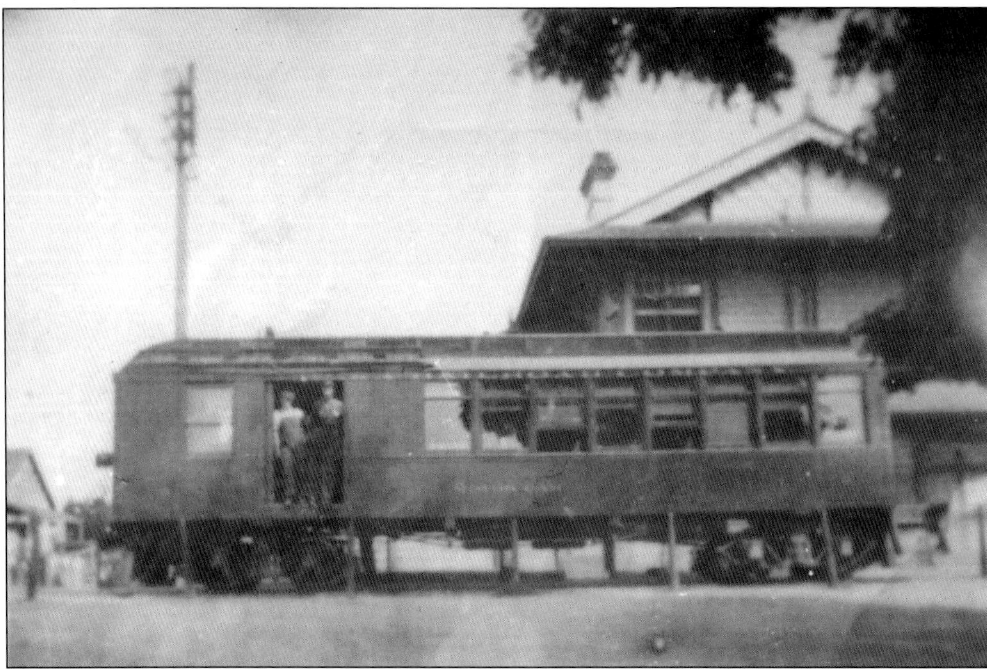

In 1909, the railroad was looking to reduce operating costs. The solution was a rail motorcar built by Hall-Scott. This car would be the first ever built by Hall-Scott. The motorcar was essentially a self-propelled passenger and was used on days when the steam locomotive didn't have any freight to haul. The savings were good enough to pay for the motorcar to pay for itself in few years.

Two

Reincorporation and Receivership

When the city of Yreka bought back the Yreka Railroad, it was more a matter of public pride than financial return. The city put a man named Robert H. DeWitt in charge of the railroad. He ran the railroad for eight years, but no return was made on the railroad, and it is unclear as to how the railroad managed to stay in business. On February 27, 1928, eighty-five percent of the stock was sold for $22,000, plus $18,000 in debts, to the Klamath River Holding Company, which was run by Harry A DeVaux. However DeVaux was not as credible as was originally perceived, and he lived his life on flamboyancy and flash. He also proposed on building the extension to Scott Valley along with a branch up the Klamath River to Happy Camp to serve the Gray Eagle copper mine. However, the Depression hit, and in December 1929, the ICC turned down the proposal for the extension, stating that is wasn't economically feasible. In 1931, DeVaux was relieved of his position as president of the Yreka Railroad after he filed a petition to abandon the railroad without consulting the board of directors. The board removed the petition to abandon the railroad and made M. A. Bressalo president. Later in 1932, DeVaux was charged with five accounts of embezzling funds from the Yreka Railroad, but he was found not guilty.

In January 1932, the railroad was foreclosed on and auctioned off on the steps of the Siskiyou County Courthouse on July 12, 1933. It was sold to Carl W. Faucett, a trustee for the bondholders. The bondholders formed a new company to take over the railroad from Faucett and incorporated it as the Yreka Western Railroad Company on August 24, 1933, with Faucett named president. The ICC approved acquisition of the Yreka Railroad by the Yreka Western Railroad Company on April 18, 1935.

In August 1935, the Southern Pacific Railroad forced the railroad into receivership, with O. G. Steele being named as the receiver. He set out to make the railroad profitable again.

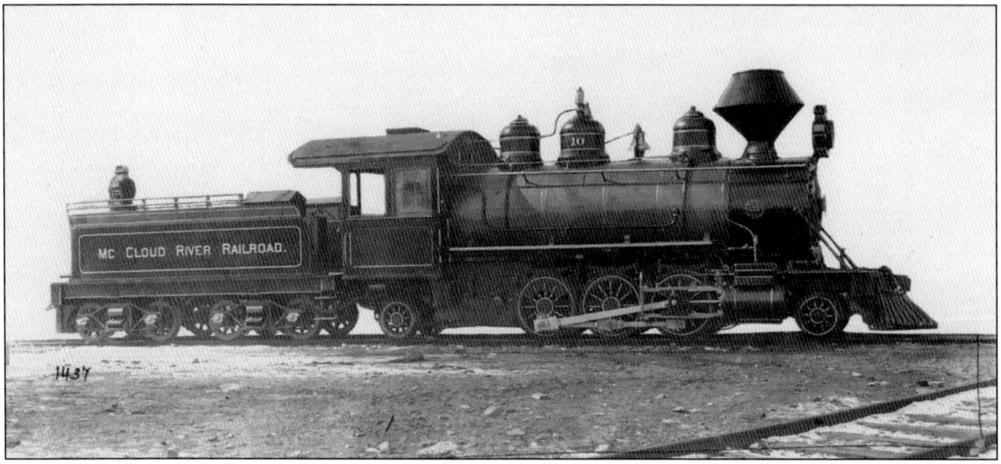

No. 10 was a Baldwin 2-6-2 weighing 107,000 pounds and built in 1901 for the McCloud River Railroad and sold to the Yreka Western in 1925. For reasons that were never clear, the engine was rarely used after 1931 (most likely the engine was in poor shape and not enough money was available to fix it), when the railroad started leasing locomotives from the Southern Pacific. It was scrapped in 1944 at Yreka. This builders photograph was taken shortly before it was delivered to McCloud. (Courtesy Jerry Lamper, Jeff Moore.)

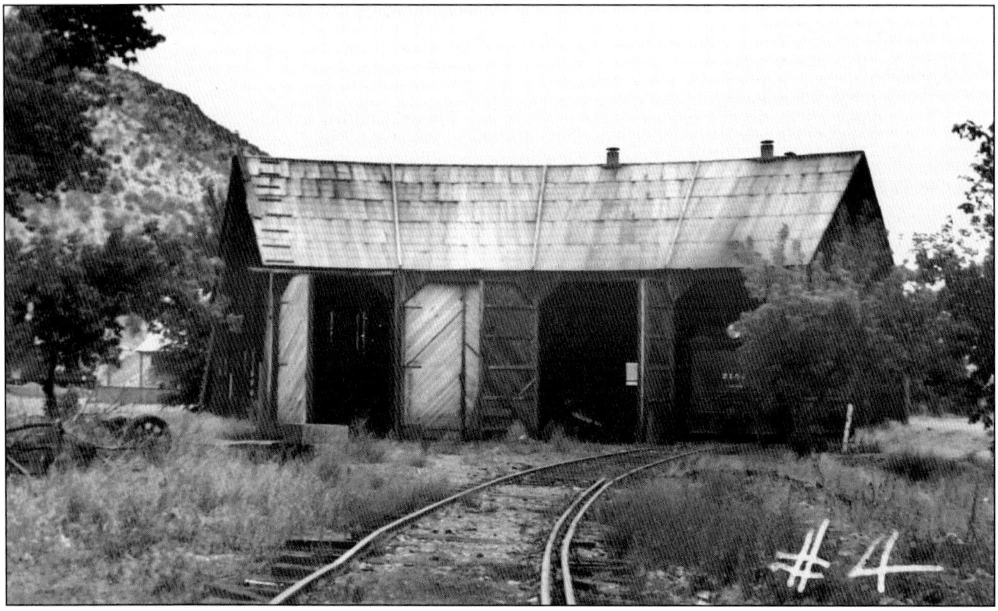

When the depot and yards in Yreka were moved to the east side of Yreka Creek, a four-stall roundhouse was constructed, rather than another two-stall engine house like that at the original site. As the years went by, the other rails in the roundhouse became surplus and were pulled up, as seen in this photograph taken sometime in the early 1930s, with only one track remaining. Inside is Southern Pacific 4-6-0 ten-wheeler No. 2181, one of the engines the railroad leased from Southern Pacific. The Yreka Western leased this engine in 1931 and again in 1932. The roundhouse caught fire and burned down on June 19, 1939. Luckily all that was lost was some stored mining equipment and a small Plymouth diesel locomotive the railroad owned. The Plymouth was eventually repaired and sold to the U.S. Army. A two-stall engine house was built to replace the roundhouse.

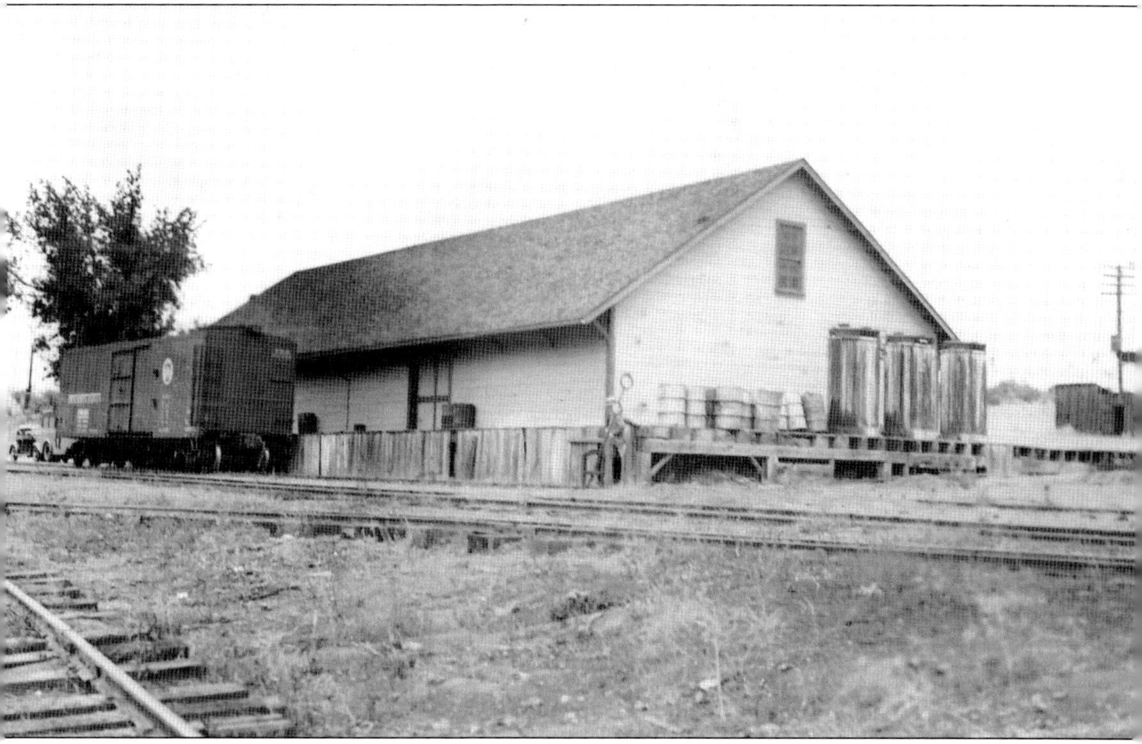

This is a shot of the Yreka depot taken on August 21, 1936, about a year after the railroad was forced into receivership and O. G. Steele was named receiver. One of the first acts Steele performed was putting an ad in the local paper, asking for everyone with unpaid bills to come forward. Once all the bills had come forward, the railroad ended up owing more $32,000. The phone bill was so high that the phone company disconnected the phone in the depot and installed a pay phone.

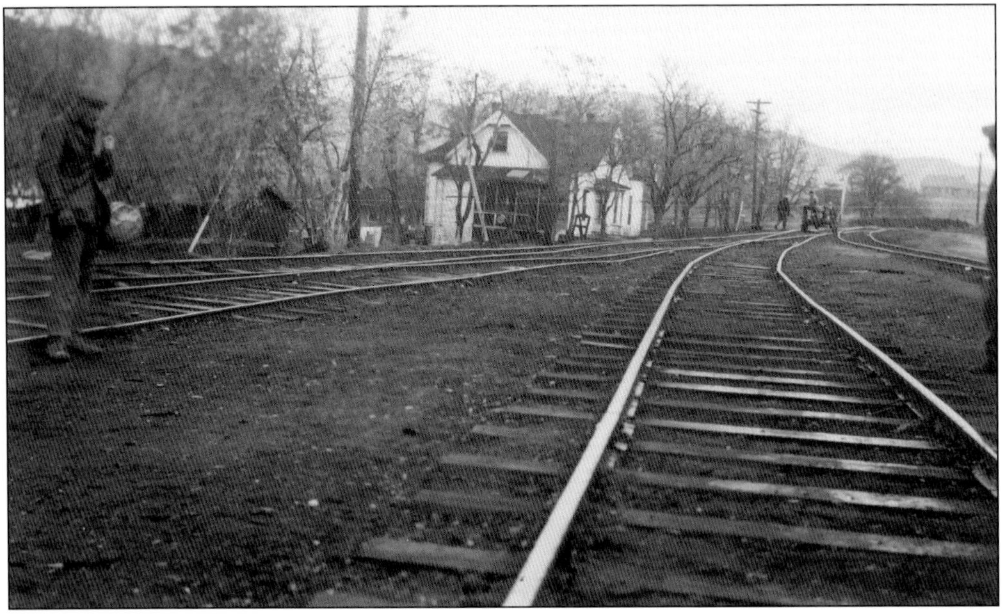

Here are two more photographs in a series of shots take in August 1936. Both these images show the deteriorated state of the railroad at that time. The rotting wood on the loading dock, below, is clearly evident, as well as the poor condition of the track in the above photograph. When Steele took over, he was quoted as saying, "I didn't know what I was getting into." And these images show just a fraction of it.

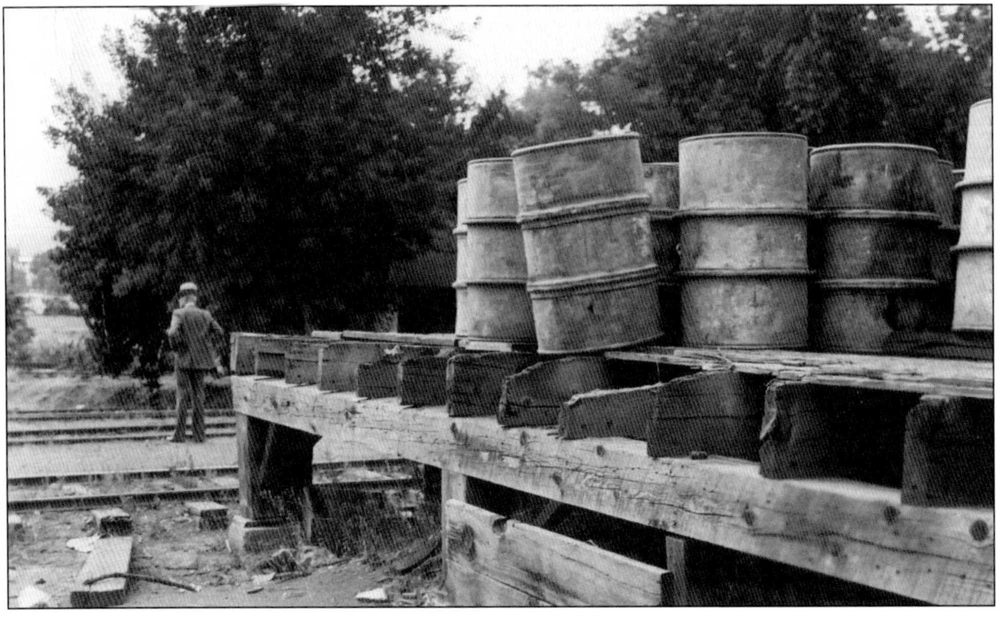

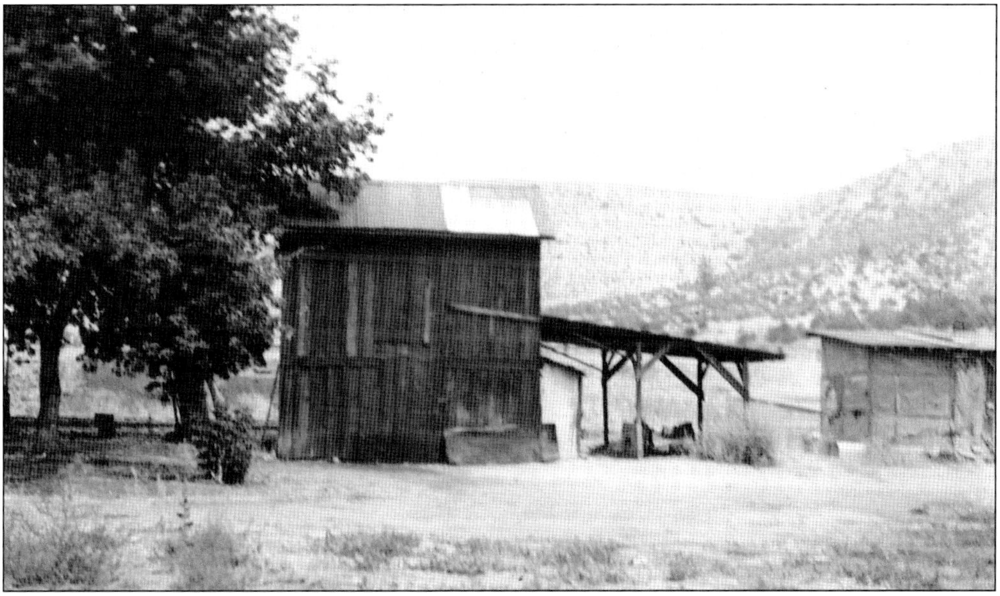

Among other structures located at the Yreka yard, besides the depot and roundhouse, were a sand house (above), which stored dry sand to be put on the locomotives for added traction, and a water softener (right) used to treat water for the locomotives to reduce scaling in the boilers.

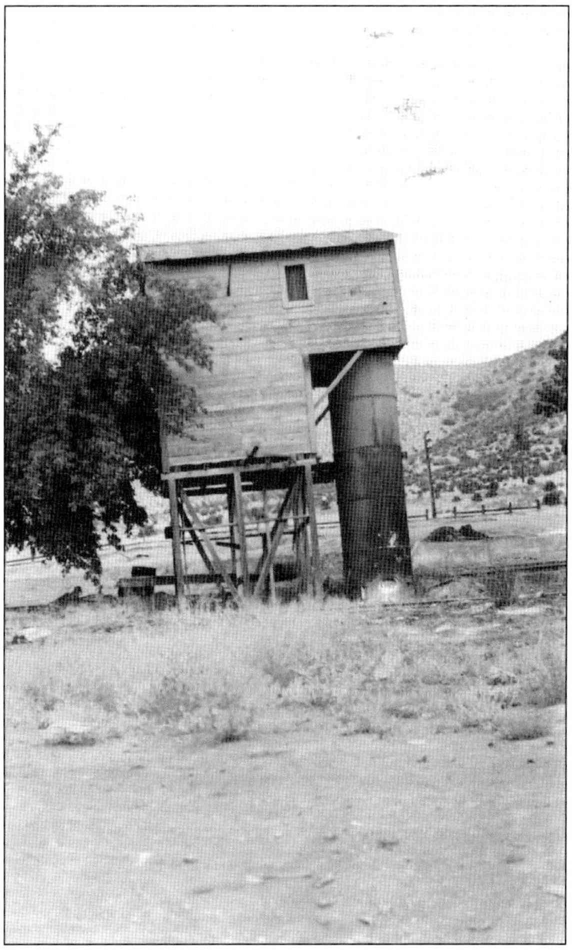

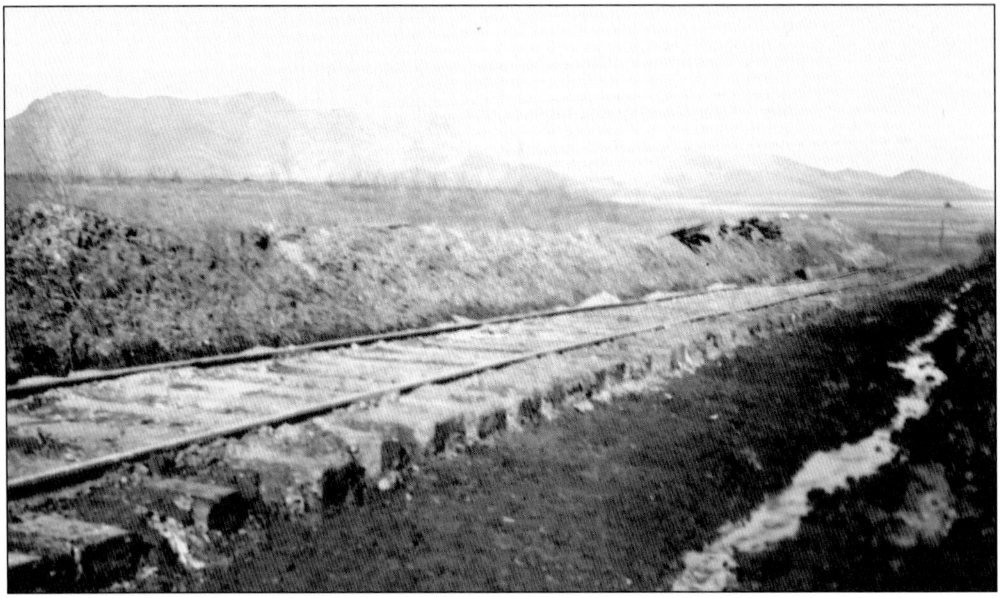

Yreka Western's mainline had suffered from years of deferred maintenance, except for some limited tie replacement during the 1920s, but even that wasn't enough. The old 40-pound rail was starting to show its age, and the ties would barely hold the spikes. Crews considered it a miracle if they could make the trip to Montague without a derailment. O. G. Steele described one of the worse trips when a light engine was sent to Montague to pick up a load of fuel oil. The engine made it to Montague without incident, but it was a week before the train made it back due so many derailments, with forward progress barely being 50 feet in one day.

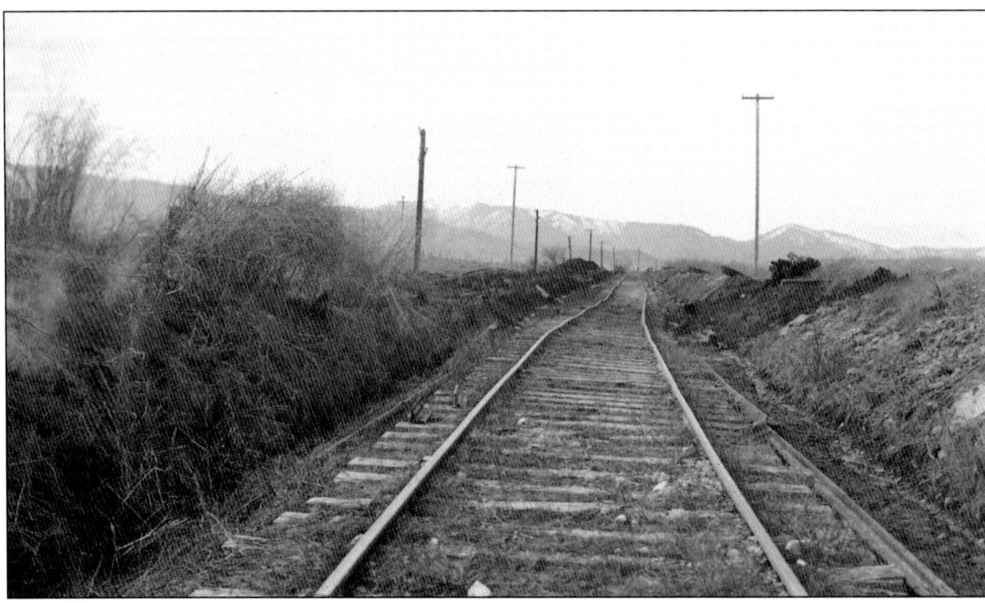

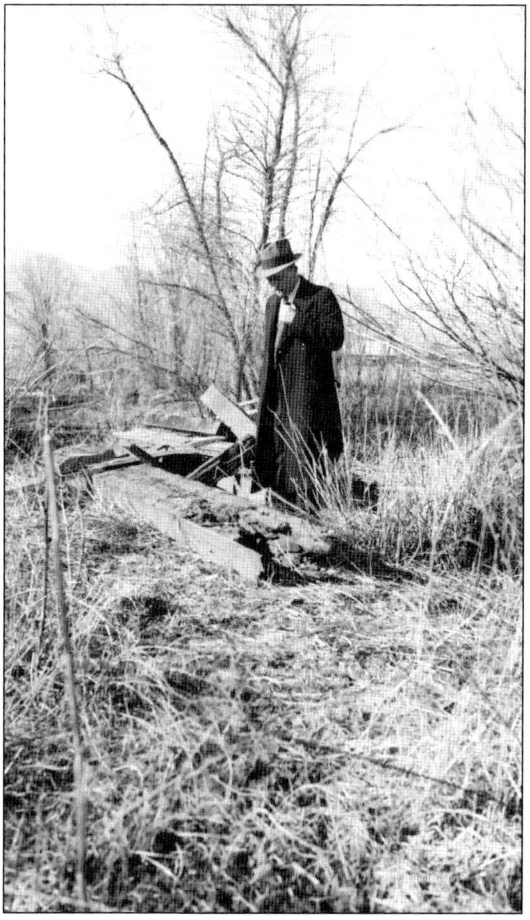

Not only were ties rotted, but bridge timbers needed to be replaced as well. To make matters worse, there were numerous places where the track was buried under several inches of dirt and mud. The worst sections of track were down by the Shasta River. In the photograph at right, new management looks over a pile of old rotted ties and bridge timbers. The piles of dirt, weeds, and mud along the track attest to the amount of debris that had covered it.

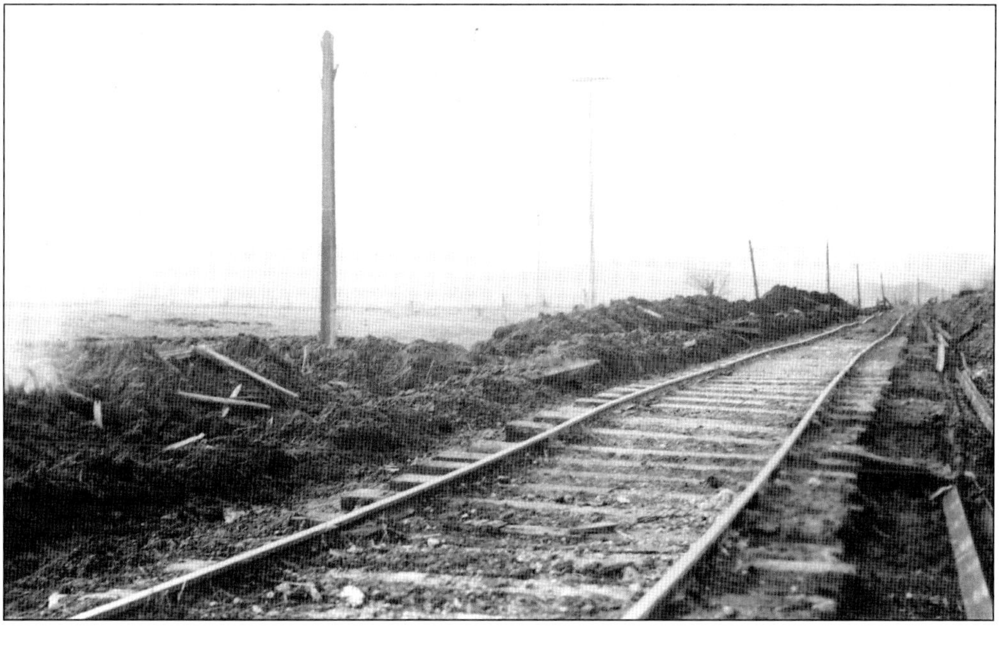

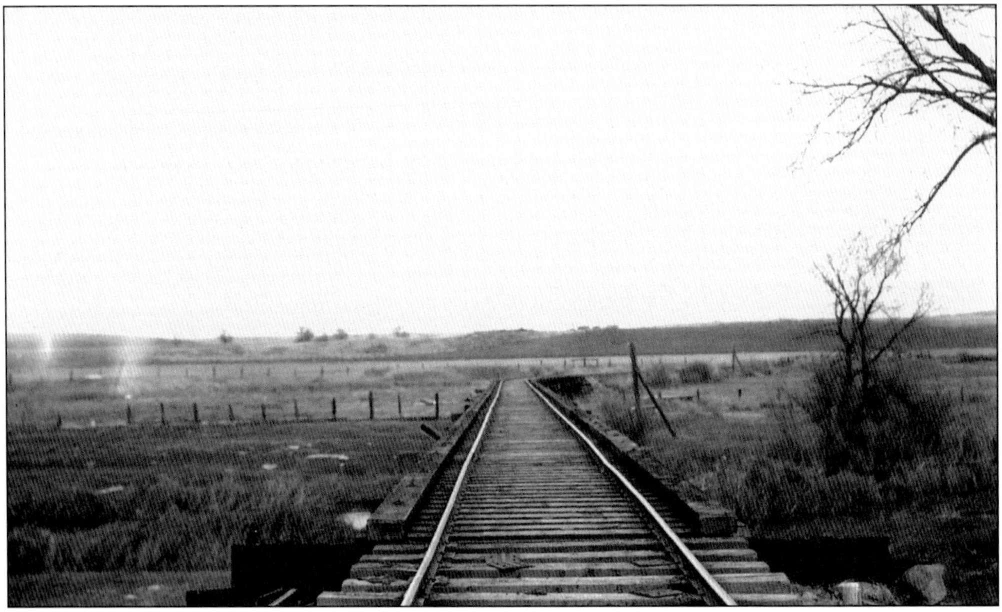

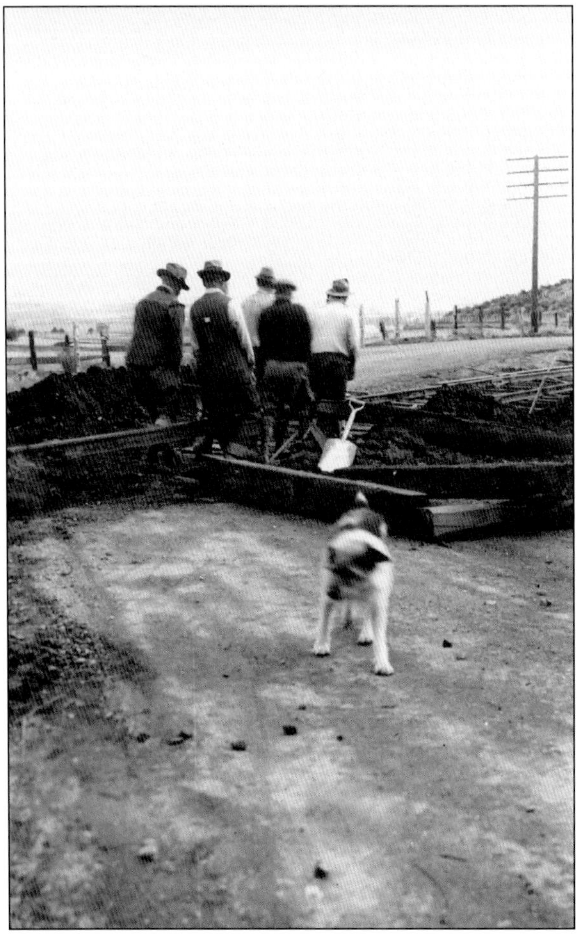

In March 1936, O. G. Steele applied to the ICC for $25,000 in receiver's certificates to improve the roadbed. The ICC granted the certificates, and Southern Pacific agreed to accept them and supply Yreka Western with new rails and ties. The railroad was relaid with secondhand, 75-pound rail and new ties with tie plates, and the buried sections were raised out of the dirt. The old dirt that was used for ballast was replaced with gravel, which helped to improve drainage. The photograph above shows new rail laid on the Shasta River Bridge, complete with new bridge timbers. Left, crews lay new rail at the railroad crossing for the old Yreka-Ager Road.

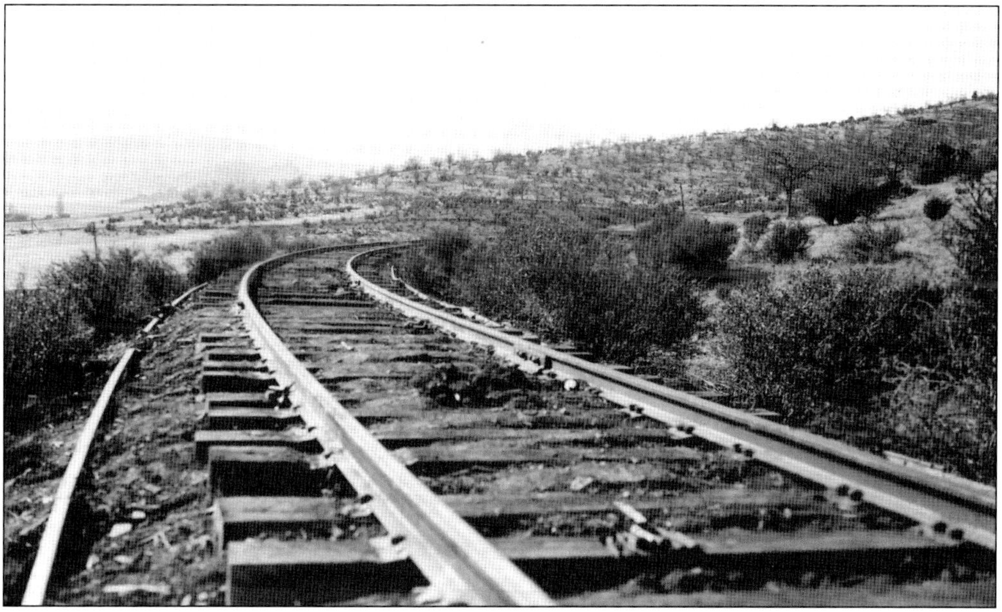

Here's a completed section of track on the east side of Butcher Hill, complete with fresh ties and newer, heavier rail. Note the old 40-pound rail lying on both sides of the roadbed.

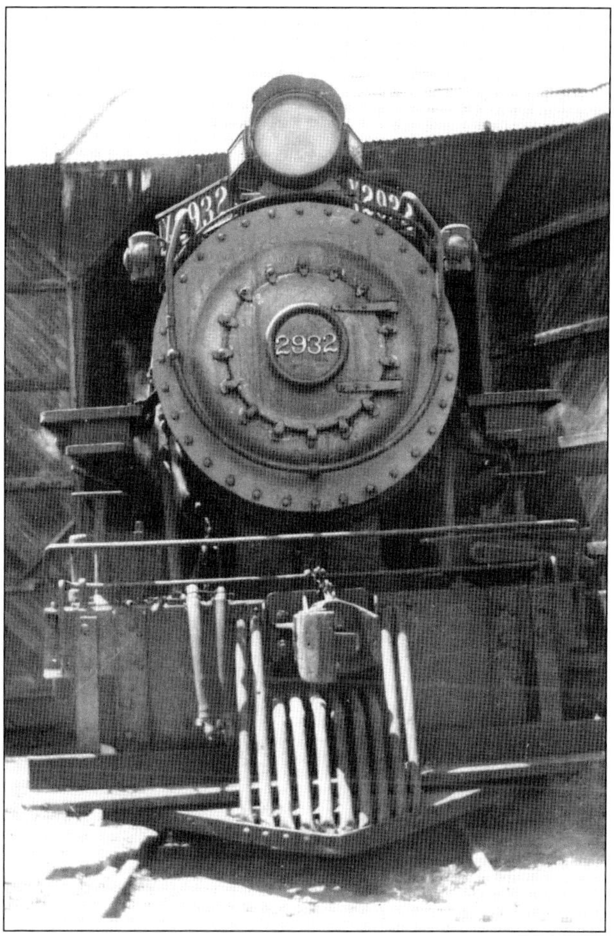

Beginning in 1929, Yreka Western started leasing locomotives from Southern Pacific. First to be leased was No. 2181 in 1931, followed by No. 2171 in 1932 and No. 2181 again in 1933. Yreka Western managed to get the No. 10 going again in 1933. By 1936, the railroad was back to leasing locomotives from Southern Pacific, with 10-wheeler No. 2178 and then 4-8-0 No. 2932 in 1937 up until 1938 when it was replaced with another 4-8-0, No. 2937. Here No. 2932 sits at the old four-stall roundhouse in Yreka.

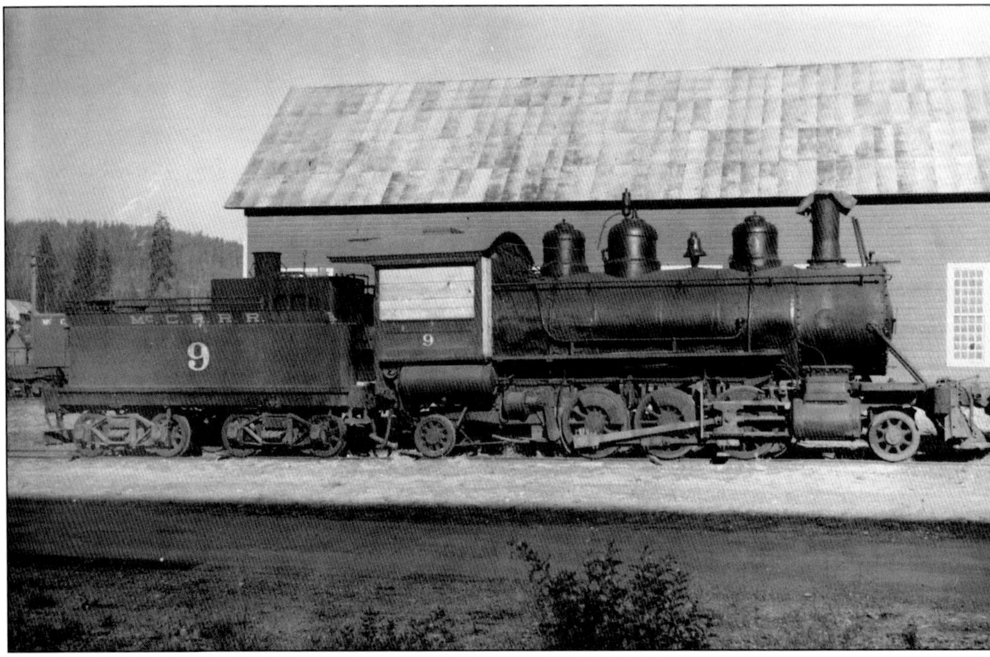

In 1939, Yreka Western again turned to the nearby McCloud River Railroad to purchase new power in an attempt to save money on fuel instead of using the leased locomotives from Southern Pacific. This time the railroad purchased No. 9, the sister engine to No. 10. The No. 9 had sat in the McCloud yard for almost a decade after becoming surplus when McCloud purchased newer power in the mid-1920s. Above, No. 9 sits stored in the McCloud yards a few years before being purchased. Below, No. 9 moves about the Yreka yard.

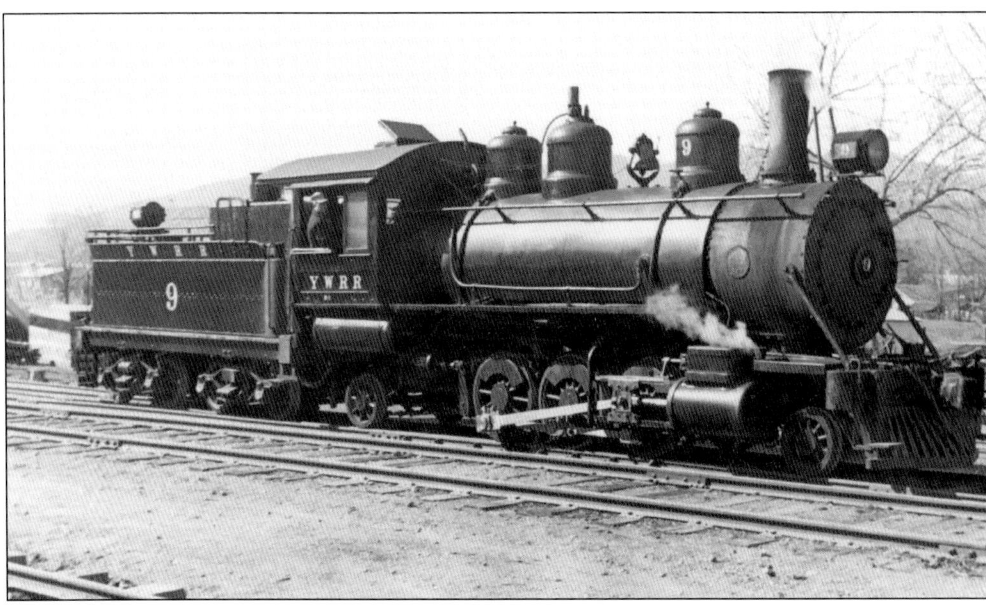

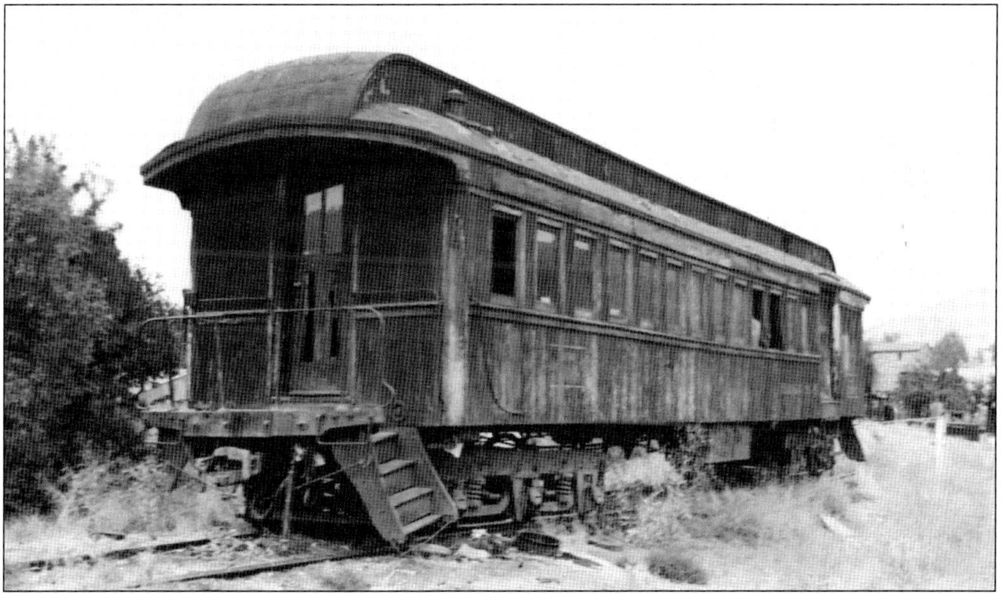

Both photographs on this page show the deteriorated condition of the railroad's two pieces of original passenger equipment. These cars have not been used in some time and spent the last part of their lives sitting on a spur track south of the depot until they were eventually scrapped in the 1940s.

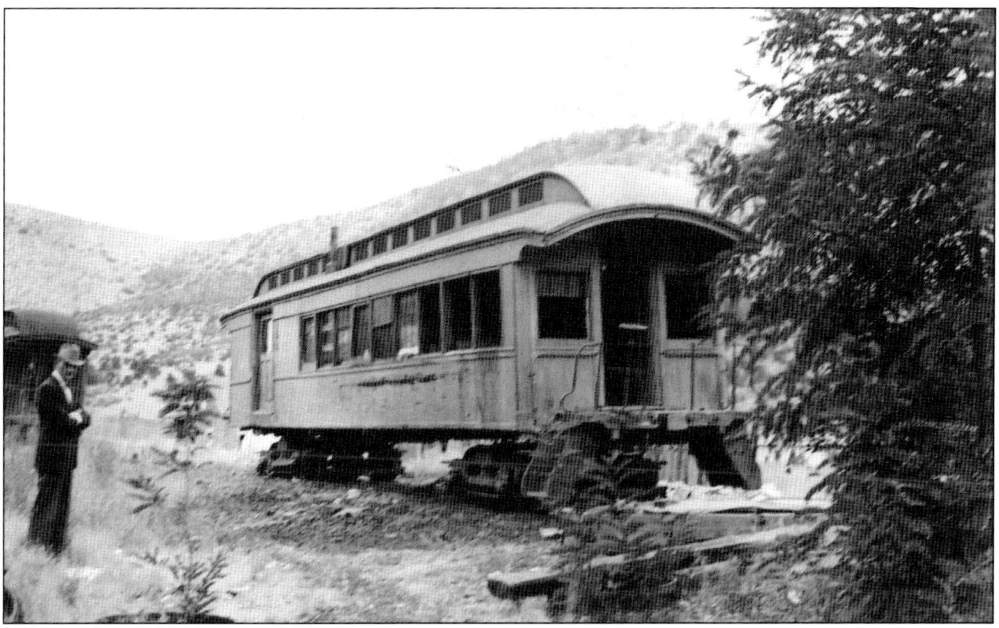

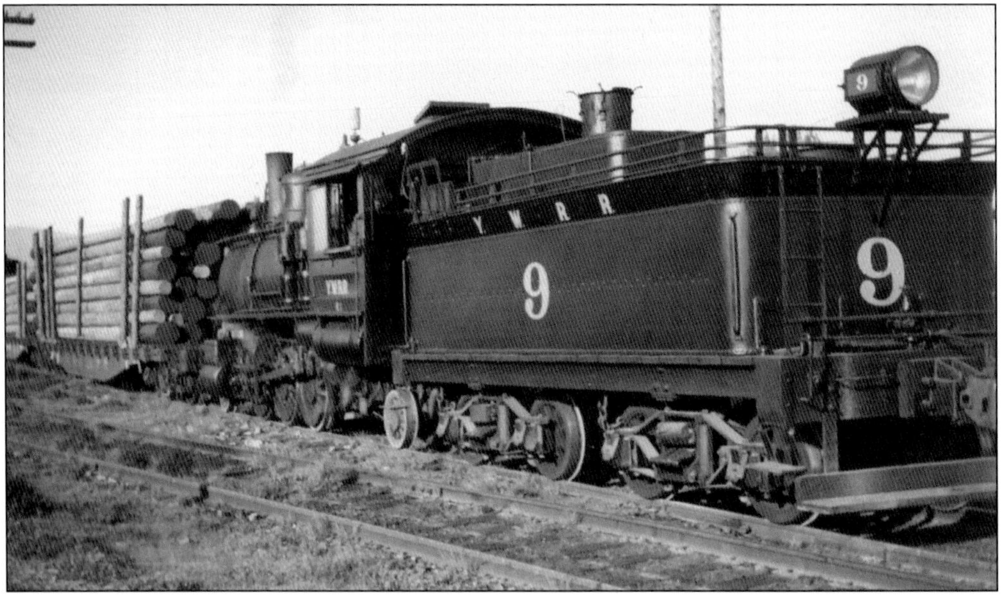

Above, No. 9 switches carloads of freshly made telephone poles in Yreka. No. 9 proved to be a very reliable freight locomotive and was well liked by the crews that ran her.

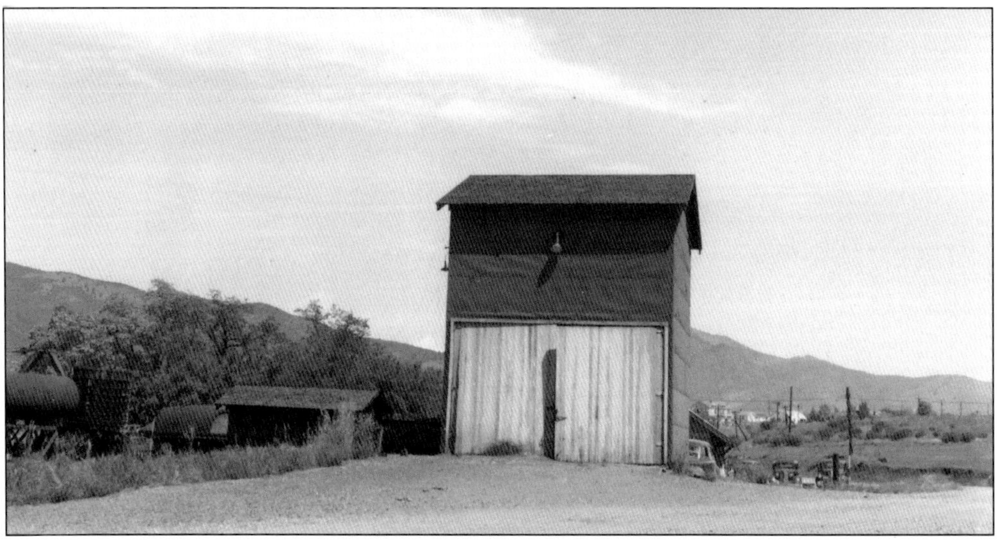

This truck-to-railcar facility was built in the 1940s to transfer ore concentrates brought in from mines in Happy Camp to railcars for their final destination.

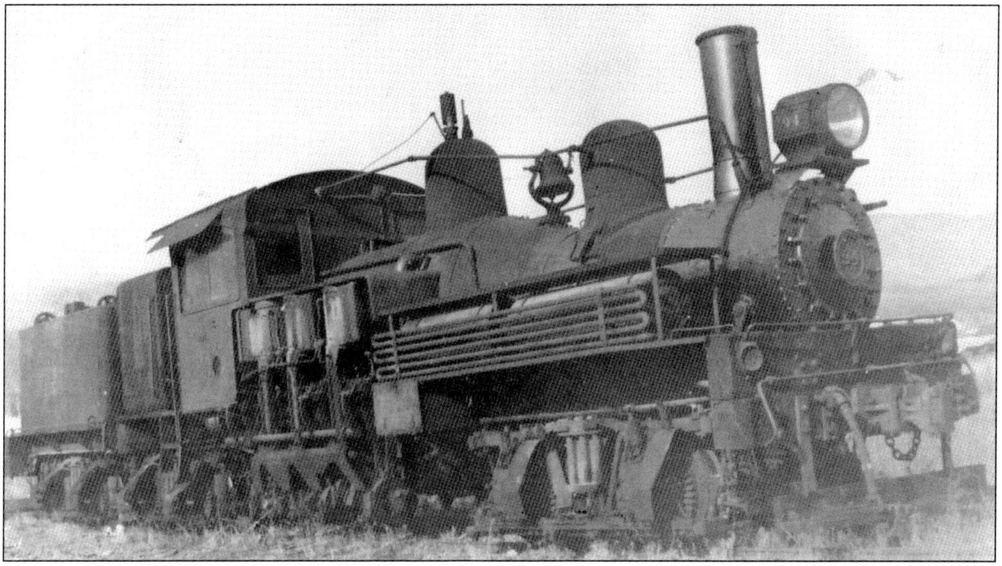

In 1943, Yreka Western purchased a three-truck Shay from Long-Bell Lumber Company's logging operation in Tennant, California, to assist No. 9 with the increased tonnage due to wartime traffic. The Shay was originally built in 1917 by Lima Locomotive Works as Builders No. 2943 for the Longville Lumber Company of Longville, Louisiana. The Shay did have drawbacks, however, it was expensive to maintain and was too slow, but it was enough to give some relief to No. 9.

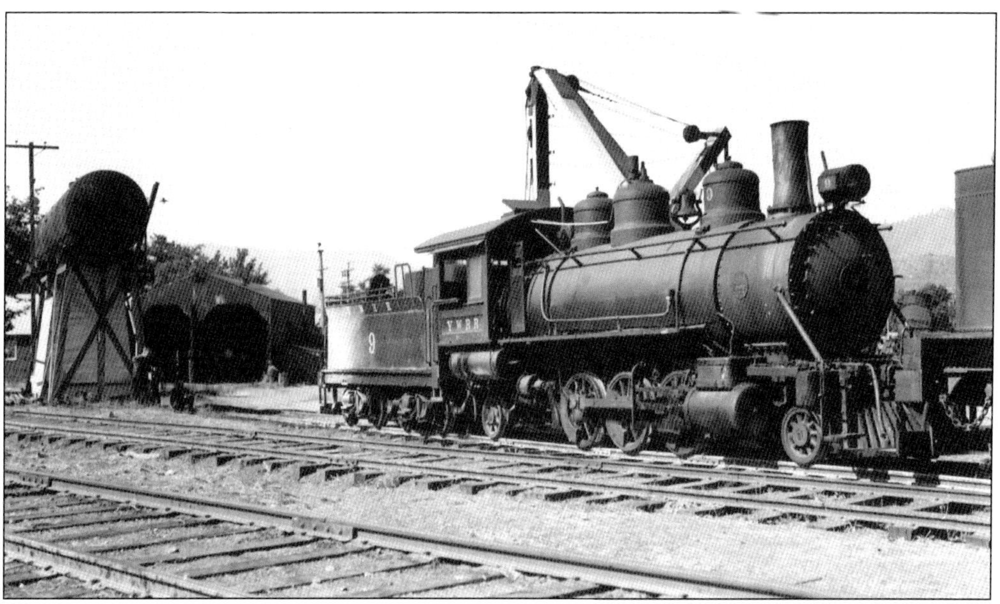

This view shows No. 9 on the shop lead in Yreka in 1943. At the very far right of the photograph is the back of No. 94's tender. The heavy tonnage being moved on the railroad was more than No. 9 could handle alone, thus, the Shay was brought in to help.

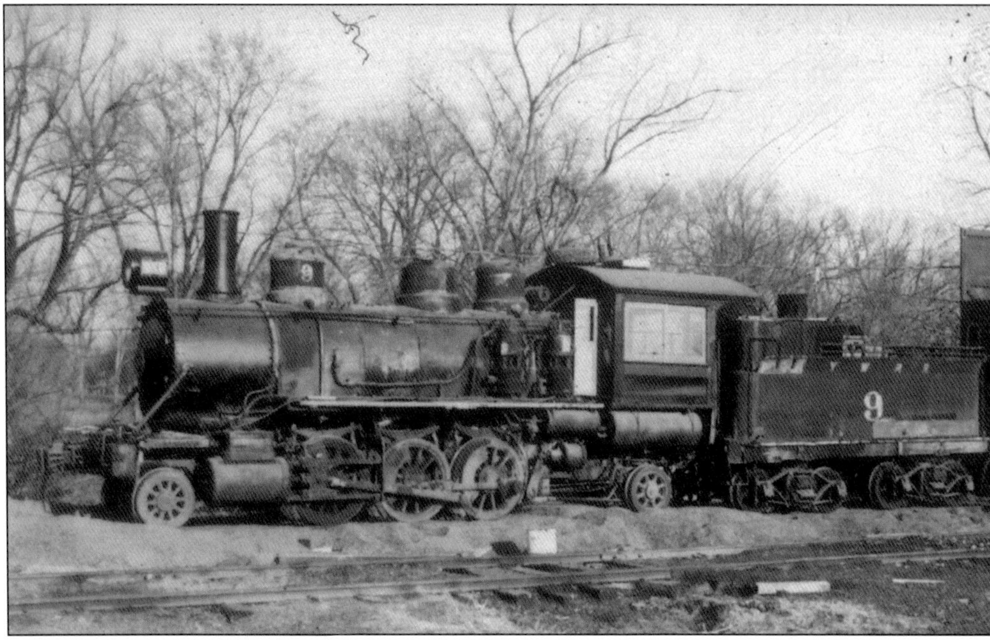

Both 2-6-2s on the property were disposed of after the arrival of Nos. 7 and 8. No. 10 was scrapped in Yreka, while No. 9 was sold to the Amador Central Railroad in Martell, California. Later it was sold to the Nez Pierce Railroad and then to the Kettle Moraine Railroad in Wisconsin where it operated until 2001, when the railroad was shut down. She now resides at the National Railway Museum in Green Bay, Wisconsin. (Courtesy Matt Starman.)

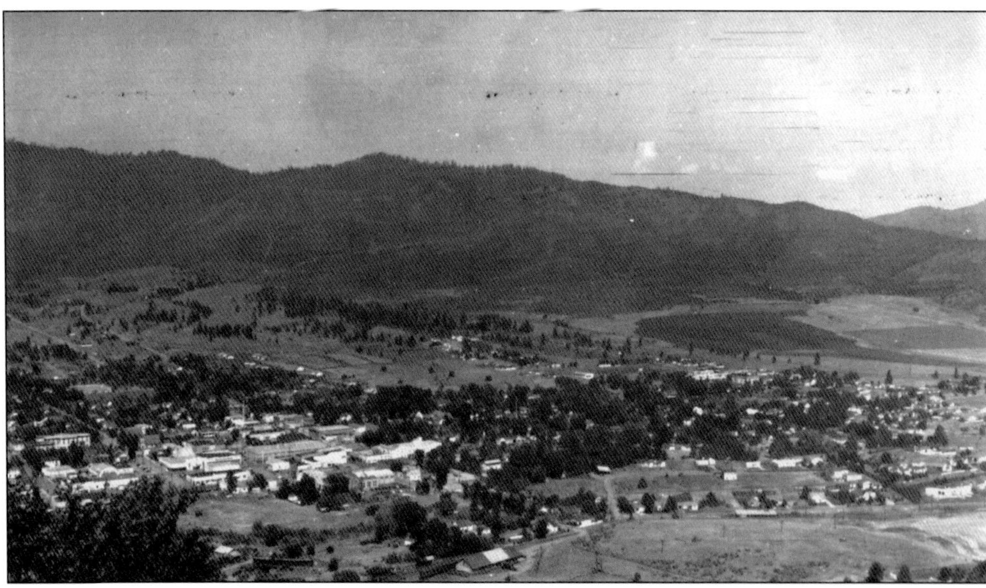

This view from the top of Butcher Hill shows the city of Yreka during the mid-1940s. The YW's depot can be seen at the bottom of the photograph.

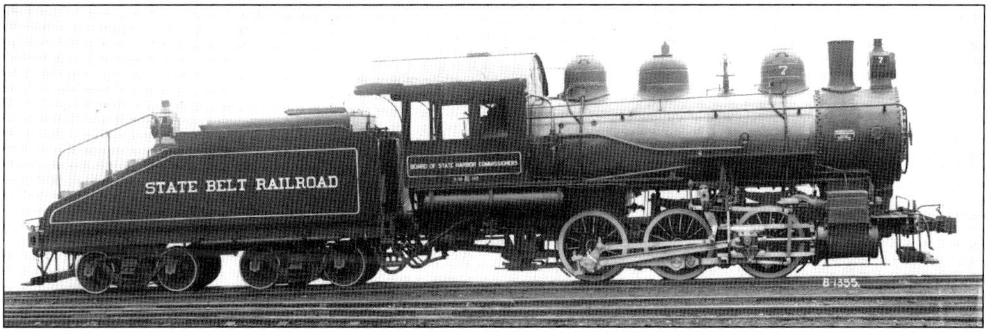

Shown above is a builder's photograph of No. 7. The American Locomotive Company built her in 1914 for the state Harbor Commissioners of San Francisco. No. 7 sported 51-inch drivers and had a tractive effort of 28,000 pounds. The image below shows No. 7, not long after she arrived in Yreka, sitting in front of the shop building.

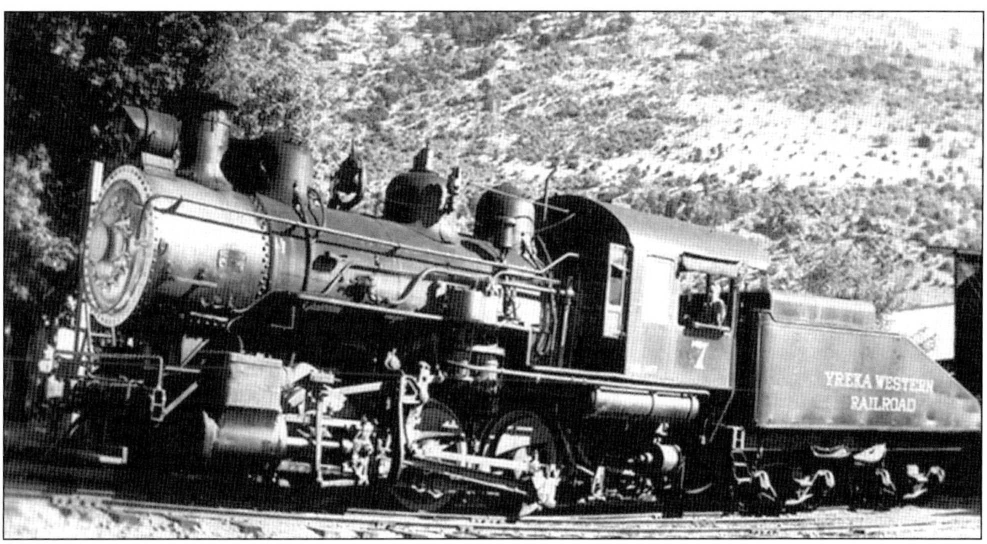

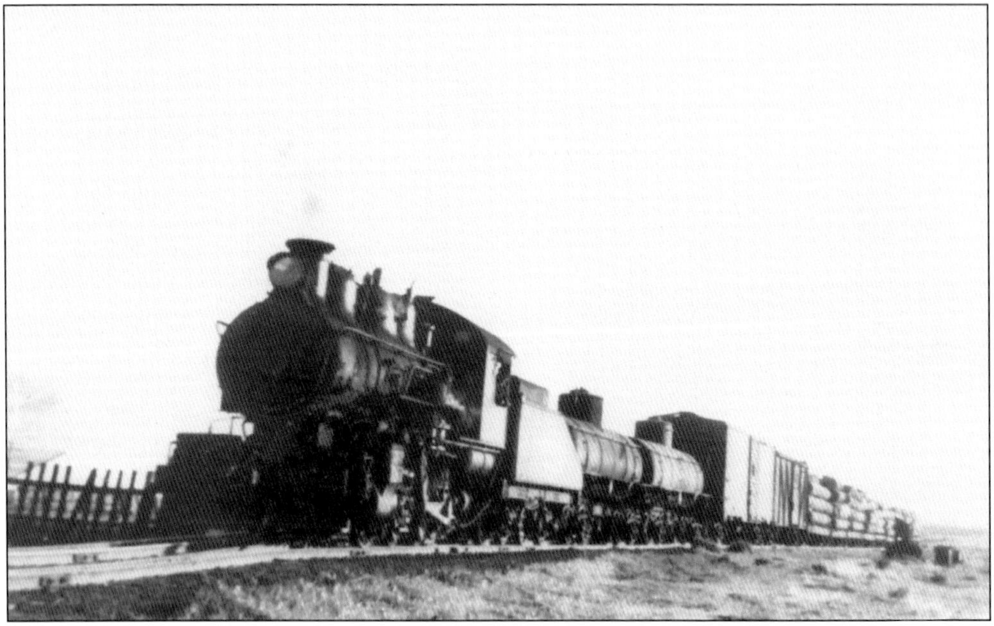

In this photograph, No. 8 is with a freight train rolling through the Shasta Valley, and below shows No. 8 on a different day with a different train approaching Montague. After arrival of the two new locomotives, the railroad was able to keep up with the ever-growing tonnage being hauled over the railroad almost daily.

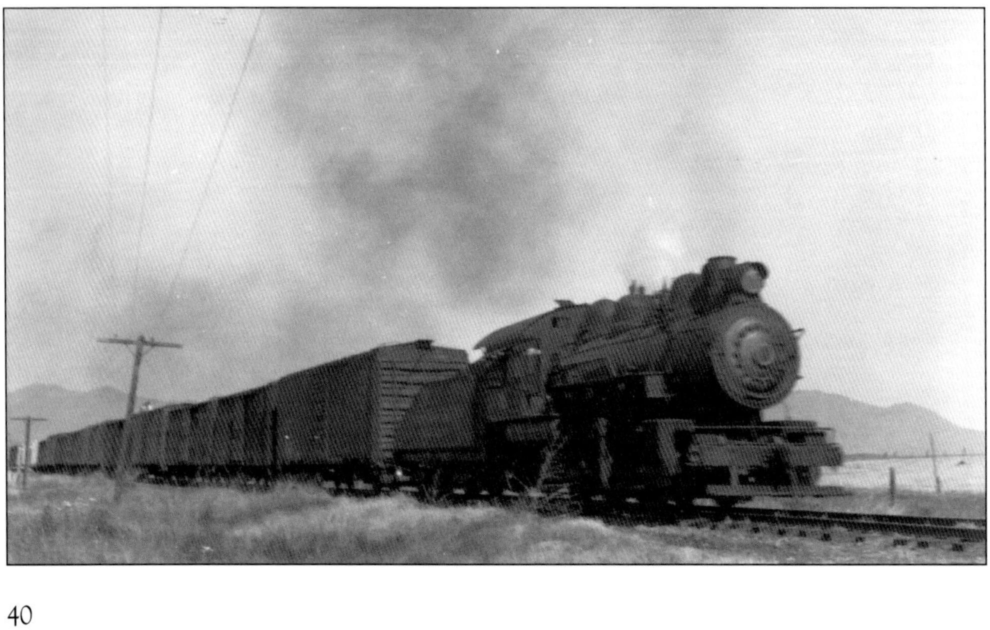

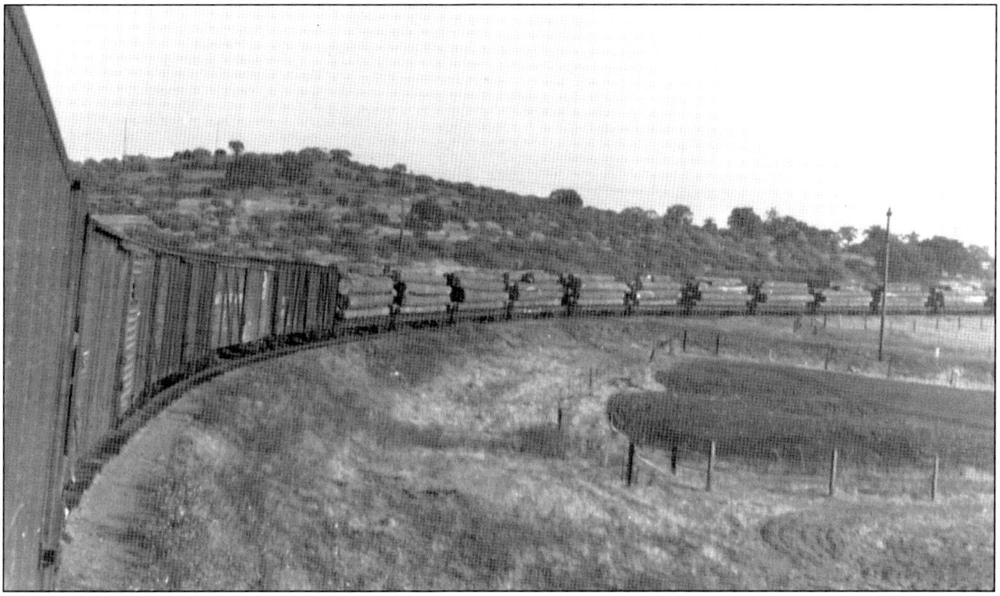
A typical sized Yreka Western freight train of the 1940s descends the grade of Butcher Hill. For several years, long trainloads of logs left Yreka due to the continuing business of the Fruit Growers Association's log reload in Yreka.

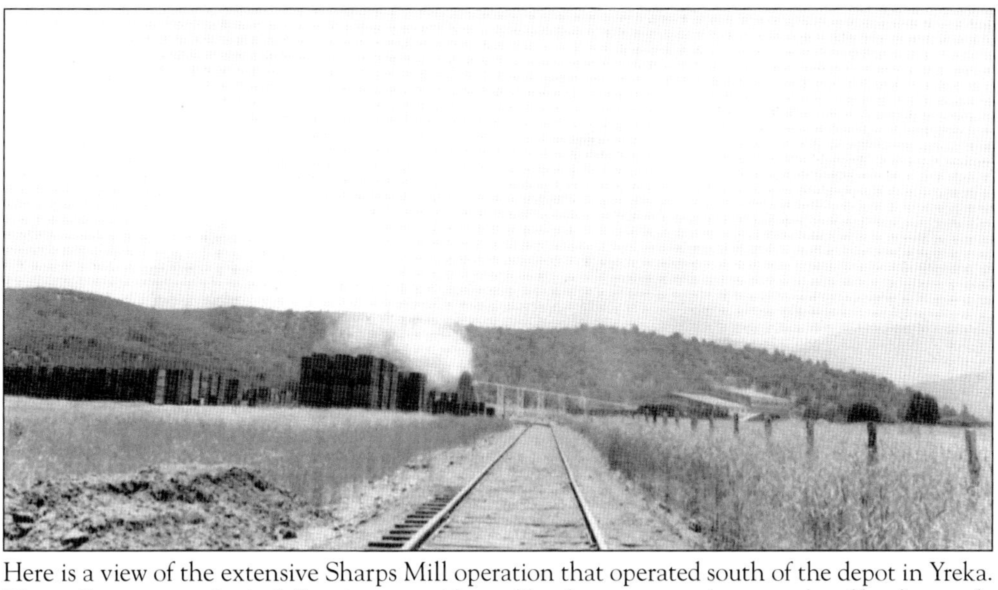
Here is a view of the extensive Sharps Mill operation that operated south of the depot in Yreka. The mill appears to be in full swing, as evidenced by the numerous large stacks of lumber ready to be shipped out and the sawdust burner creating a great deal of smoke.

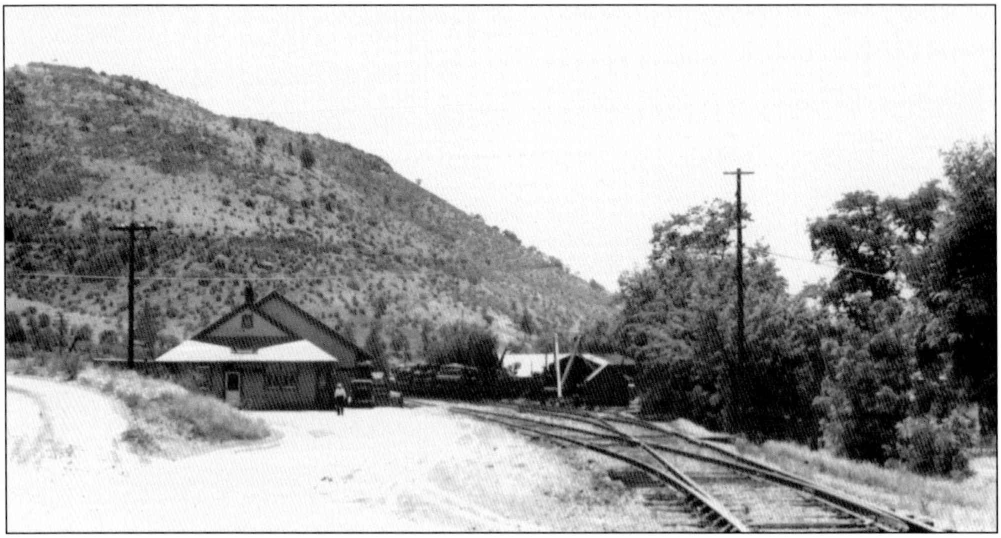

The photograph above shows the overall layout of the Yreka yards in the 1940s. A loaded log train sits in the yard waiting for the run over the hill to Montague. To the right, the water tower, shop facilities, crane, and maintenance-of-way shed are also visible. Below shows a boxcar converted into a maintenance-of-way storage shed in the yard.

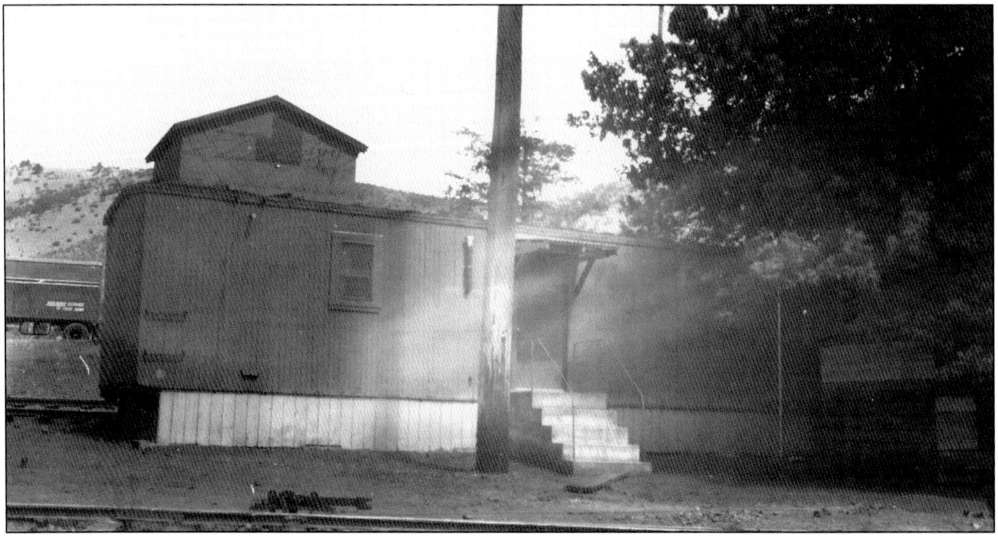

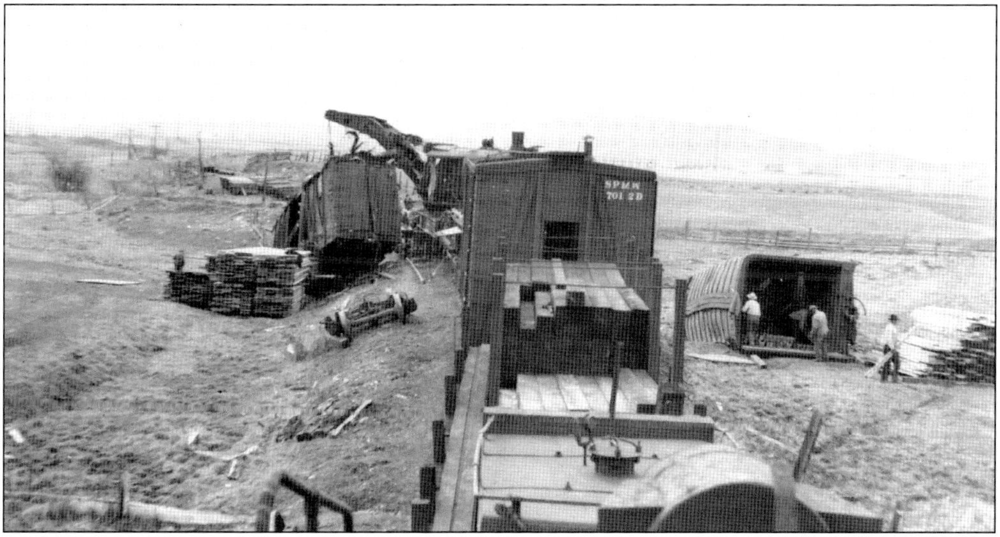

In April 1948, a bit of a mishap occurred near the Shasta River. An eastbound freight train pulled by No. 7 derailed, making quite a mess. A steam crane was borrowed from Southern Pacific (SP) to aid in cleaning up the spilled freight cars. Below, the SP crane lifts a boxcar back onto the rails. No. 7 can be seen in the far right of the photograph. Even though the track was fairly new, a mistake can still cause the inevitable derailment.

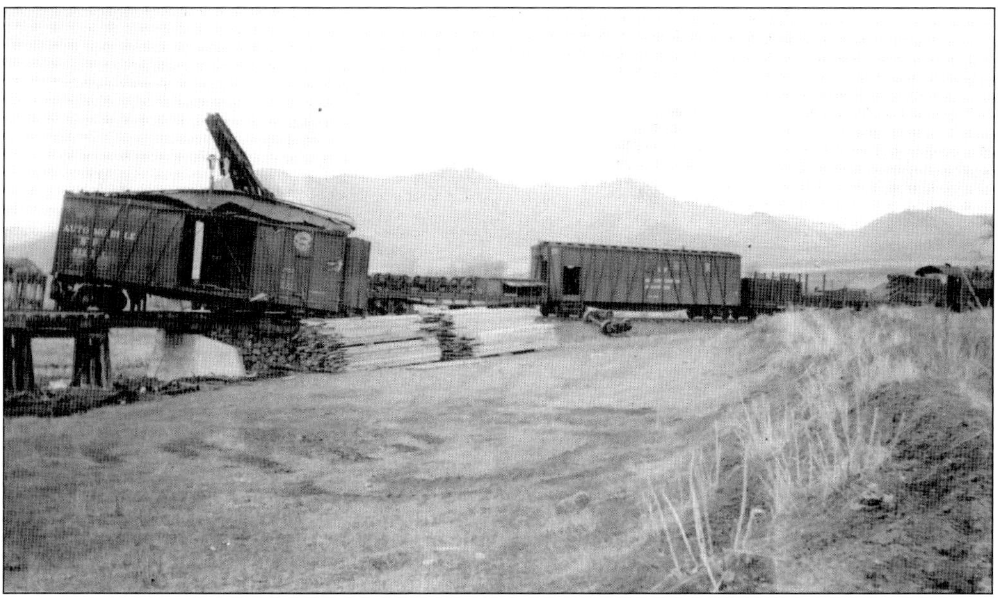

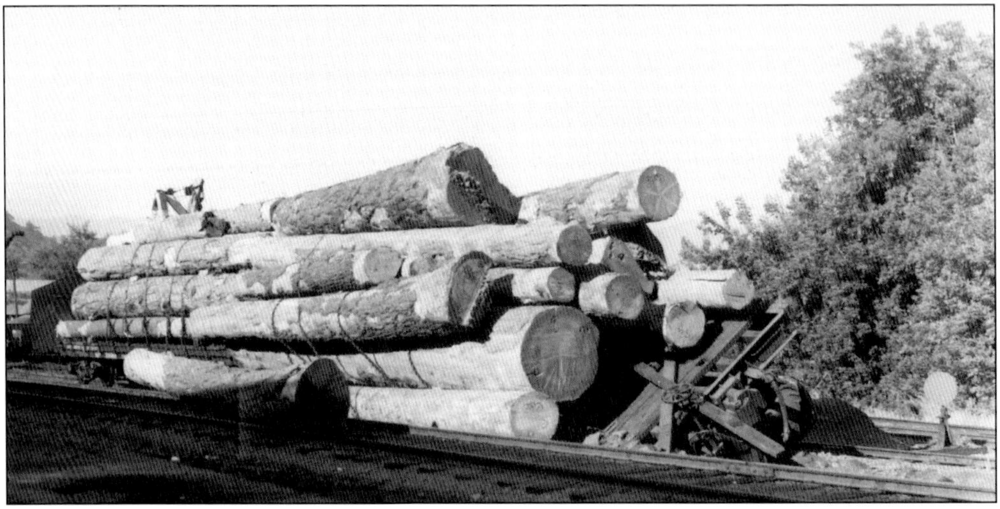

In the summer of 1951, a Fruit Growers Supply log train has run into a bit of trouble in the Yreka yard. One of the loaded log cars has tipped over and spilled its load of logs on the adjoining mainline. Below, the heavy logs knocked the rails on the mainline out of alignment and damaged other track parts.

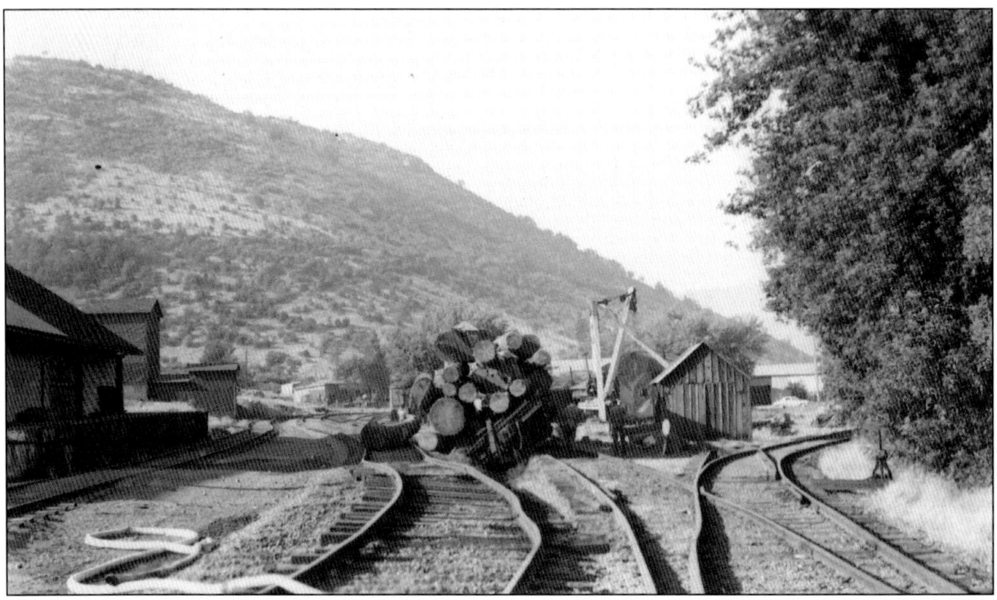

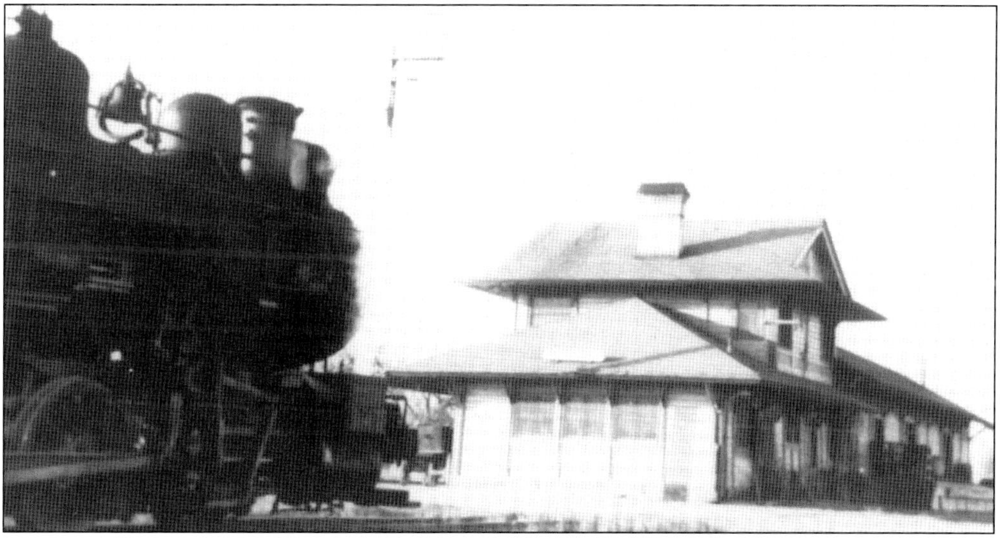

No. 7 switches in front of the depot in Montague. Long, heavy trains were being brought to the Southern Pacific interchange on a very frequent basis, keeping the railroad healthy and the locomotives and their crews busy.

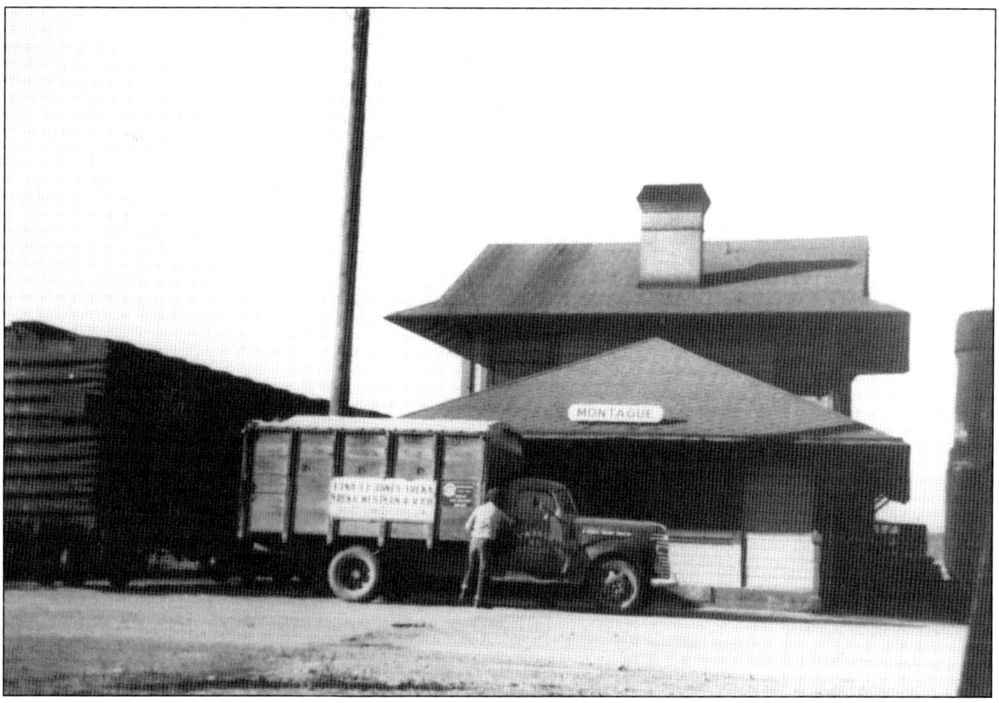

Yreka Western freight is loaded onto a truck for delivery to the mountain towns of Fort Jones and Etna. While the railroad was never able to extend to these towns, the truck line was able to connect by highway and create more freight traffic for the railroad.

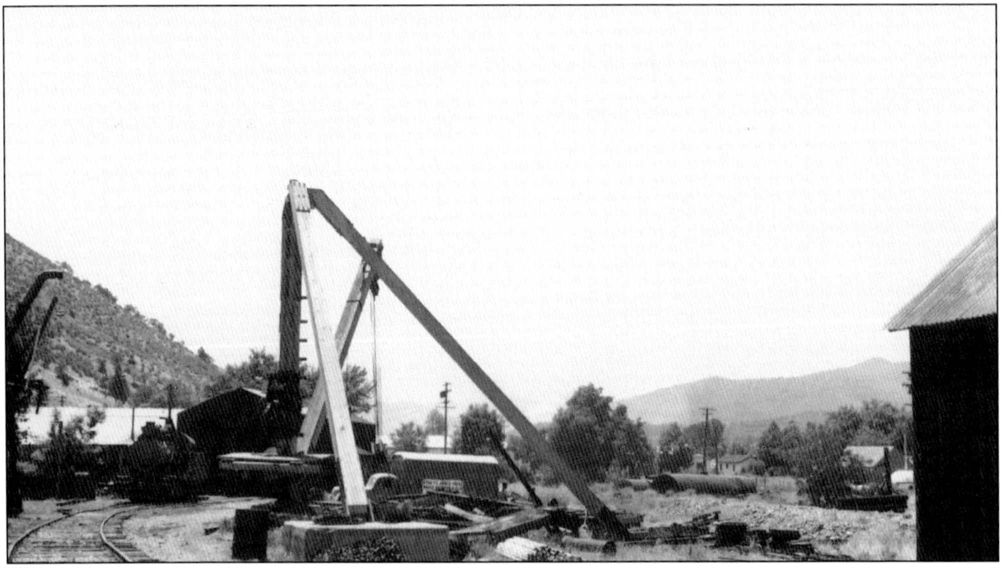

A 1940s view of the Yreka yard shows No. 8 resting in front of the shop building. Also visible to the right is another one of Yreka Western's freight trucks. The crane in the middle of the photograph was used to load and unload cargo from trucks to railcars. It still stands in the yard to this day.

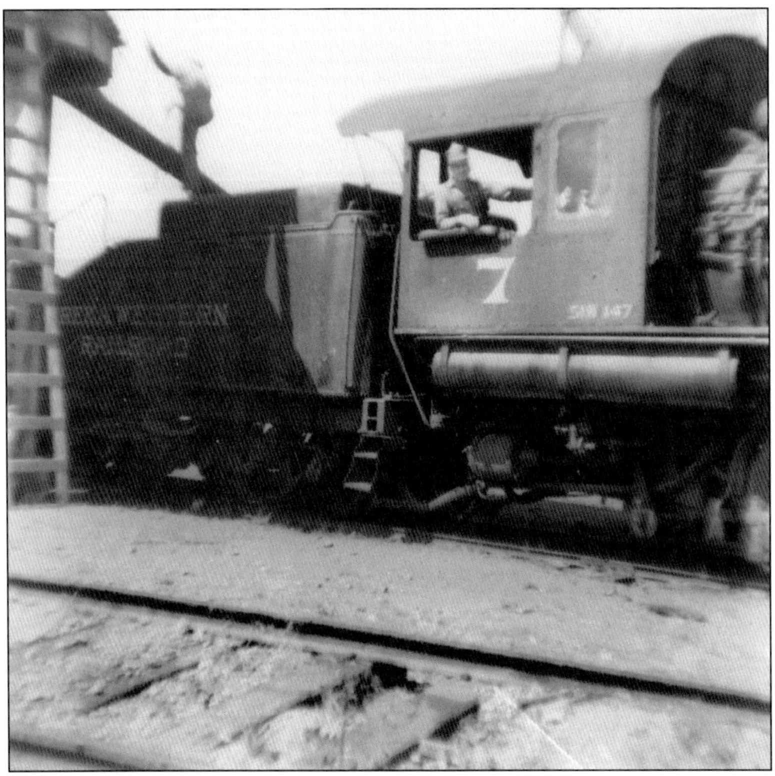

No. 7 takes on water in Yreka in the mid-1940s before heading out for the day's work. While the fireman fills the tender with water, the engineer strikes a classic railroad pose for the photographer.

Three

A Siskiyou Short Line

Economically, World War II and the postwar years were a growing time for Yreka Western. The increase in tonnage moved over the railroad resulted in the YW making a large profit. With this capital, Steele was able to pay off all of the debts, and the railroad was beginning to show a consistent profit from its outbound tonnage. The Siskiyou County Superior Court agreed that Yreka Western's finances were now stable and that it was operating on an adequate basis. The receivership was terminated on September 30, 1948. Steele continued to act as the railroad's vice president and chief operating officer, while A. D. Schader, owner of the railroad, continued to act as president.

Throughout the years, tonnage had increased to the point where all trains had to double the hill at the grade near Shasta River and Butcher Hill. The YW again turned to the McCloud River for new motive power. Steele had originally purchased Long Bell Lumber Company No. 100 in 1953, but the deal fell through and instead 2-8-2 Mikado No. 19 was purchased and arrived at the railroad in 1953. Also at this point, No. 7 was put up for sale. Eventually, No. 100 was acquired but was determined to be too costly for repair, so it was sold for scrap in 1955. McCloud River No. 18 was purchased and arrived in 1956. After the arrival of the two new locomotives, Nos. 7 and 8 were sold for scrap. Additionally in 1956, the Yreka Western came under new ownership. Willis B. Kyle purchased the railroad. Kyle did not plan the purchase, he happened to be in the bank on the day that the railroad was auctioned off as part of an estate sale after A. D. Schader had passed away in 1954. Kyle put in a bid for $140,000, however it was rejected for being too low. But one week later he received a call from the bank to negotiate. The final price was set at $141,000 and exceeded an offer by a local junk dealer whose intention was to scrap the railroad. The ICC approved the ownership change, and Kyle found himself in the railroad business. As Kyle wasn't a resident of Yreka, he left the daily operation of the railroad to Steele until he retired in 1957. Steele's successor was Lynn T. Cecil, who had gained experience with the Apache Railroad. Kyle knew that no railroad could survive without on-line shippers, and one his first moves was buy 600 acres of land next to the railroad and offer it free of charge to any lumber company or other manufacturer that would use the railroad to ship its products. In just five short years, the YW had six new customers and was again operating in the black. Additionally in 1957, the railroad decided to enlarge its existing trucking business by purchasing the Klamath River Freight Line. Eventually an application was filed with the California PUC asking for a common carrier permit for the entire state of California. The application was approved, and Yreka Western was given a statewide trucking permit.

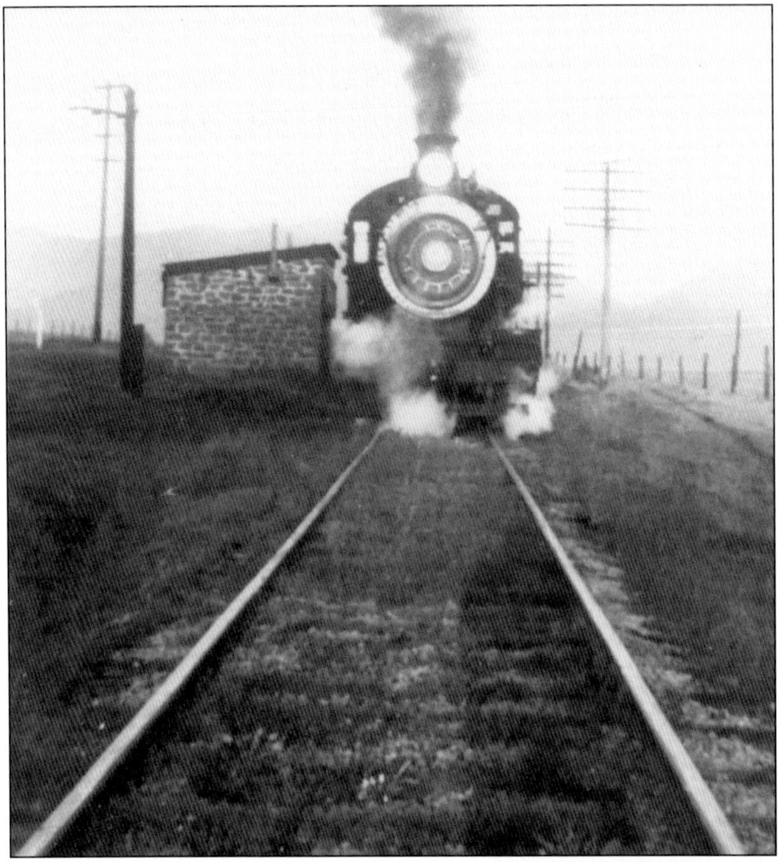

No. 8 leads a train up Butcher Hill and past one of the abandoned powder houses that existed there.

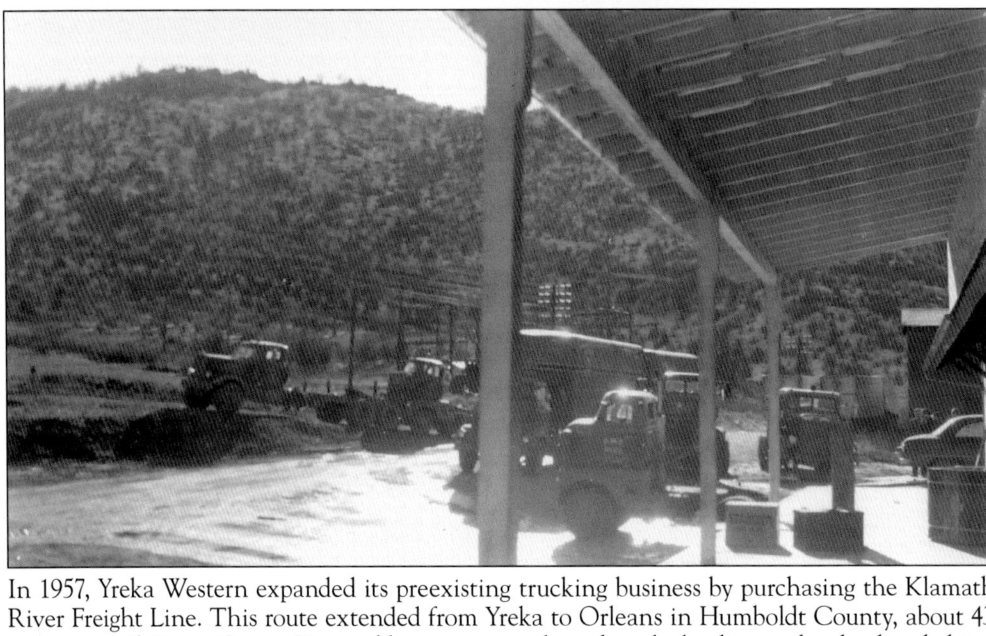

In 1957, Yreka Western expanded its preexisting trucking business by purchasing the Klamath River Freight Line. This route extended from Yreka to Orleans in Humboldt County, about 43 miles west of Happy Camp. Pictured here are a number of trucks loading and unloading behind the depot.

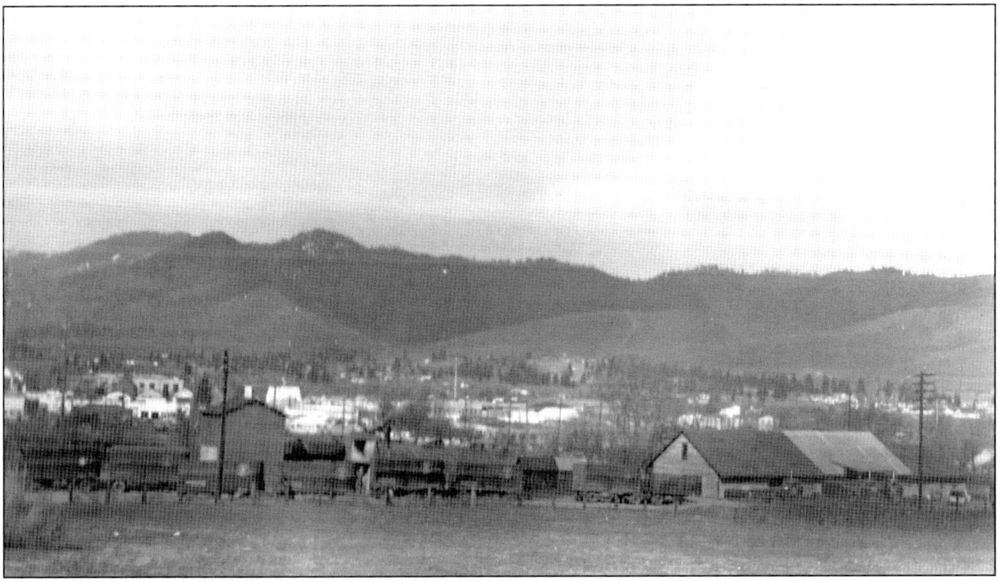

A view from on top of the hill shows the depot, as well as a good number of trucks in the loading docks.

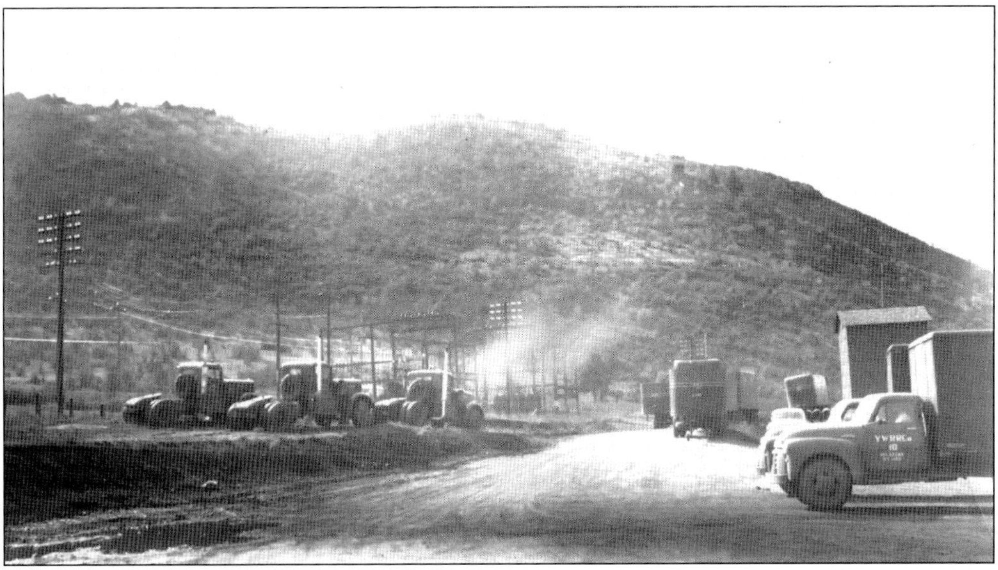

By the 1960s, Yreka Western's trucking line was still expanding. Here, just a small portion of the railroad's truck fleet is visible in this early 1960s view.

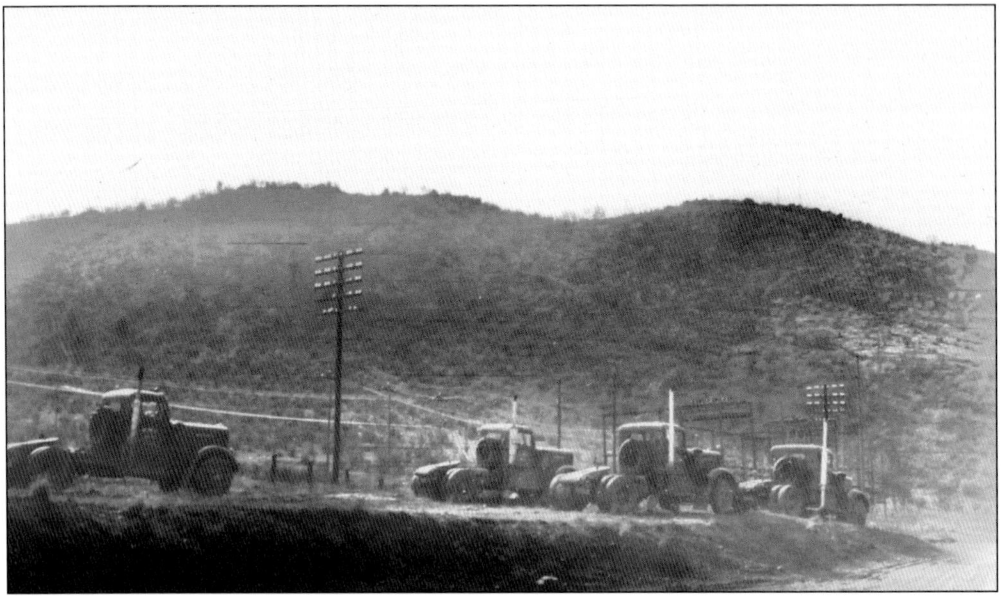

This shot shows some the trucks that ran out of Yreka for the Yreka Western. The trucks were leased from Pacific Motor Transport, which was a subsidiary of the Southern Pacific.

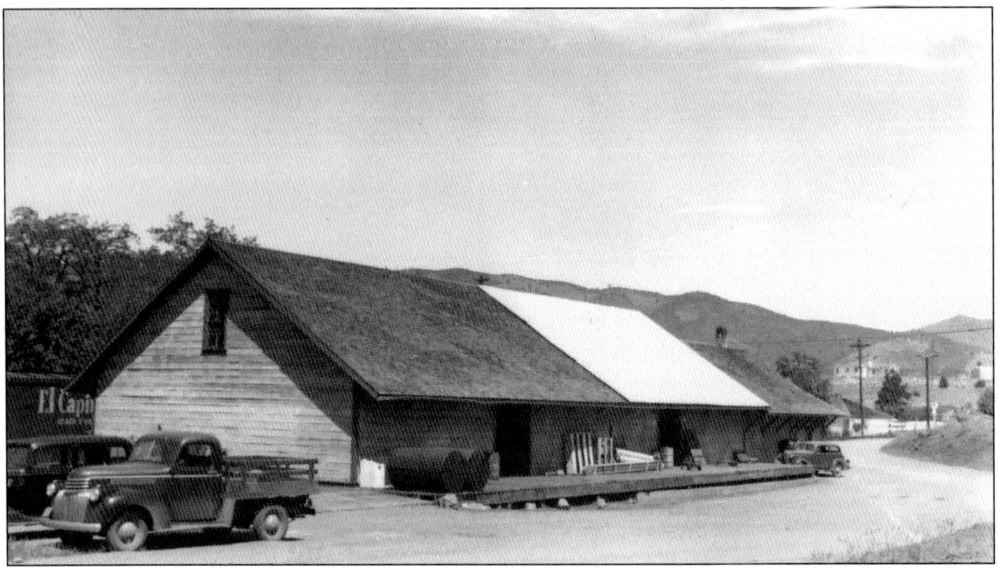

This postwar shot shows some of the merchandise being moved out of the depot. Much of the items moved were less-than-carload freight, but an occasional flatcar of tractors and farm equipment would be unloaded here.

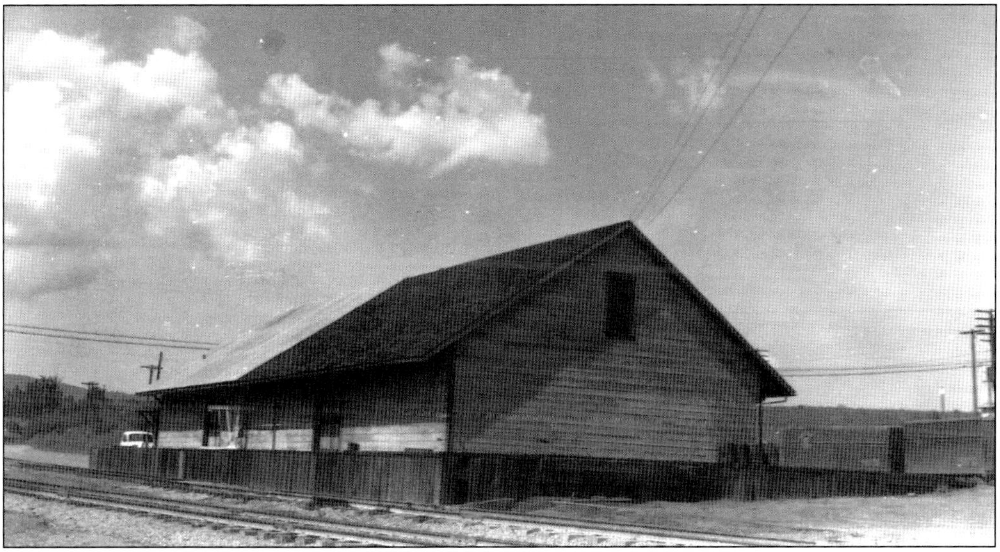

This is a view of the front of the Yreka depot as it appeared in the 1950s. Also visible behind the depot is more of the truck fleet owned by the railroad.

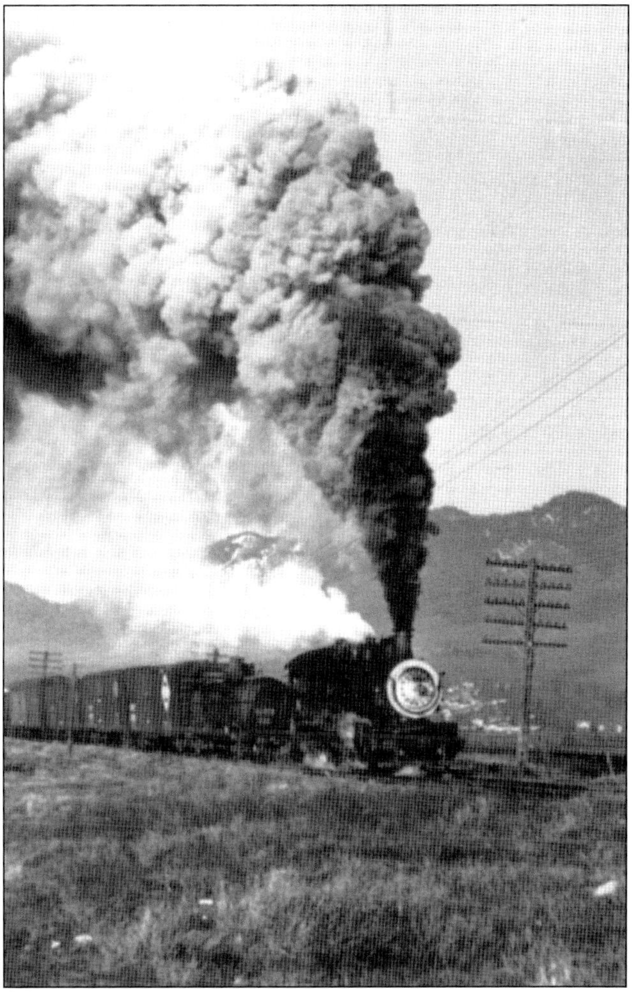

No. 8 charges up the grade, leaving Yreka with a full train in tow. With steep grades and heavy trains, the 0-6-0s really had their work cut out for them.

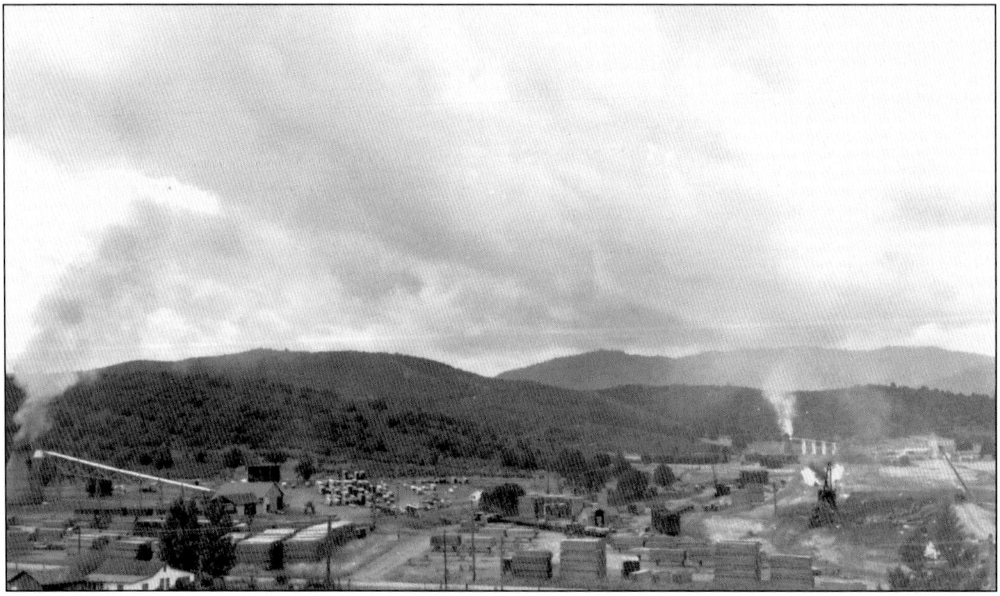

Postwar Yreka once had 13 mills operating in the area, with 7 of them being served by the Yreka Western. The two photographs here show the Oberlin and Sharps Roads area of Yreka where a majority of these mills were. Fruit Growers Supply's log reload can be seen on the left side of the picture below.

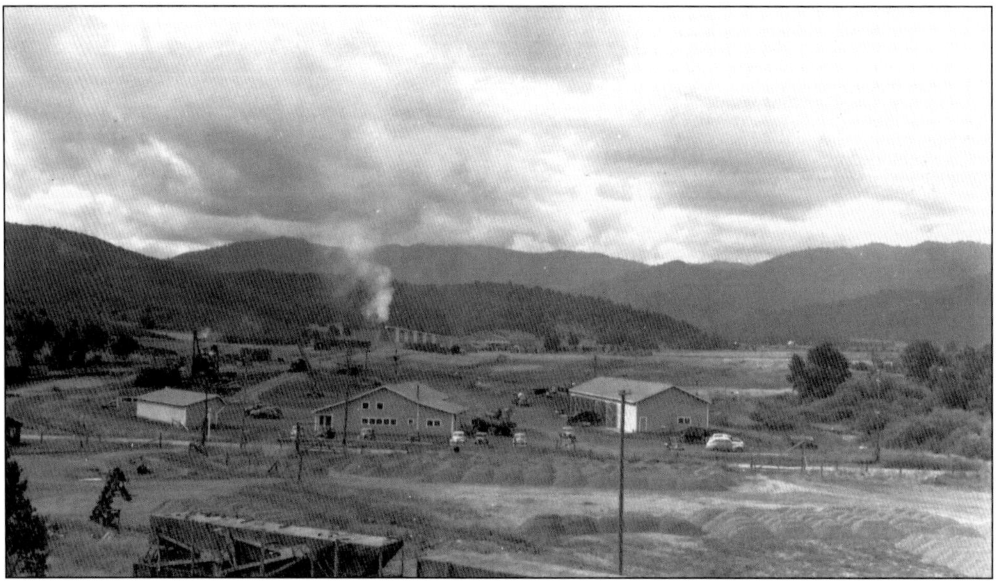

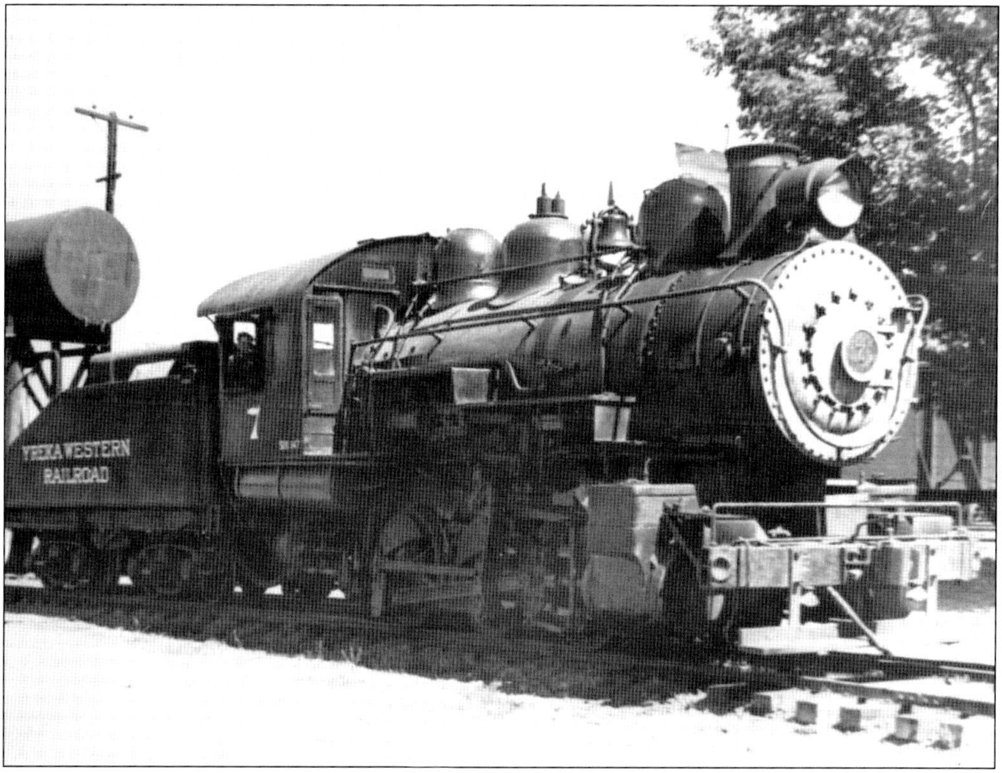

No. 7 poses for a photograph in the Yreka yards in the late 1940s. (Courtesy Jeff Moore.)

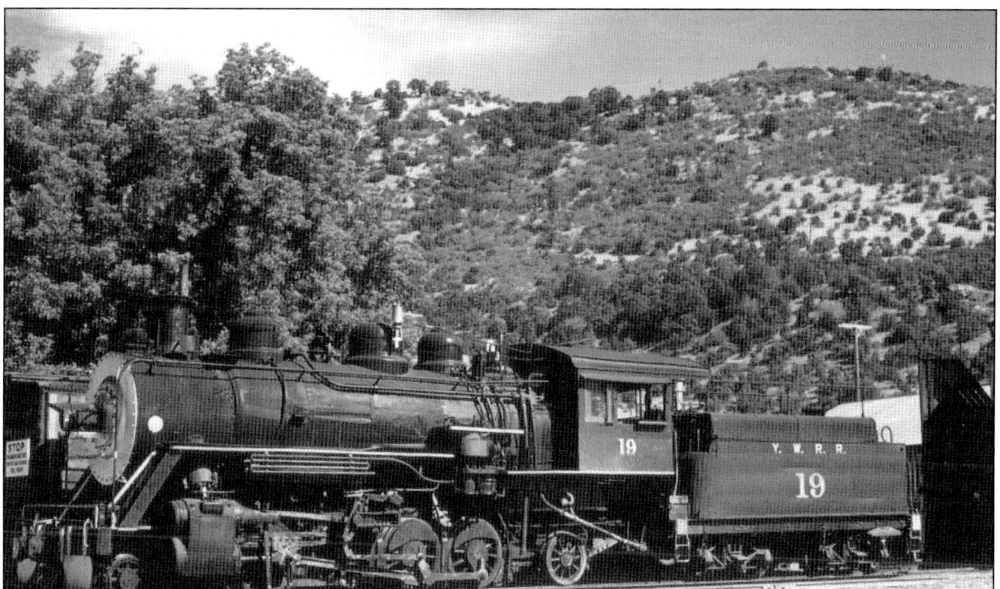

In 1953, the Yreka Western purchased No. 19 from the McCloud River Railroad. The tonnage being hauled by the railroad at the time was becoming too much for the 0-6-0s, and heavier power was needed.

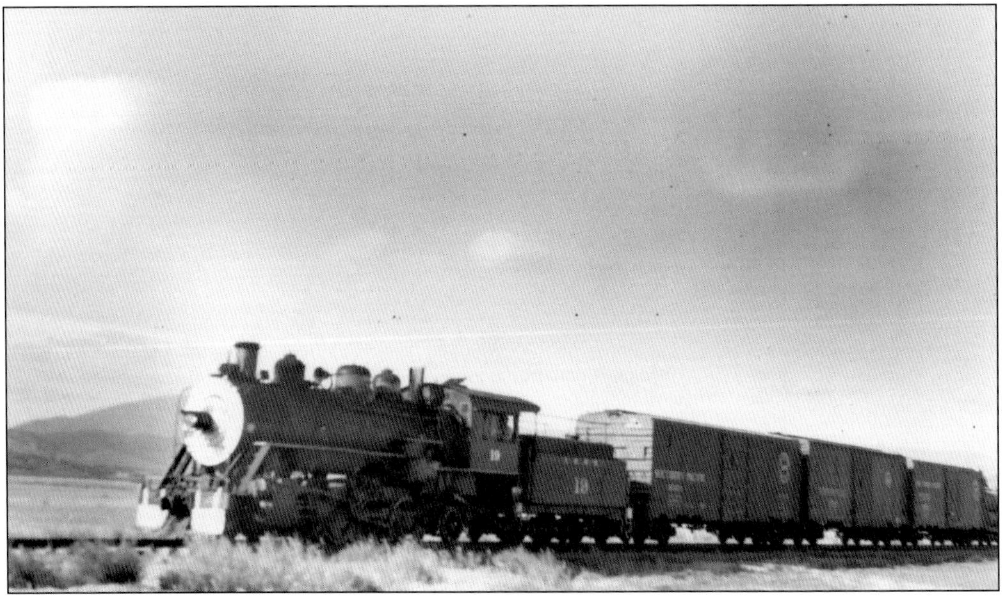

These two shots show No. 19 with the regular freight bound for Montague. An average train at this time typically consisted of loaded log cars and boxcars full of finished lumber.

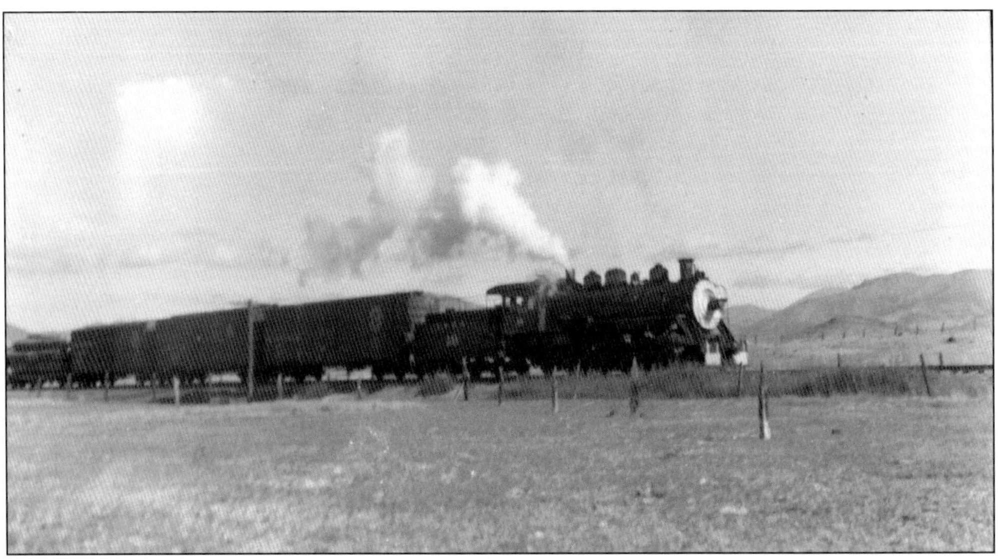

In August 1957, No. 19 pulls loaded cars that were just swapped out with the empty cars at the mills in the Oberlin Road area. No. 19 will then take the cars to Southern Pacific in Montague.

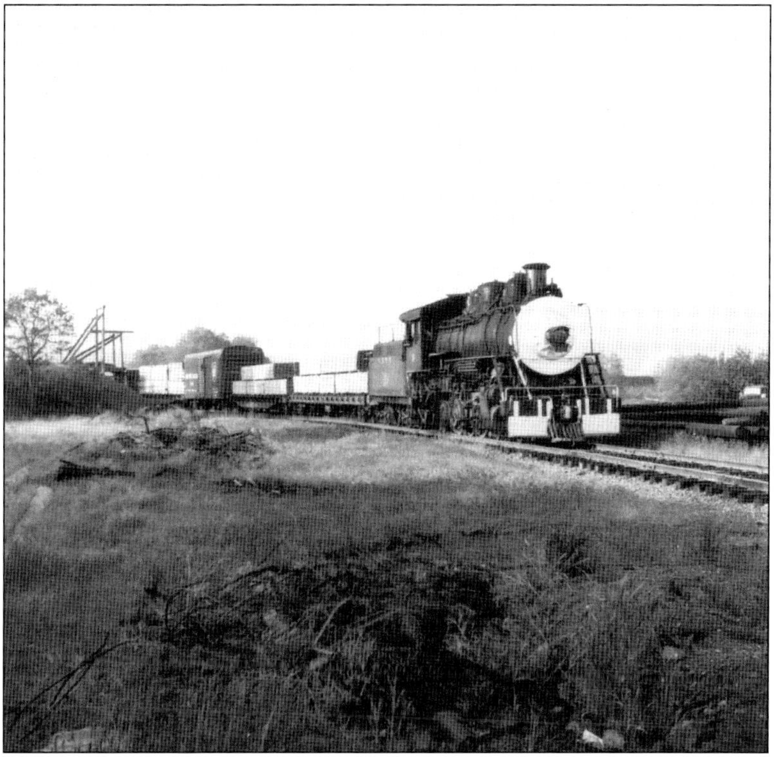

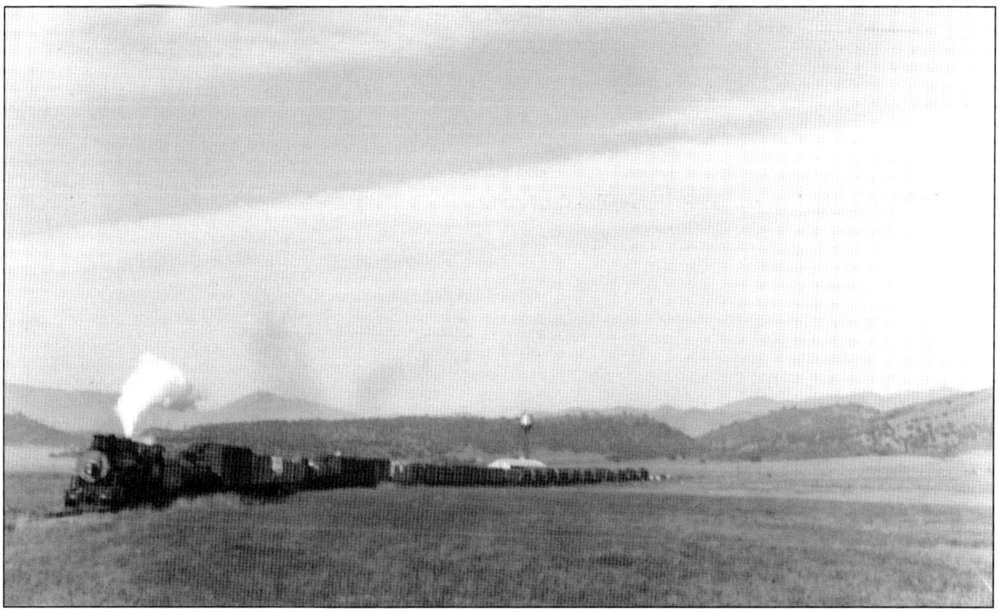

Here No. 19 is with freight, showing what typical train lengths were during the 1950s. There are 29 cars on this train, most of them with loads expect for the few tank cars, which were usually empty when outbound from the oil dealership in Yreka.

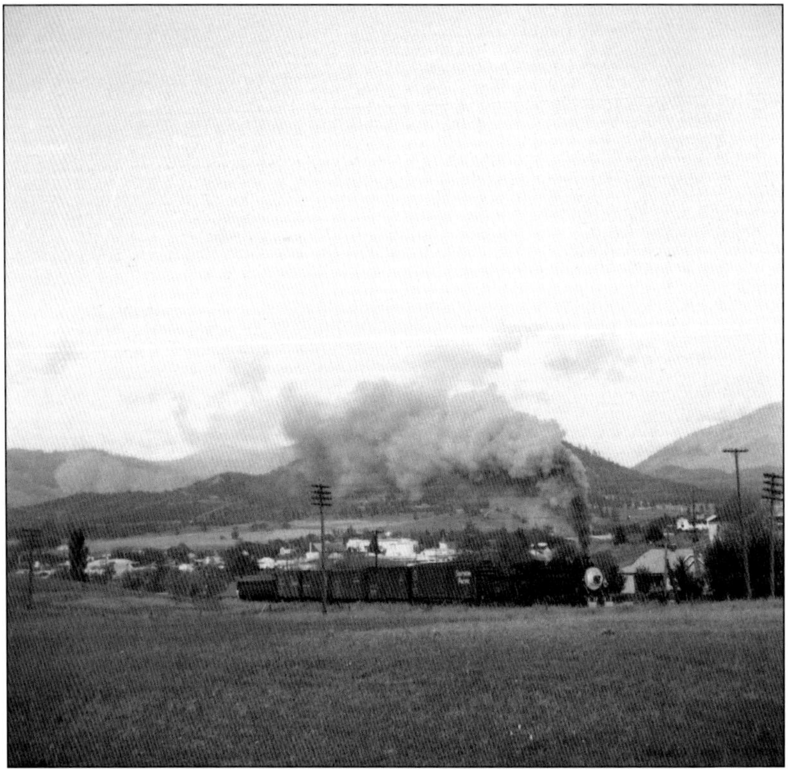

In August 1957, No. 19 is pulling a short train out of Yreka and up Butcher Hill, with a coach tacked onto the rear end. This was more than likely part of a railfan excursion. The Yreka Western hosted a number of these excursions throughout the 1950s and 1960s.

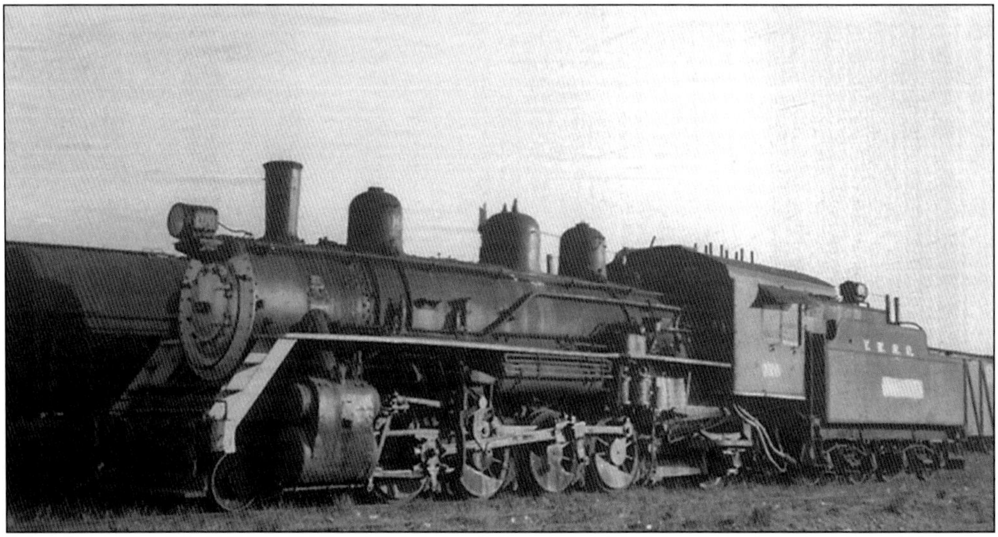

Pictured here is Yreka Western No. 100. This 2-8-2 Mikado was purchased from the Long Bell Lumber Company out of Tennant, California, in the spring of 1955. After arriving in Yreka, the railroad began repairs in the shop. It was soon determined that the repairs needed would be too extensive and not worth the time it would take. She was sent to the South San Francisco scrap yards in November 1955. (Courtesy Matt Starman.)

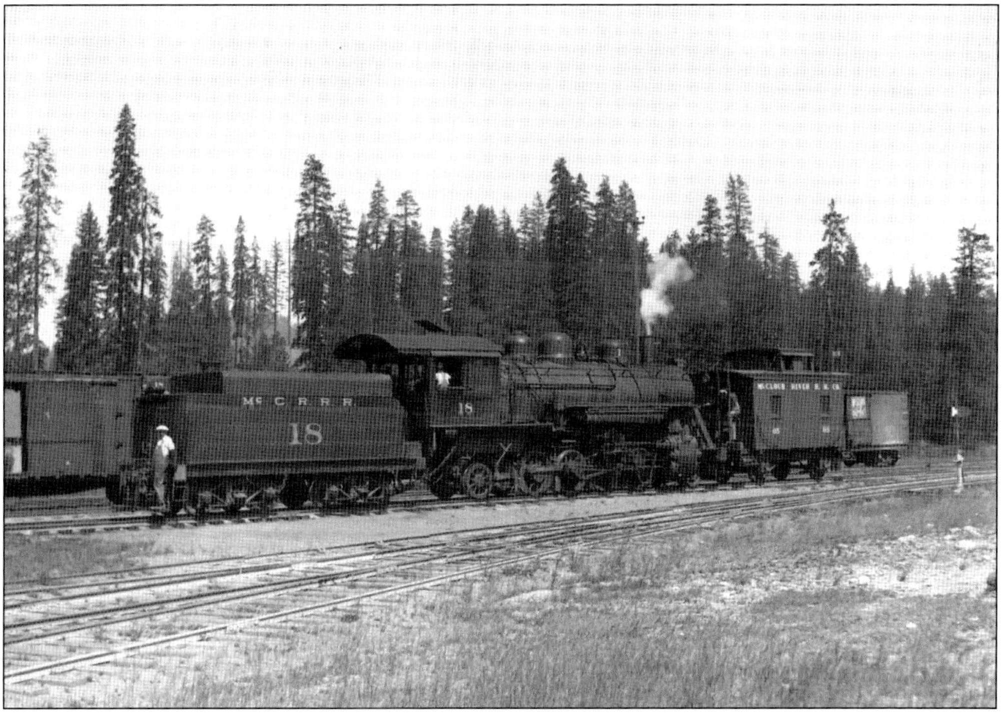

In early 1956, McCloud River No. 18 arrived on the property as replacement for the ill-fated No. 100. No. 18 is a 90-ton logging 2-8-2 that was built in 1914 by Baldwin Locomotive Works for the McCloud River Railroad. The above picture shows No. 18 working the McCloud yard around 1938. Below she is seen, not long after arrival, near the upper end of the yard in Yreka.

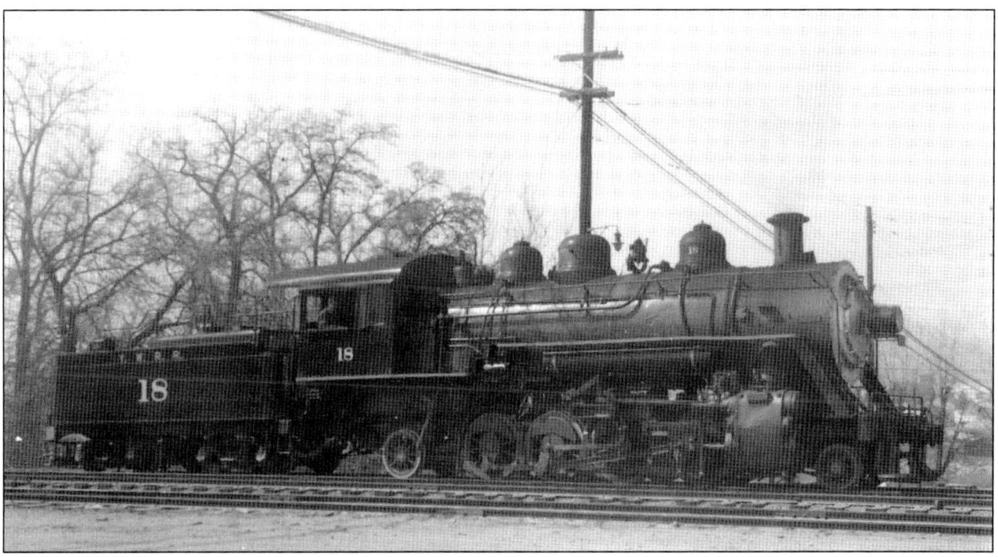

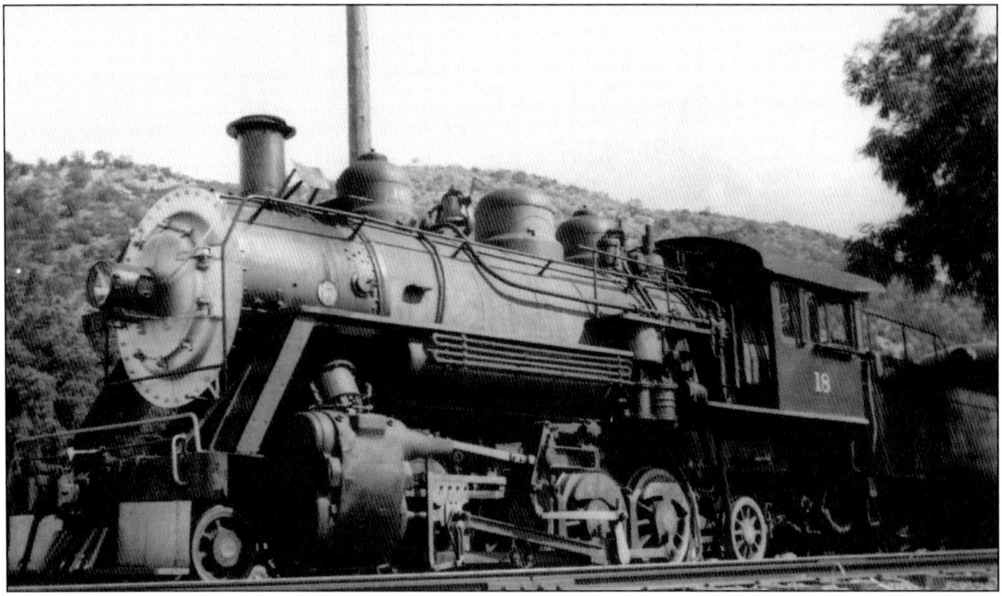

Here No. 18 sits on a siding in the Yreka yards. There has been some debate over how close of a relationship Nos. 18 and 19 share besides both being McCloud River locomotives. There is speculation that No. 18 was originally built for Caddo River Lumber but that Caddo River ran out of money to purchase the locomotive, and with McCloud River eventually purchasing the unfinished locomotive from Baldwin, it would become their No. 18.

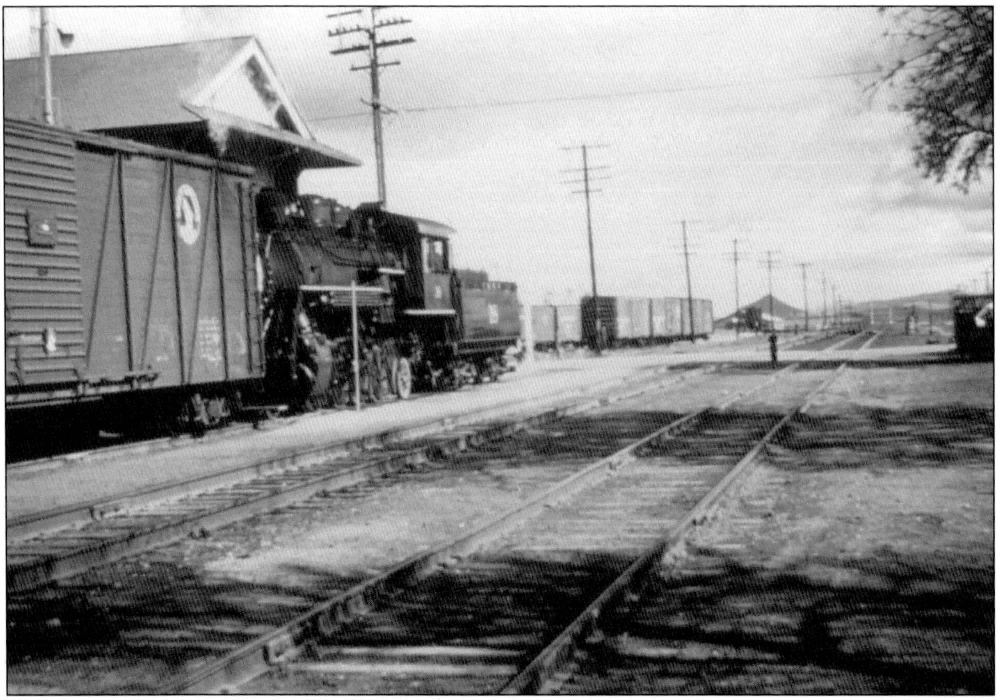

In 1956, No. 18 is switching freight in Montague. Southern Pacific's Siskiyou Line is in the foreground. This view is looking north toward Ashland, Oregon. (Courtesy Jeff Moore.)

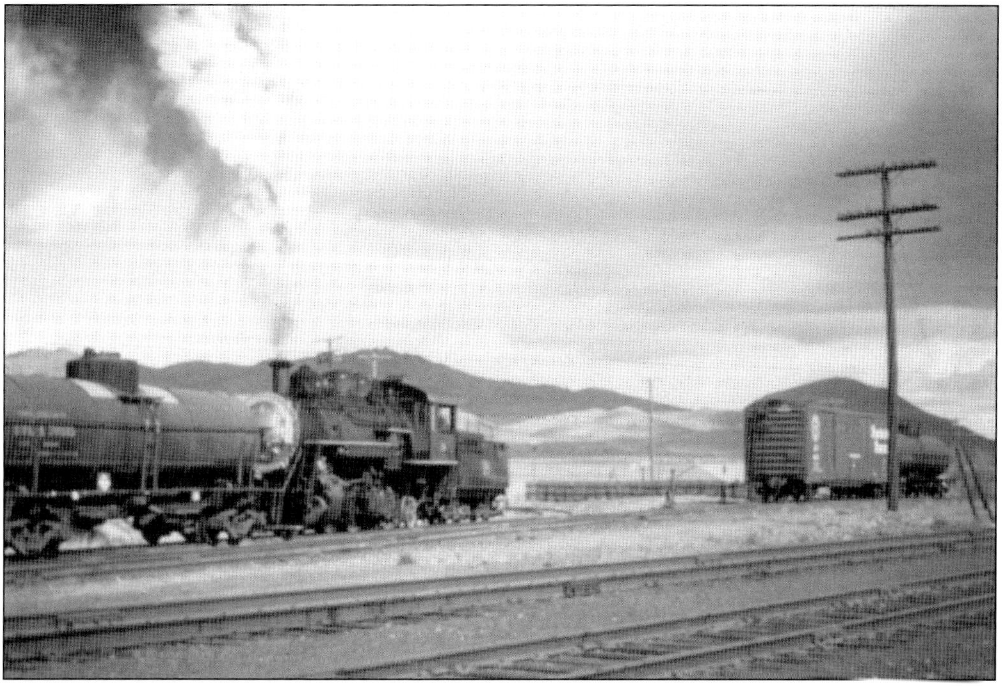

After completing her switching chores, No. 18, along with a carload of fuel oil, begins the return trip to Yreka. (Courtesy Jeff Moore.)

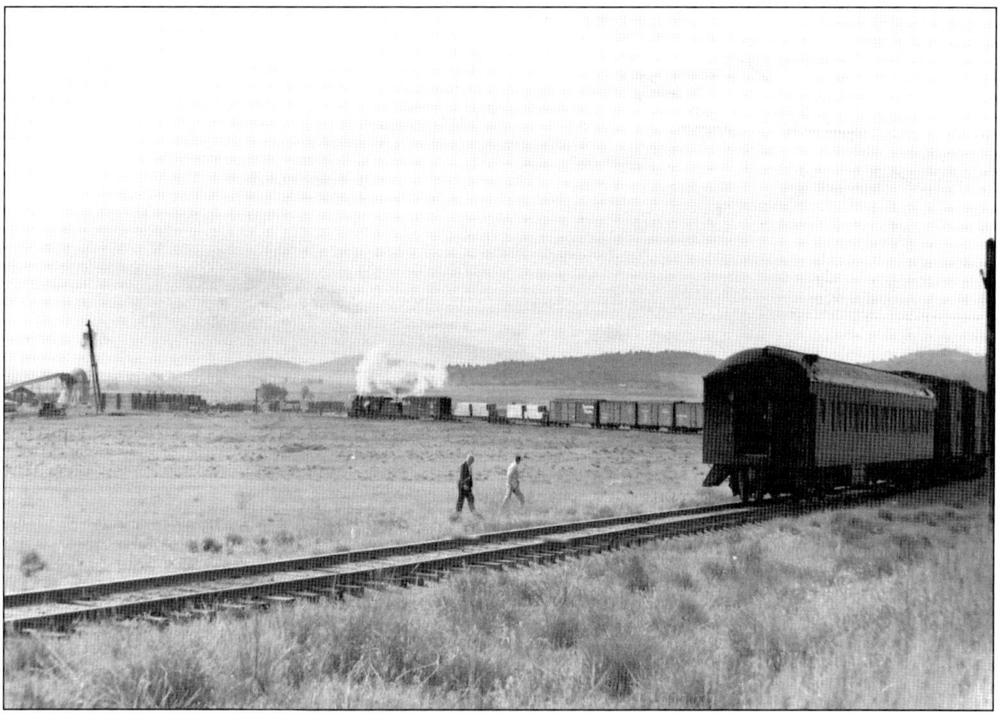

In May 1957, No. 19 and train are on a railfan excursion, as evident by the line of photographers in the distance. The two men in the foreground were both very influential people to the Yreka Western. On the left is O. G. Steele, and on the right is Lynn Cecil.

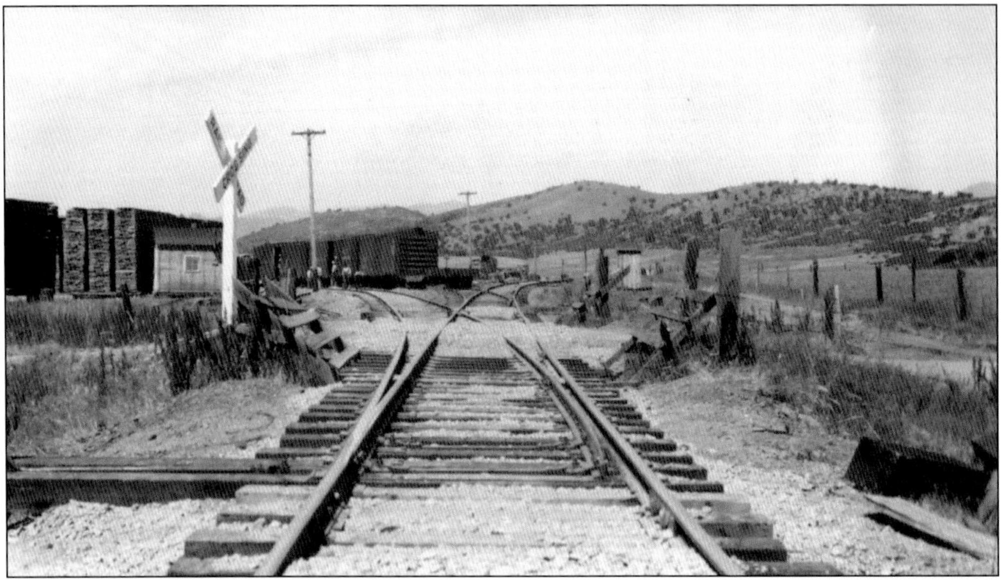

Depicted here are the newly completed spur tracks into the Eastlick Mill located about halfway between Yreka and Montague. The land this mill is on was one of several parcels purchased by the railroad and offered free to any industry that would ship using the railroad. Below, track workers are putting the finishing touches on one of the new spur tracks into the Eastlick Mill while the other track is already being put to use.

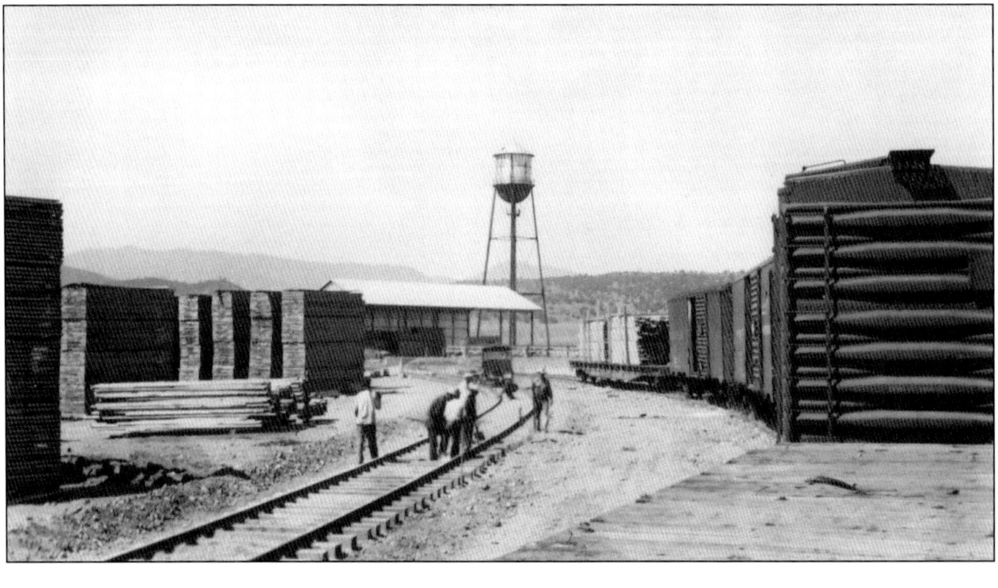

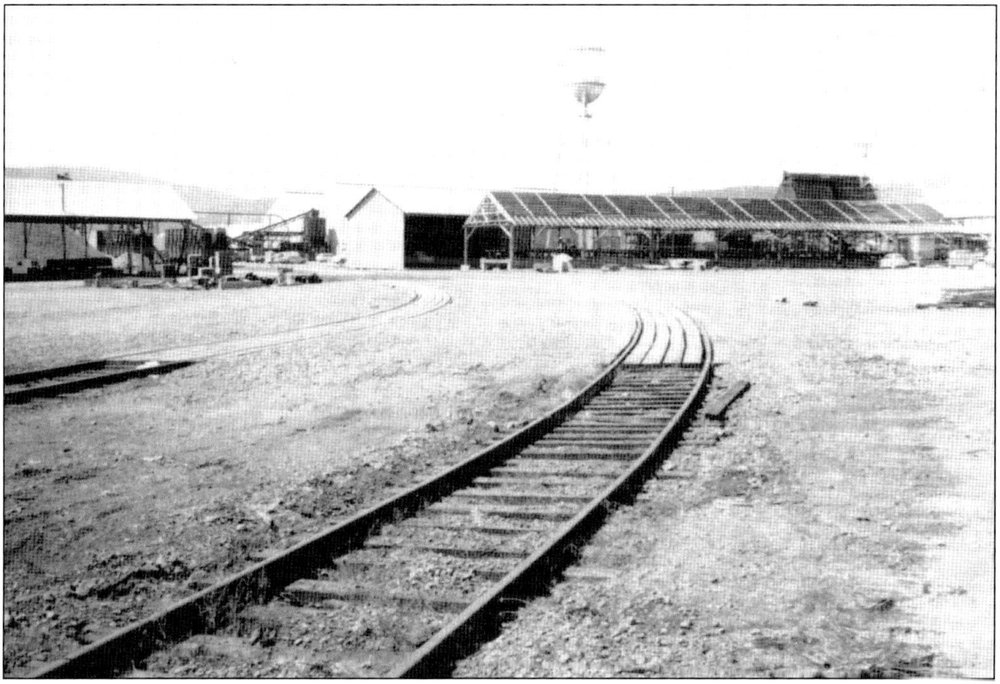

Here is a shot of the spurs leading into the Eastlick Mill. This mill would change ownership several times. Later on, the mill would be owned by Sierra Pacific Industries and then by the Hi-Ridge Lumber Company until it closed in 1999.

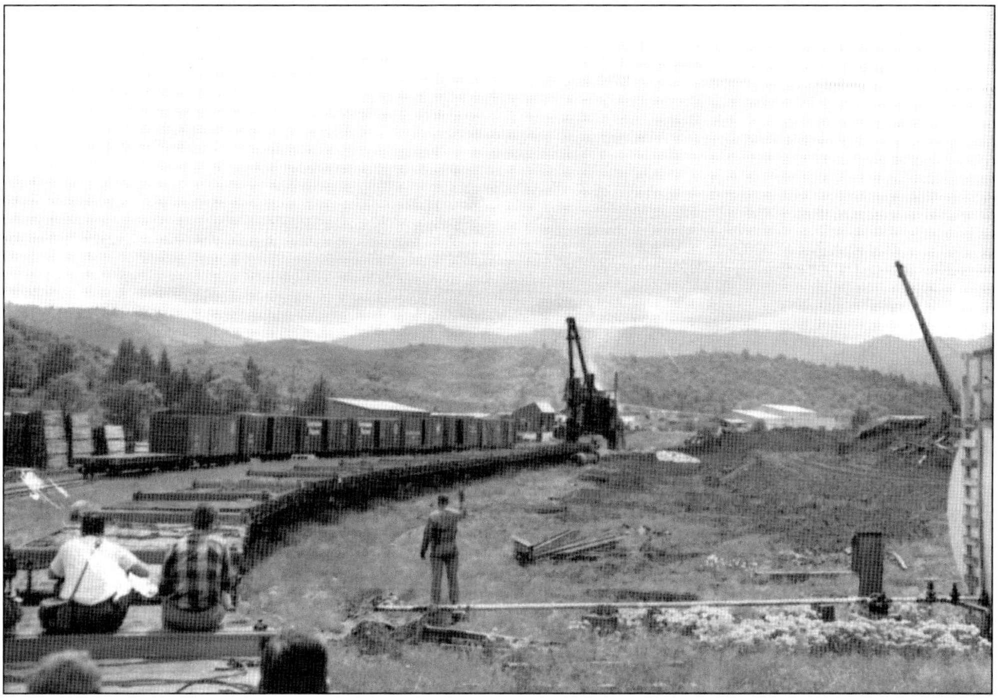

Railfans observe the process of loading logs at Fruit Growers Supply's reload in Yreka as the train backs the log flats through the McGiffert loader in August 1957.

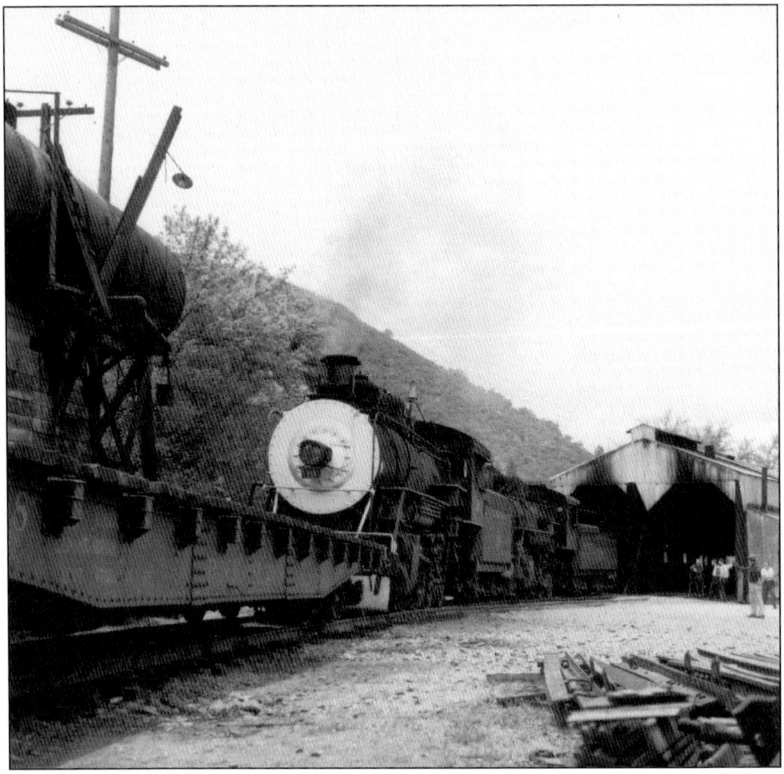

Nos. 19 and 18 are steaming up in front of the shops to prepare for a railfan excursion in 1957. A great number of the excursions were often run as doubleheaders with both steam locomotives.

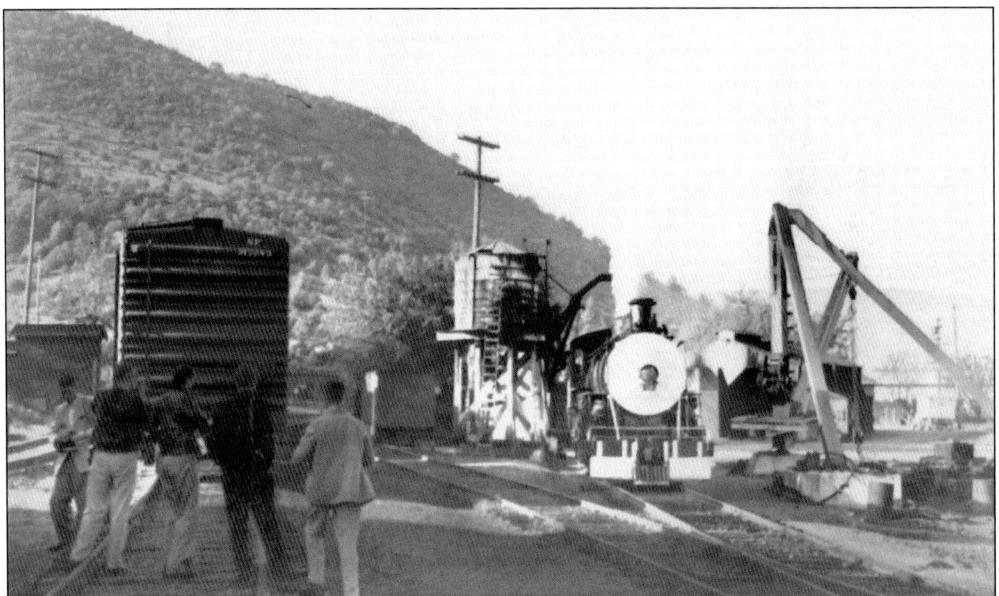

A group of railfans talk trains while No. 19 is serviced and readied for the day's run in front of the water tower.

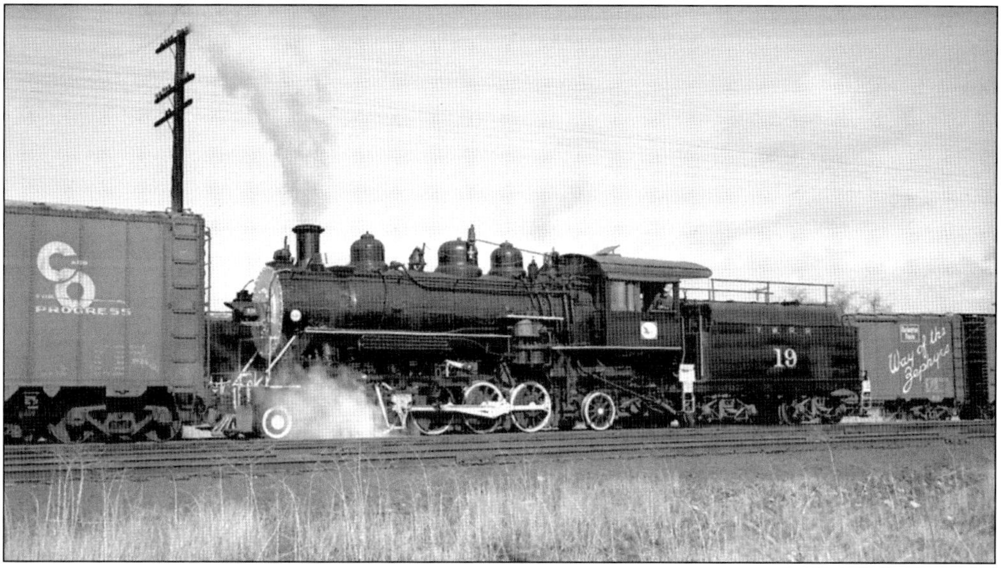

No. 19 switches cars at the interchange with Southern Pacific in Montague prior to taking the empties to the mills in Yreka. (Courtesy Don Hansen.)

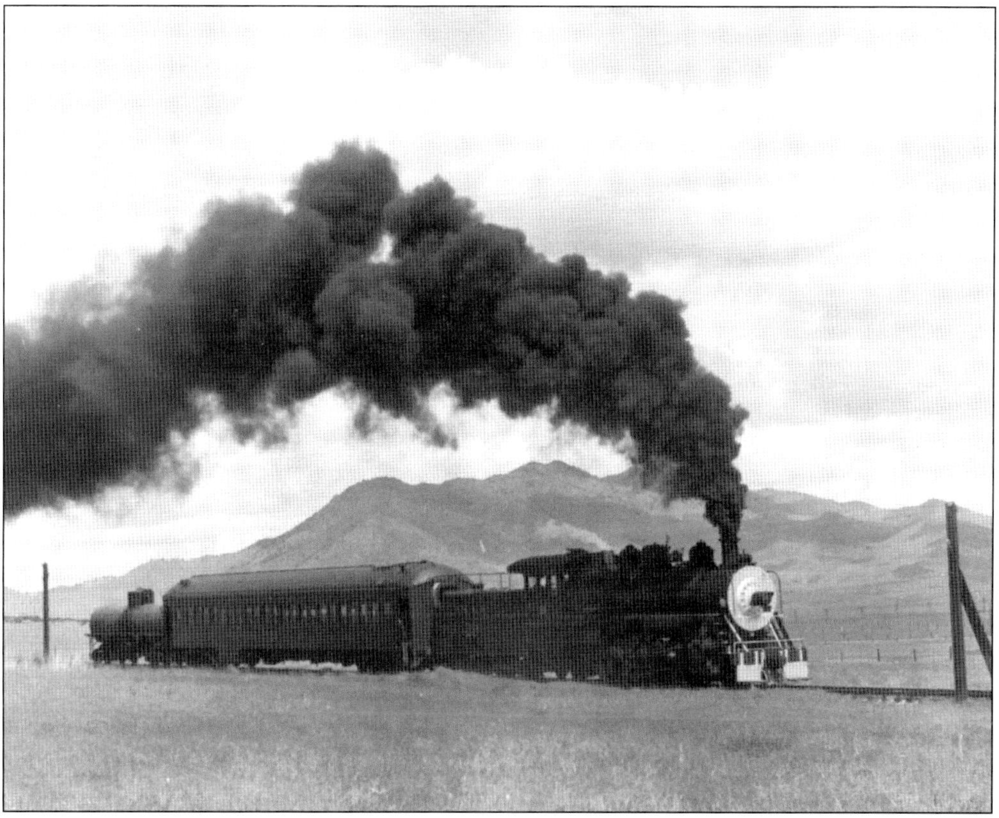

No. 19 does a run by for photographers as she rolls across a field near Montague sometime in the late 1950s. This was one of the many excursions performed during this time period.

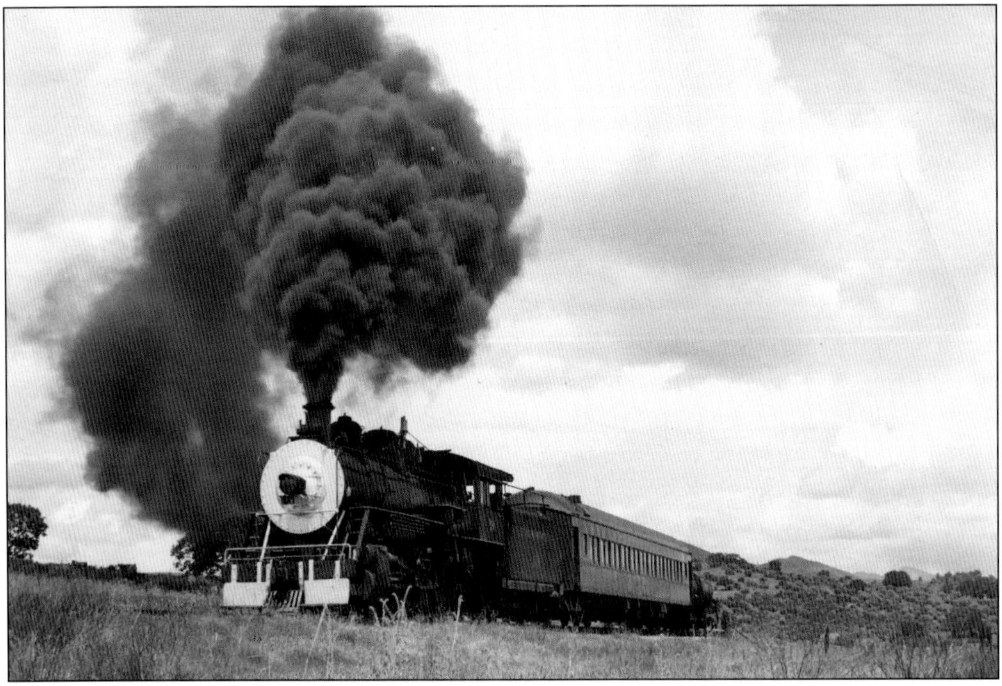

No. 19 does another run by on an excursion near Montague. This image was taken on the same trip as the previous photograph.

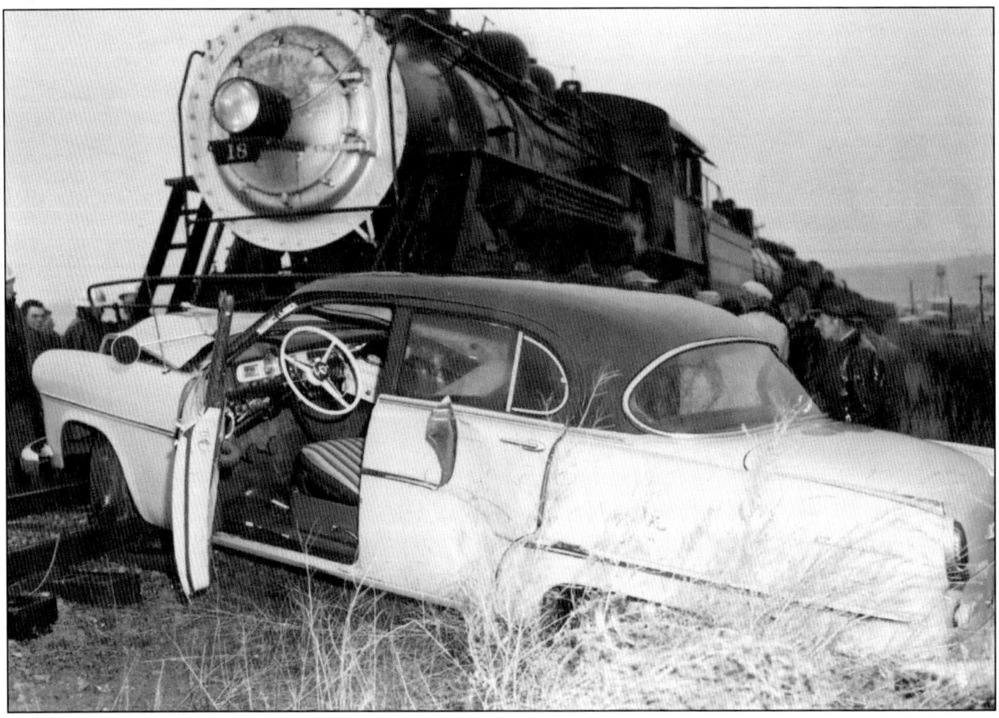

It's October 23, 1957, and No. 18 has run into a bit of trouble at the Highway 3 grade crossing. A vehicle attempted to beat the train to the crossing and obviously didn't make it. The aftermath is shown here.

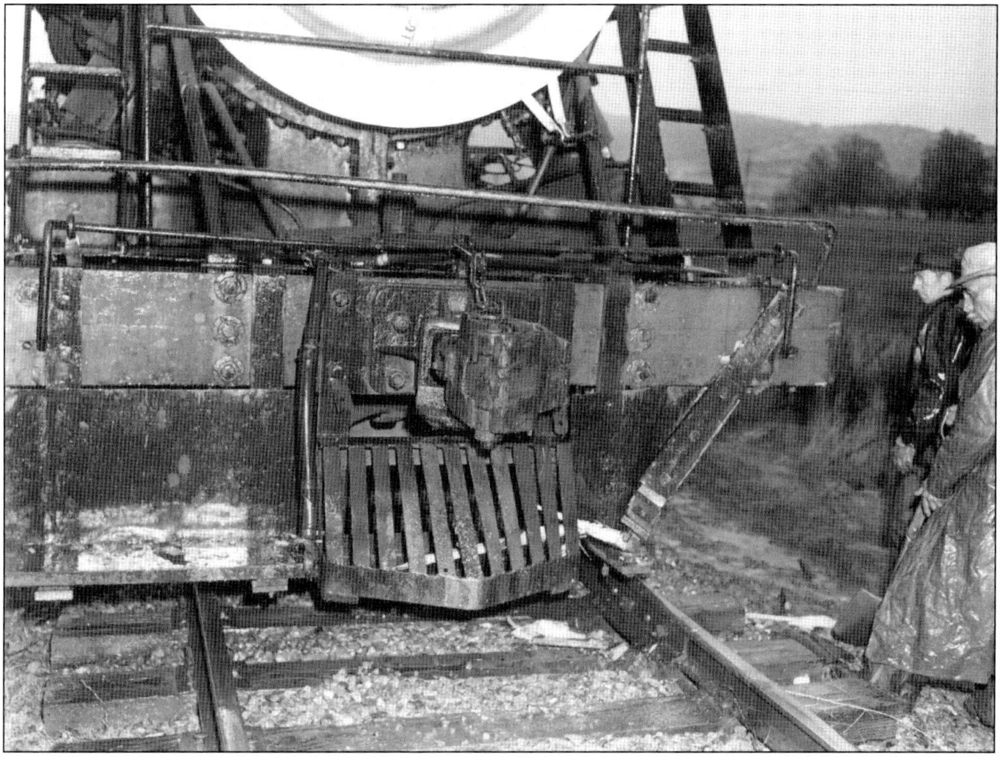

The damage to No. 18 was quite minor, resulting in a bent footboard on the fireman's side of the locomotive. The vehicle, on the other hand, was not so lucky and was considered a complete loss.

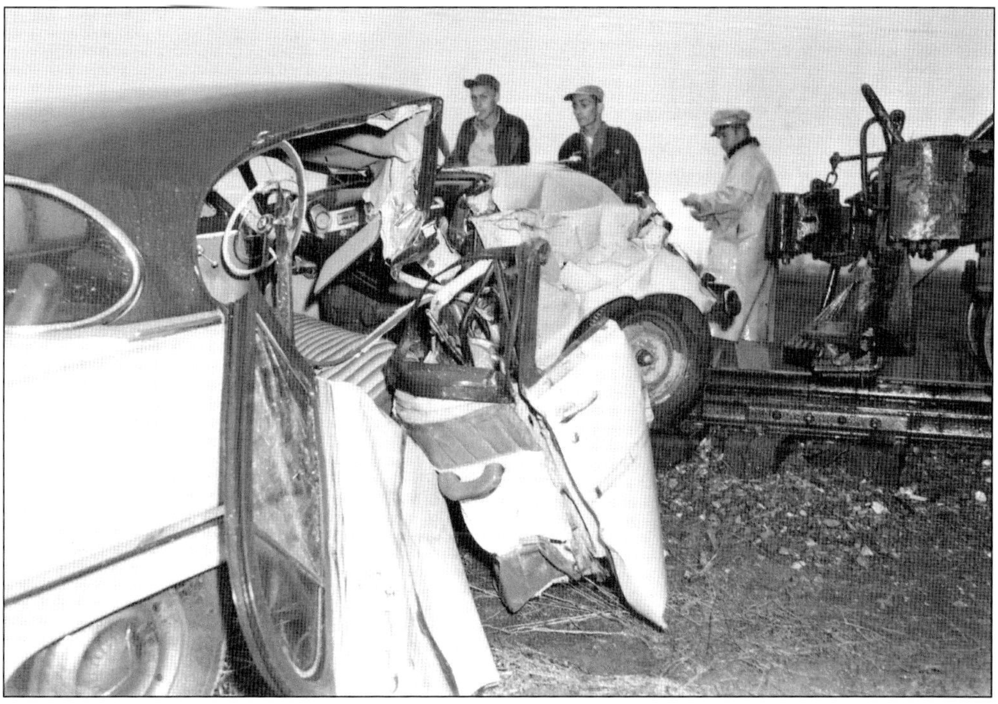

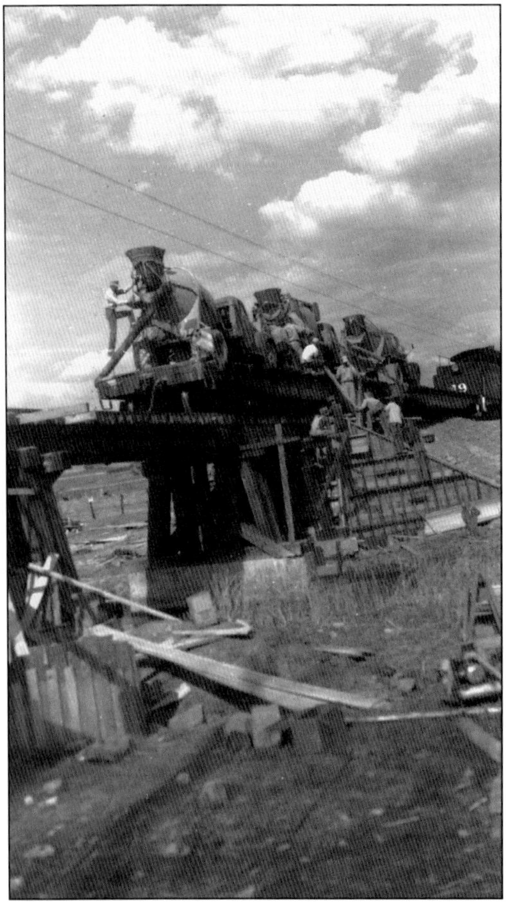

In April 1955, the railroad elected to replace and rebuild the Shasta River Bridge. The bridge was filled in at both ends, and a shorter steel bridge was built over the river. The photograph at left shows crews pouring cement for the new bridge abutments. The image below shows crews removing the old wooden bridge timbers.

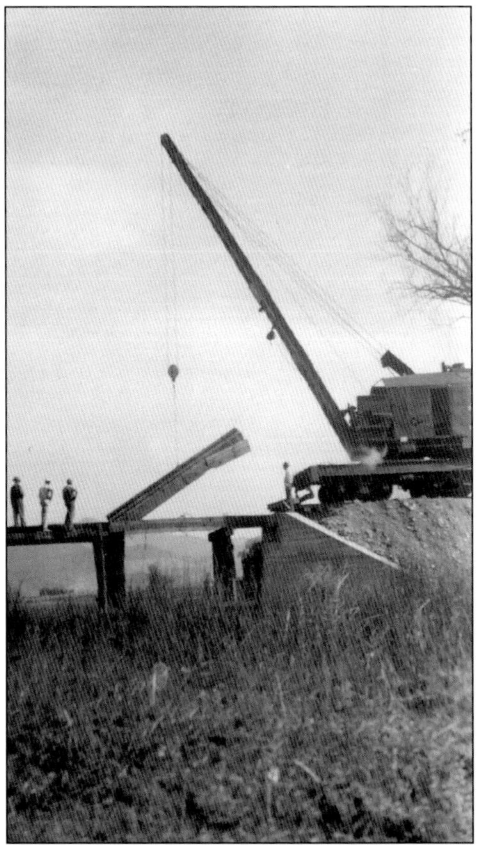

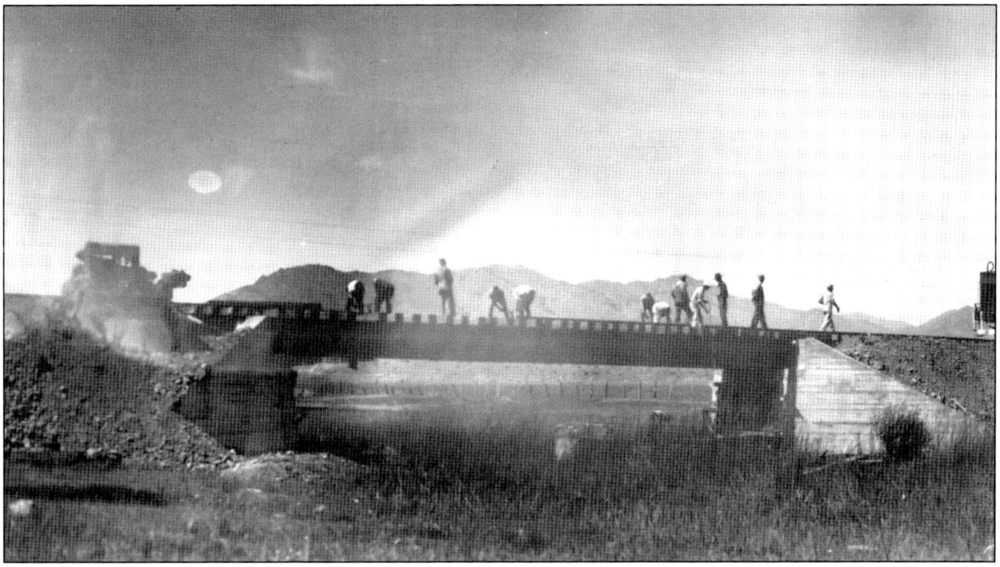

The new bridge is nearing completion, and the crews are spiking down the rails to the bridge deck. The back of the tender of No. 19 is just visible at right.

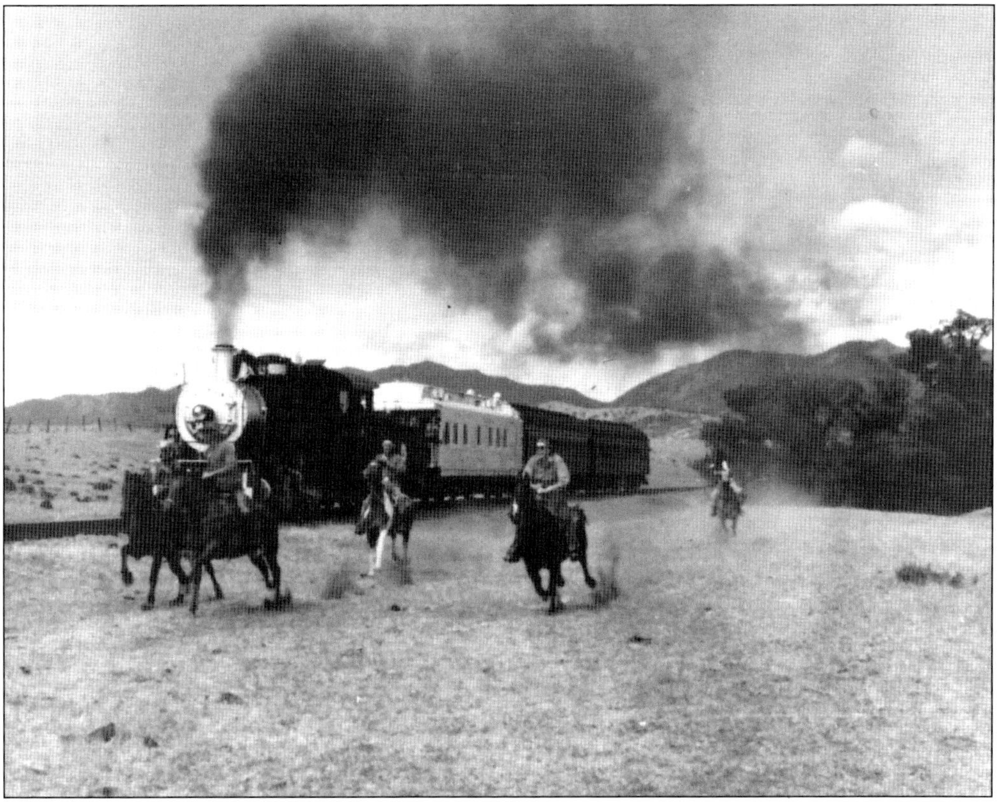

No. 18 takes an excursion train through the Shasta Valley. Riding alongside is a group of cowboys on horseback who were set up just for this photograph.

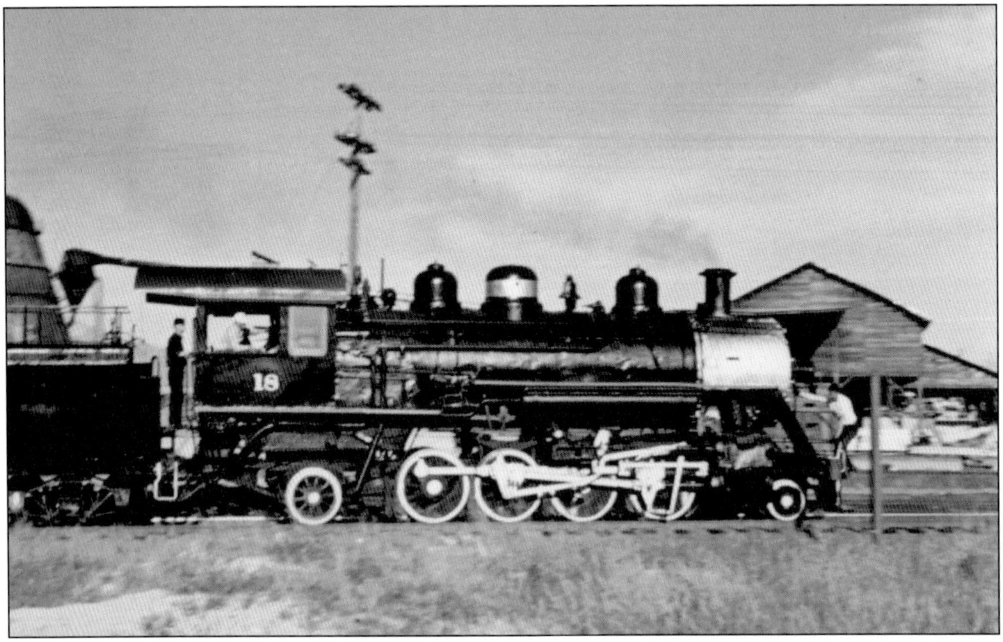

No. 18 and her crew switch cars in Montague in the late 1950s. (Courtesy Tim Stricker.)

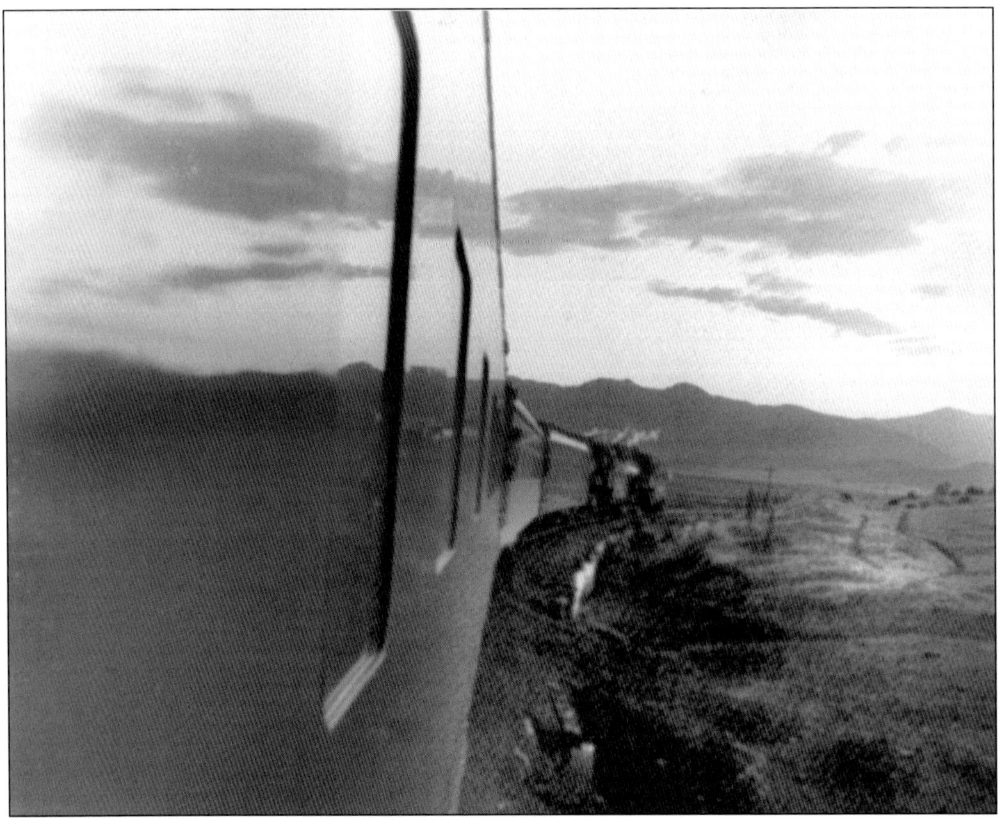

Nos. 18 and 19 lead an excursion train back to Yreka, just outside of Montague. The two locomotives ran as a doubleheader numerous times during passenger excursions.

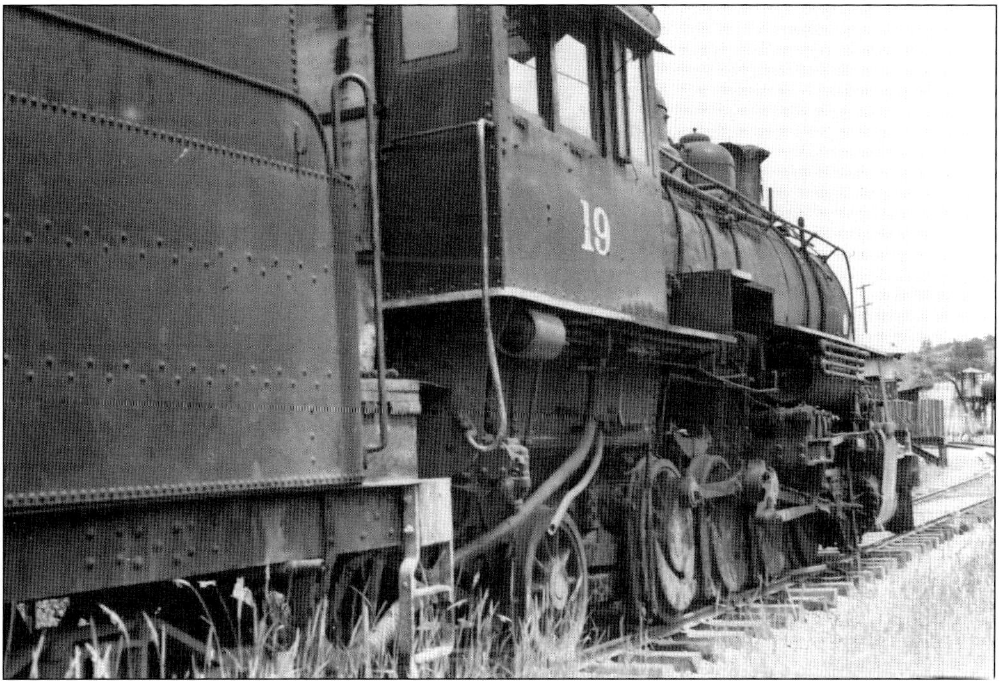

No. 19 rests on a spur track in the Yreka yards next to the shops. This track no longer exists after a rearranging of the yard tracks in later years, which was mostly caused by the construction of Interstate 5. (Courtesy Jeff Moore.)

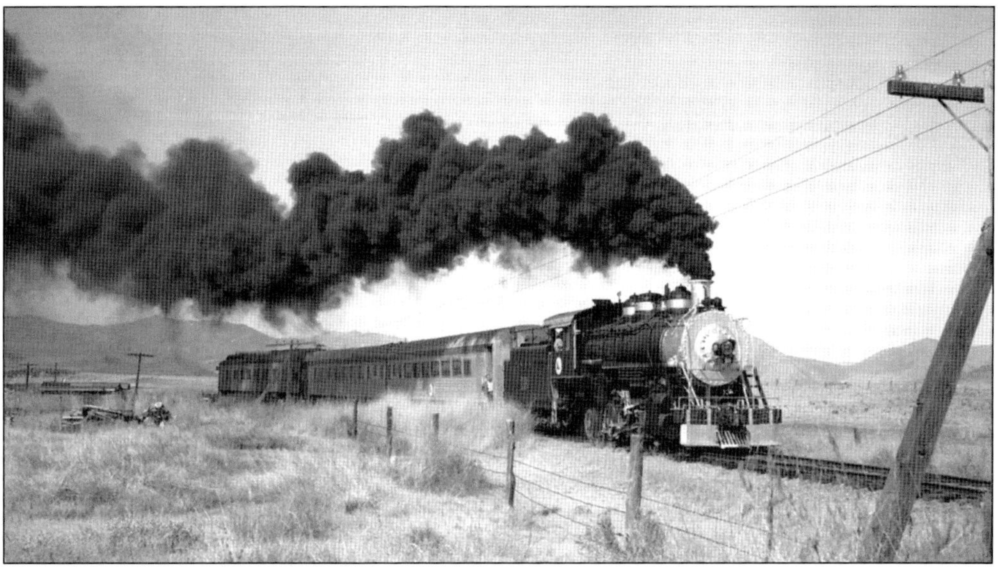

No. 19 leads an excursion train into Montague in 1970. The fireman puts out a nice black plume of smoke for the photographers. (Courtesy Don Hansen.)

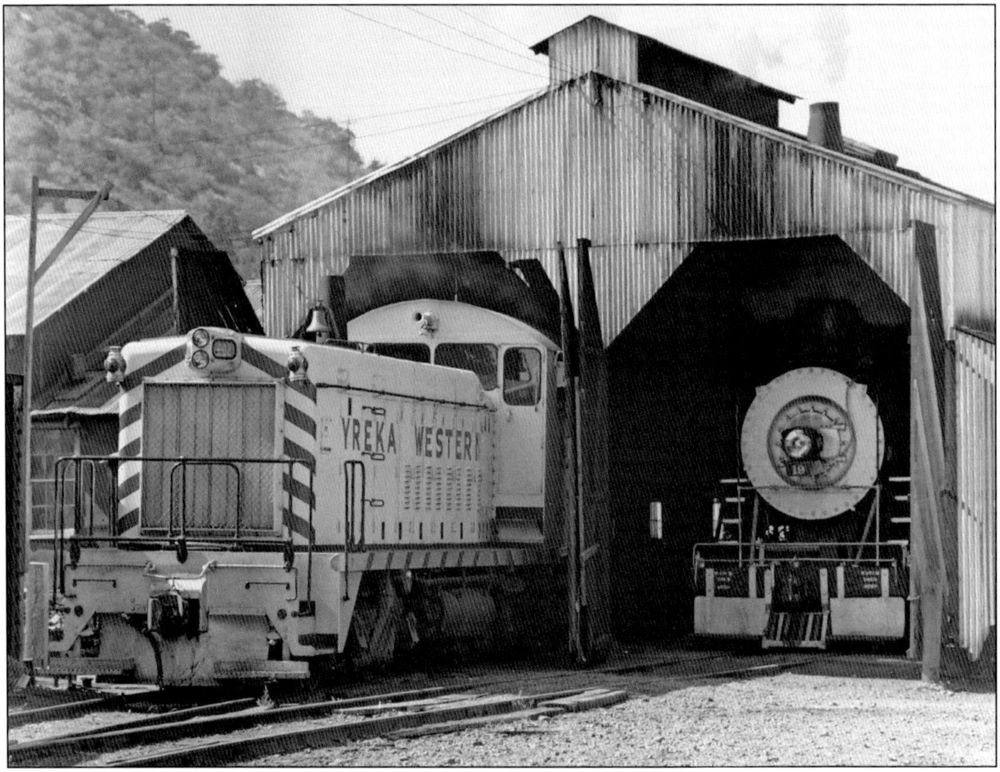

In 1962, Yreka Western's SW8 No. 602 leaves the engine house to perform its freight duties while No. 19 continues steaming up in the shop, preparing for a special run for the Siskiyou County Fair. Below, No. 19 backs her special fair train towards Yreka near milepost 4. (Both photographs courtesy Bob Morris.)

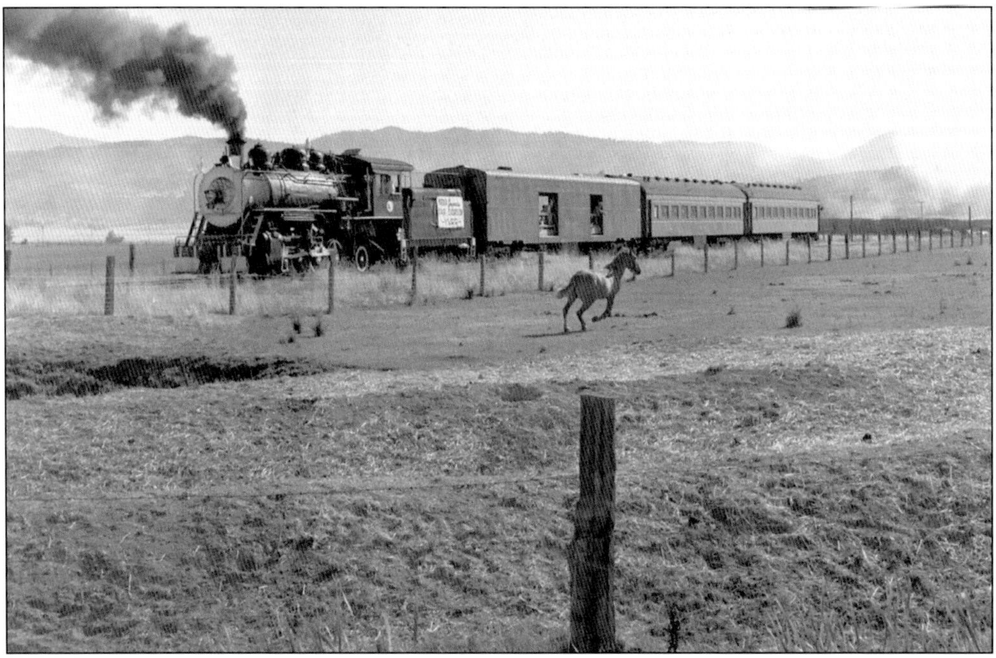

Four

DIESELIZATION

In 1958, the Yreka Western purchased its first diesel locomotive, No. 602, an SW8. This effectively put both steam locomotives on standby status, except for pulling passenger excursions. Eventually, the railroad acquired two additional diesel locomotives in 1963, thus ending regular steam freight operations on the Yreka Western. Traffic peaked in 1966 with 3,000 carloads moved outbound and 500 to 700 miscellaneous carloads inbound. The annual number of cars moved over the railroad remained steady around 2,000 carloads a year, with traffic peaking in 1978 and 1979 with 2,500 carloads moved. However, the 1980s brought with it a decline in the timber industry and a rise in environmental issues. The result was the closing of several mills along the railroad. The railroad hit a low of 324 cars moved in 1986 and was down to just two employees. Rumors of abandonment began circulating around Yreka. In 1986, the city approached the railroad about starting an excursion train, and in June 1986, the Blue Goose Excursion Train was launched. The excursion train may have helped save the railroad from the dark times of the late 1980s.

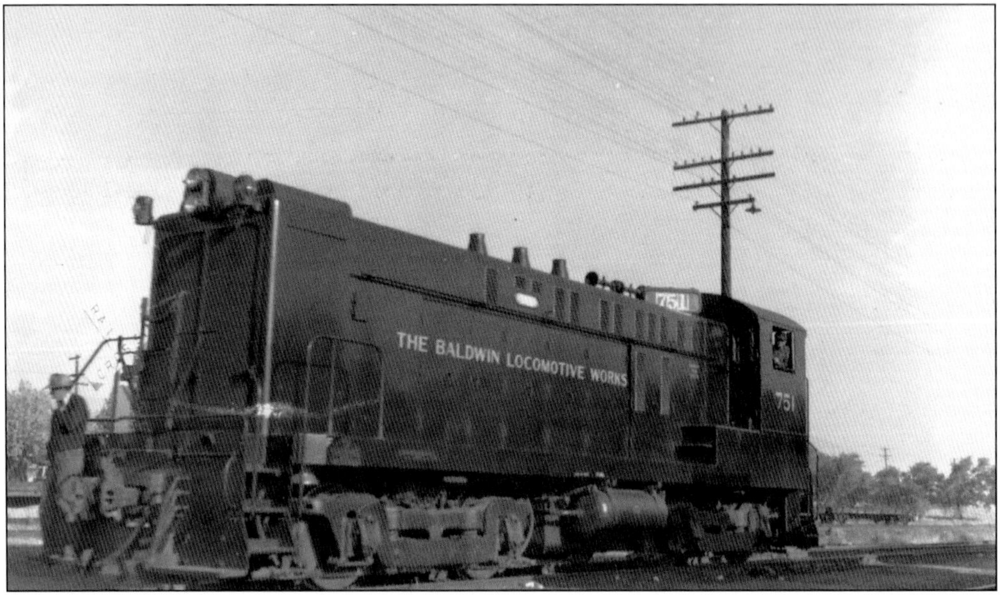

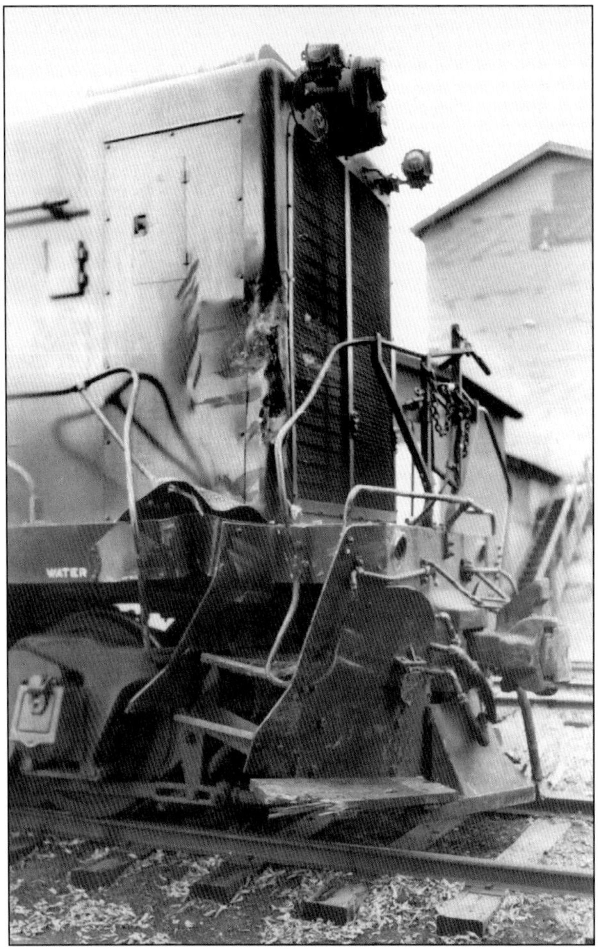

In October 1950, Yreka Western evaluated buying a diesel locomotive. The result was two demonstrator units from Baldwin Locomotive Works. They were DS4-4-750 models numbered 750 and 751 and were rated for 750 horsepower. Shown above is No. 751 on a trial run in Montague. However, as shown at left, one of the trial runs did not end well. No. 750 hit a log truck that attempted to beat the train to the crossing. The locomotive sustained some damage, but the truck was destroyed and the driver was killed.

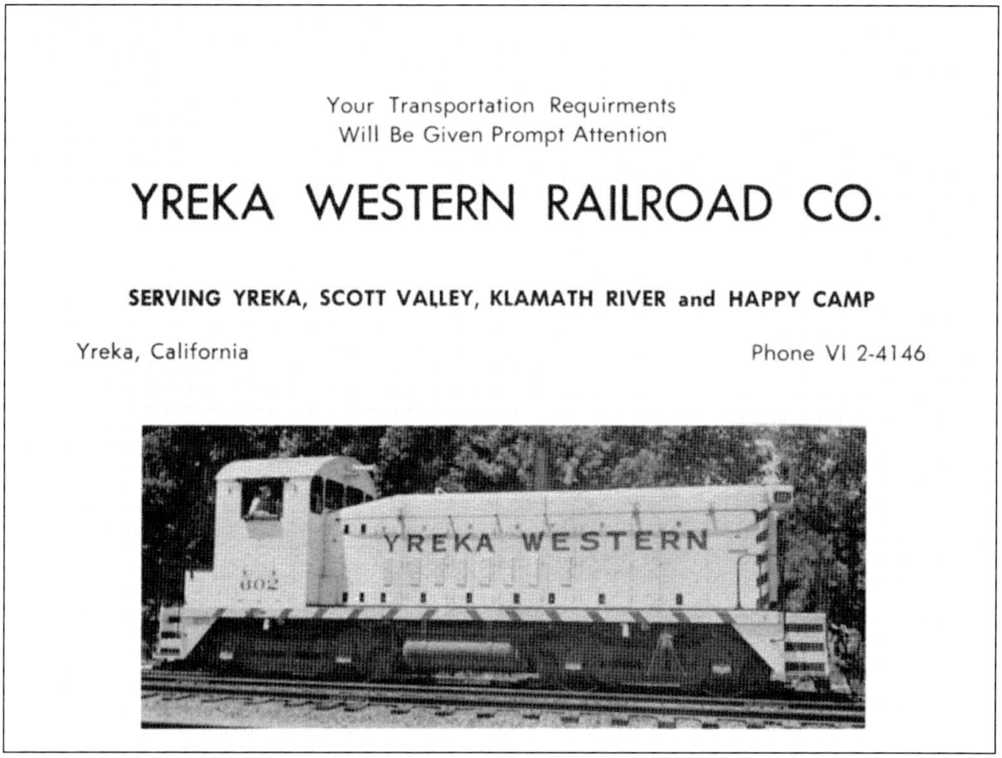

Yreka Western Railroad ran this ad in the 1962 yearbook at Yreka High School, promoting the growing freight business and acquisition of more modern diesel locomotives. (Courtesy Jeff Moore.)

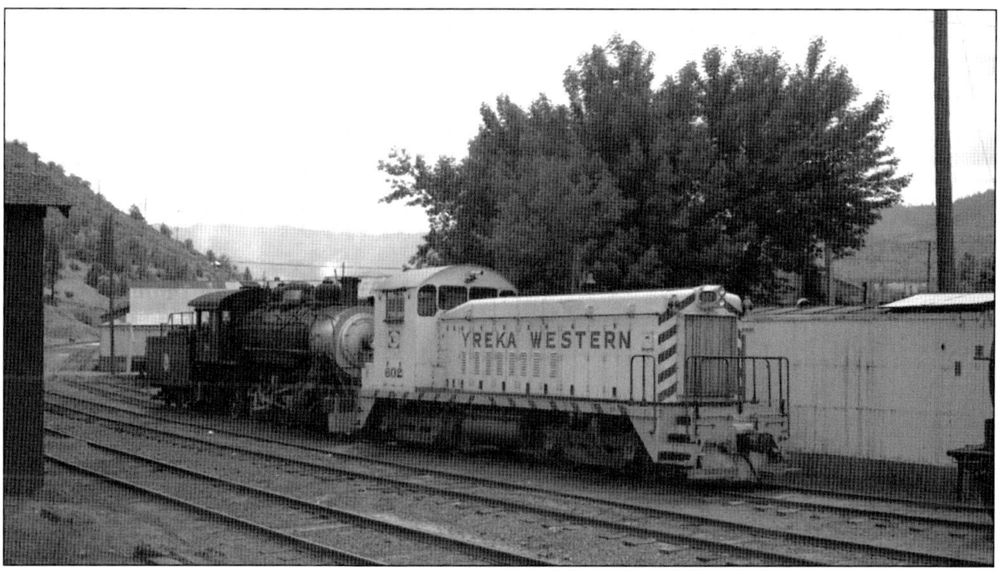

On June 20, 1964, No. 18 and No. 602 are residing in the yard at Yreka. No. 602 was an SW8 purchased from the Bamburger Railroad in Utah, arriving at Yreka Western in 1958. It was the first diesel locomotive to replace steam on the railroad. (Courtesy Don Hansen.)

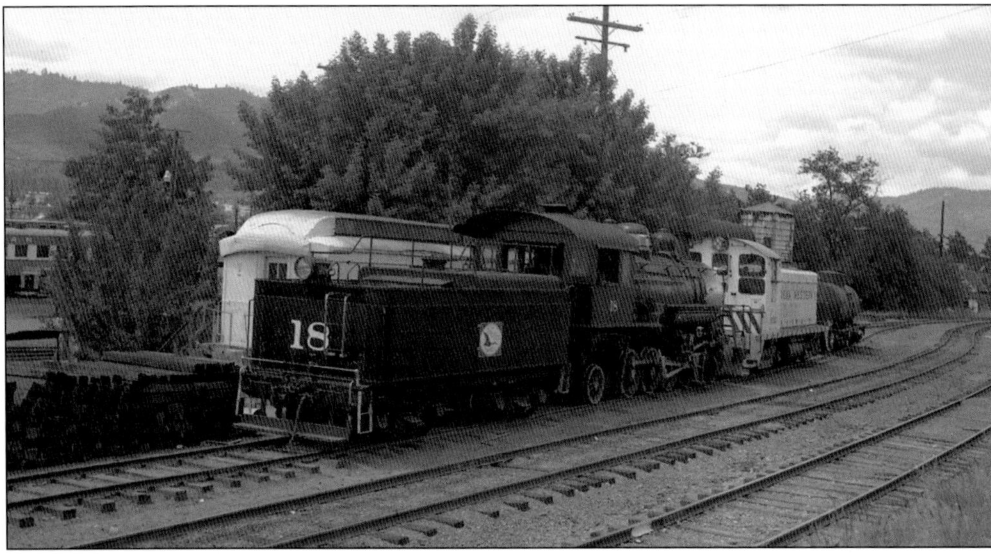

A tank car of fuel oil sits just ahead of the two locomotives on June 20, 1964. Also visible to the far left is the Yreka Western's business car known as the *Goose Nest*. It was originally built for Great Northern Railway's president James J. Hill. Also visible in the middle of the photograph is the passenger car Willis Kyle bought and kept in the yard to use as his accommodations when he travelled to and from Yreka. (Courtesy Don Hansen.)

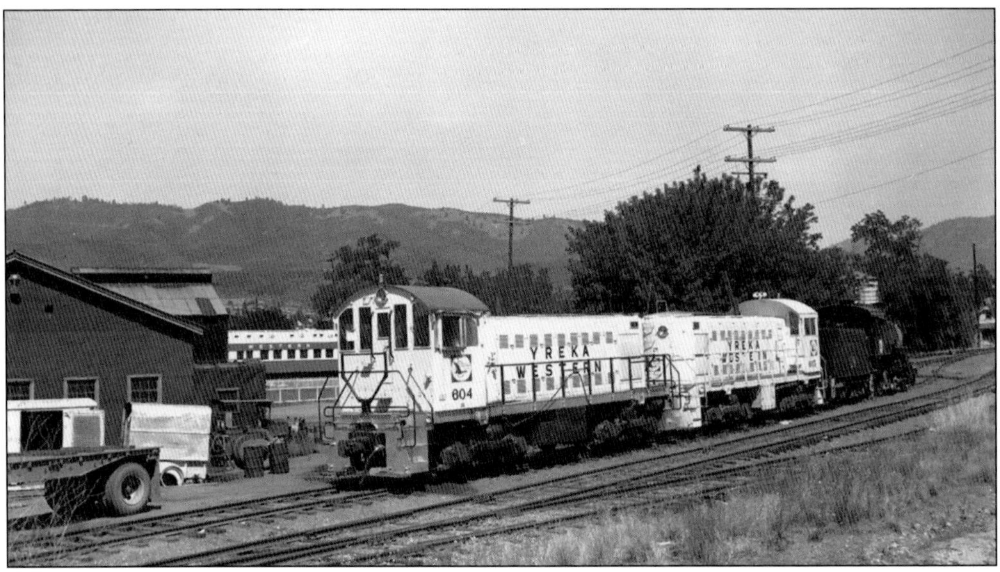

It's August 15, 1965, and Nos. 604, 603, and 19 sit in the Yreka yard. Nos. 604 and 603 are both Alco S1s that were purchased from the Portland Terminal Company in 1963. The acquisition of these two locomotives affectively ended all regular steam-powered freight operations on the Yreka Western. (Courtesy Don Hansen.)

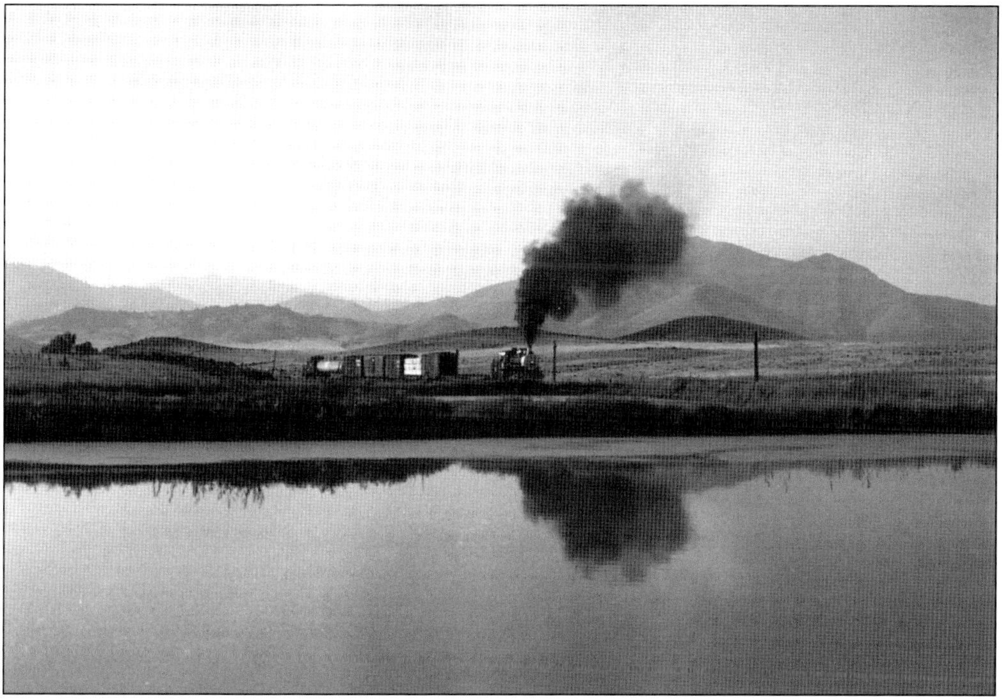

Even with the purchase of the diesels, the railroad didn't sell off or scrap the steam locomotives like most railroads did. Instead they were kept and used for excursions and railfan trips.

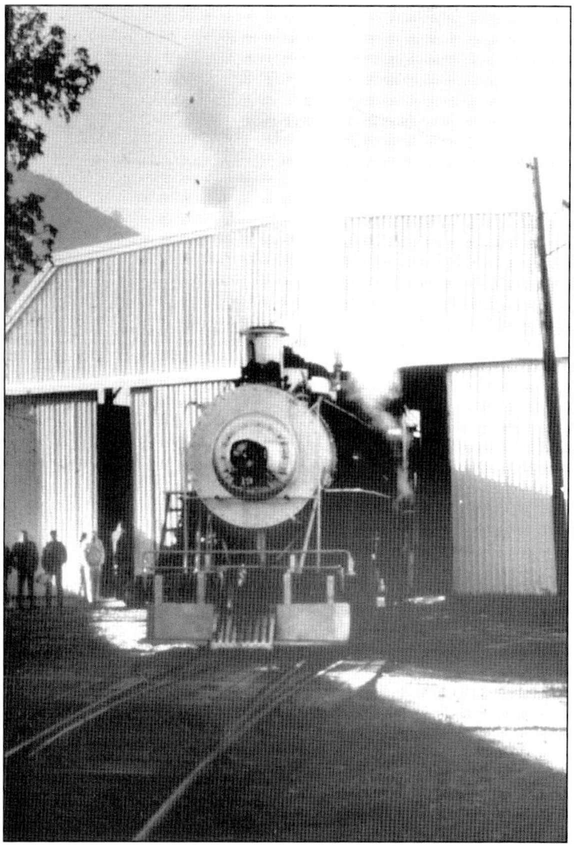

Here No. 19 steams up in front of the shop building before going out to perform for the photographers during a 1960s railfan photograph freight. A group of railfans can be seen observing the fire up procedures.

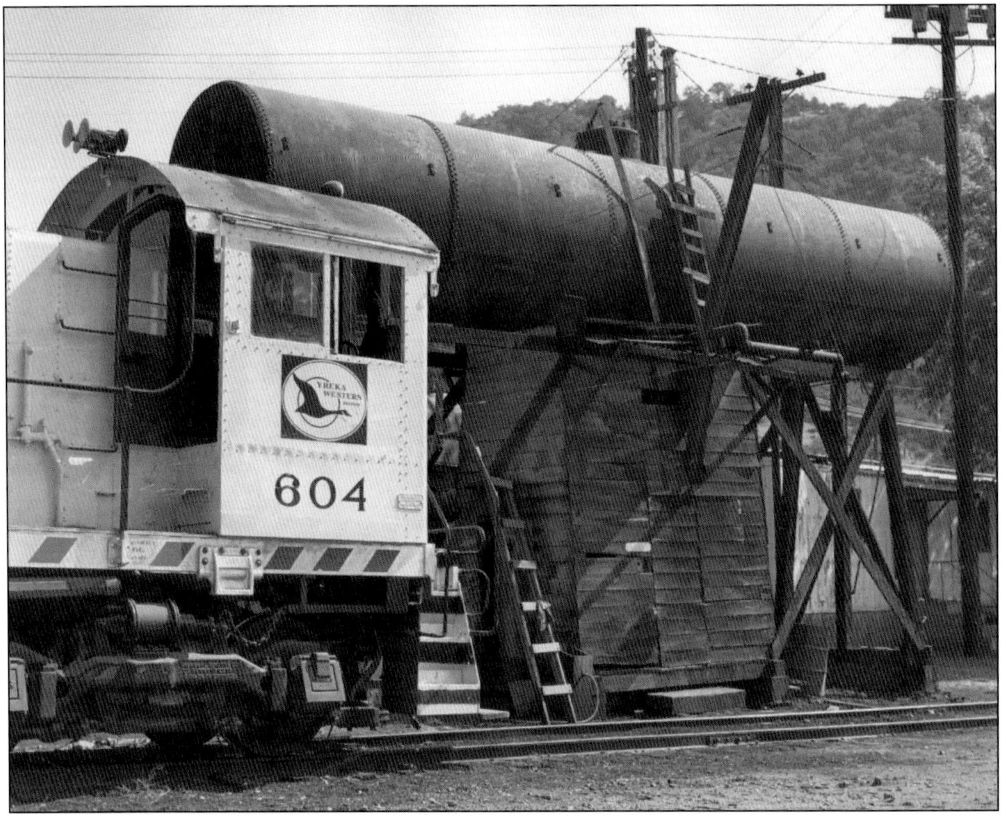

S1 No. 604 sits in front of the fuel oil tank by the shop building in Yreka. This locomotive was eventually sold to the Port of Tacoma Railroad in 1974.

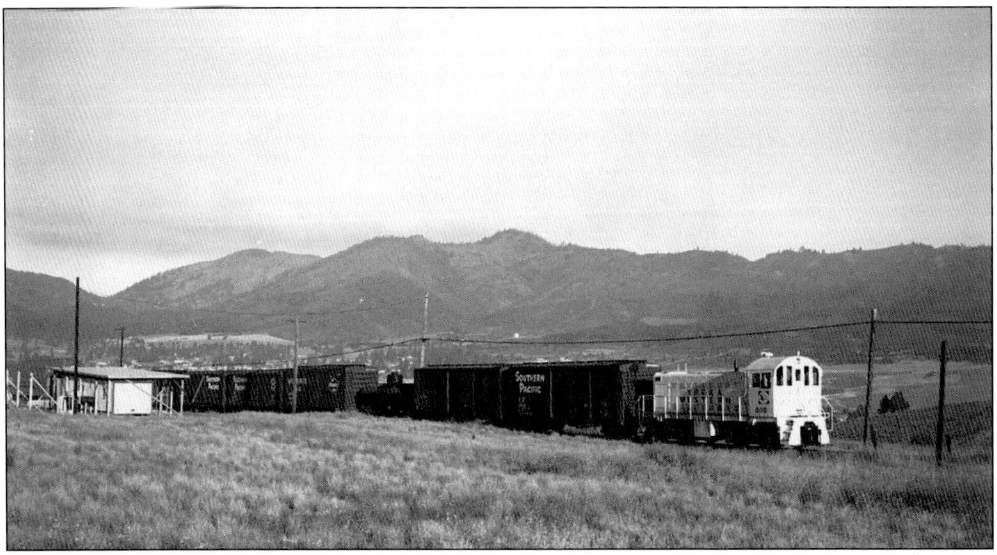

No. 603 leads a typical freight of the 1960s up Butcher Hill and out of Yreka, as shown here on the morning of August 4, 1964. (Courtesy Don Hansen.)

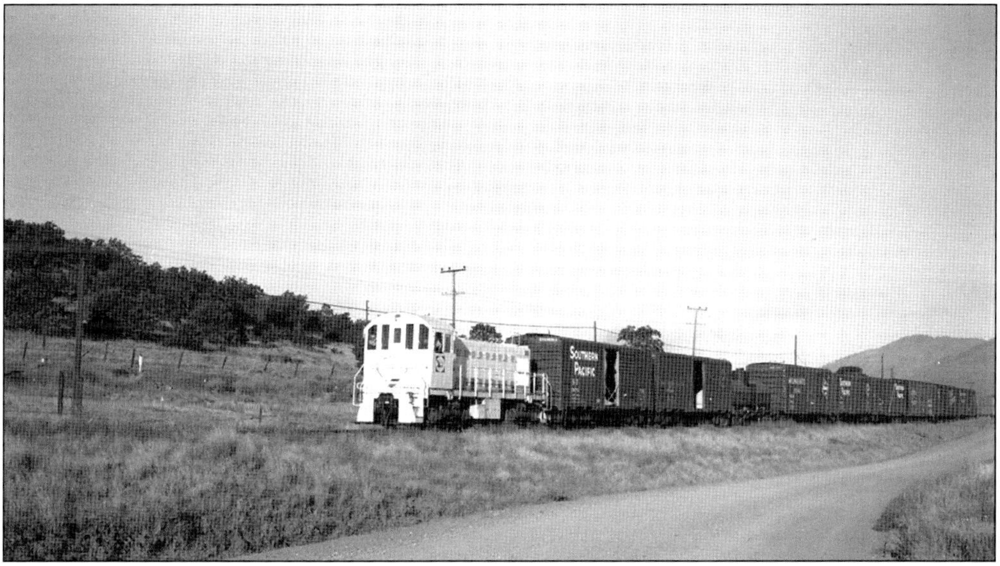

The train has reached the top of Butcher Hill and is beginning its descent down the side to the mill. In the foreground is the old Yreka-Ager Road. (Courtesy Don Hansen.)

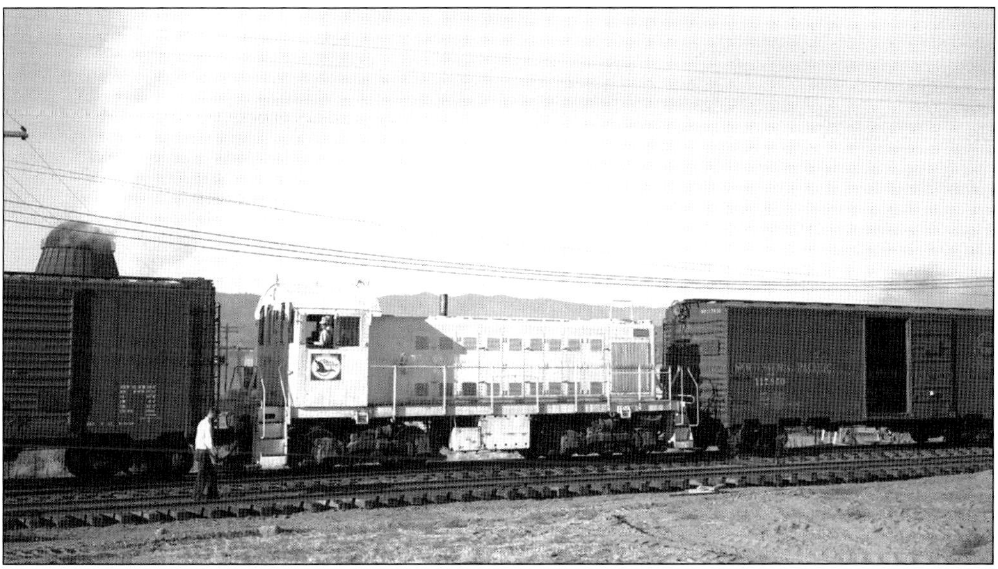

Once at the mill, the crew has a bit of switching to do. No. 603 is sandwiched between two cuts of boxcars as the engineer backs the first cut into the mill siding. (Courtesy Don Hansen.)

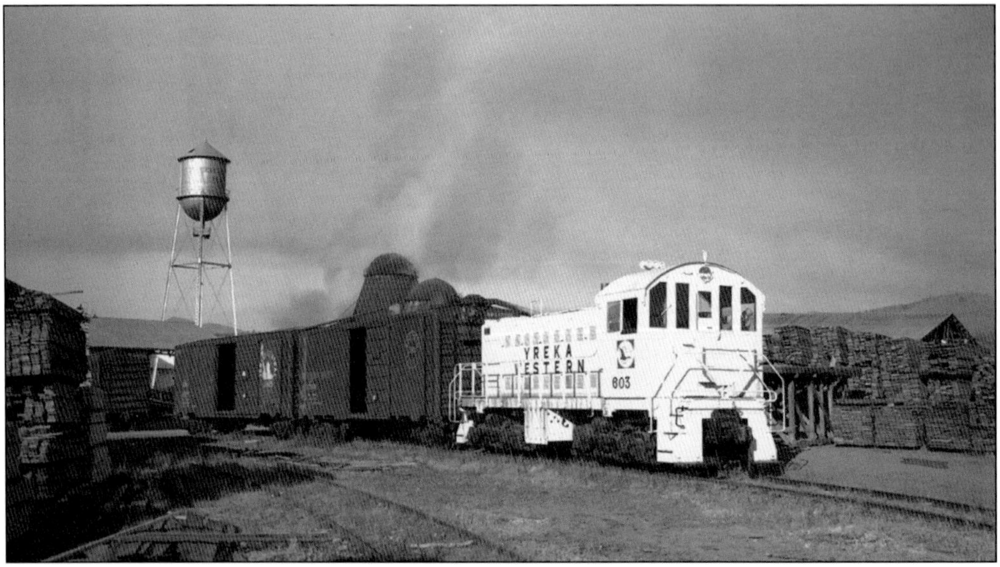

The 603 goes about her switching chores at the Eastlick Mill that was located about halfway between Yreka and Montague. The numerous stacks of finished lumber indicate the healthy state of the timber industry at this time. (Courtesy Don Hansen.)

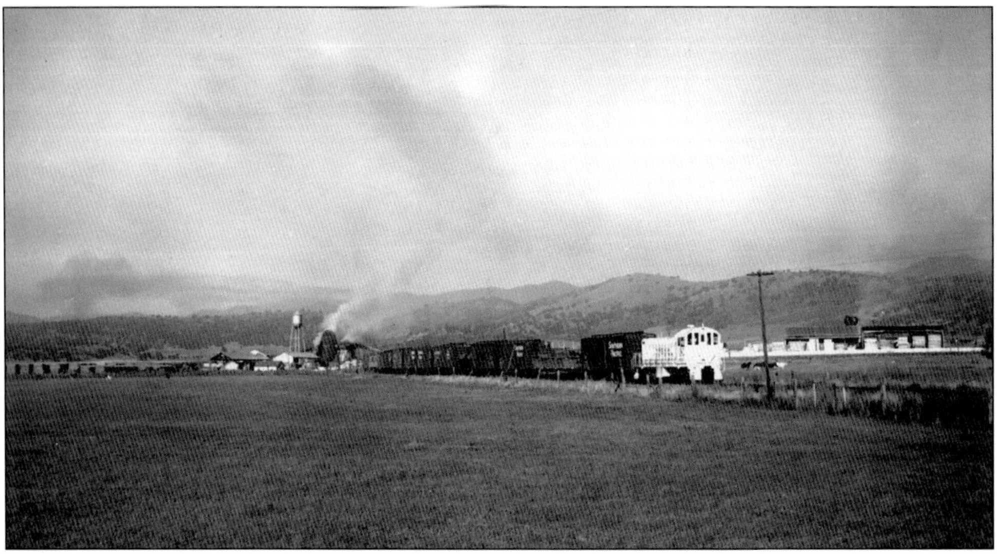
With all of its switching complete, 603 and her train cross Highway 3 and roll through the field toward Montague to interchange loads for empty cars at Montague with the Southern Pacific. (Courtesy Don Hansen.)

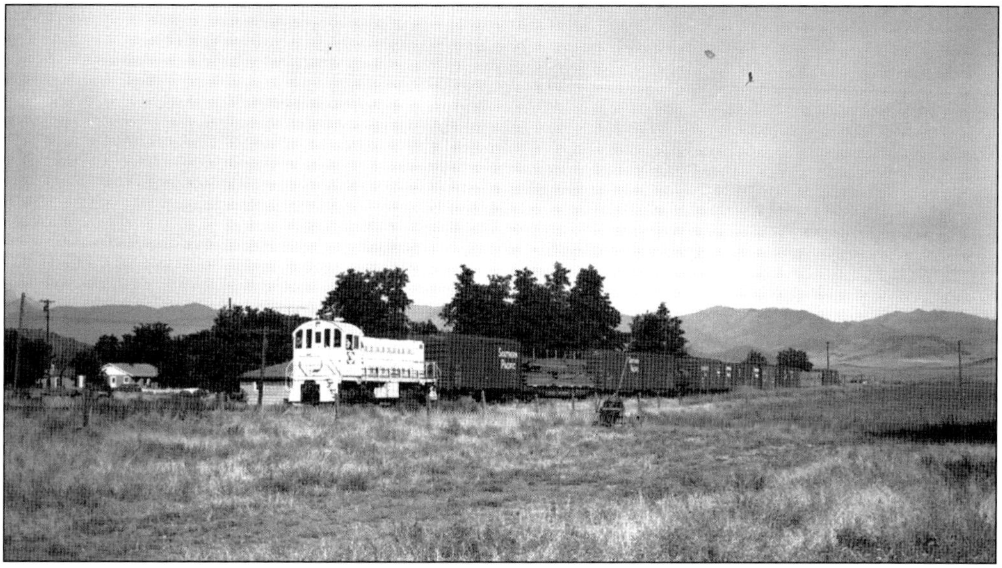

Later on that day, the 603 rolls into Montague, approaching the North Eleventh Street crossing. The house in the background is part of the city of Montague. (Courtesy Don Hansen.)

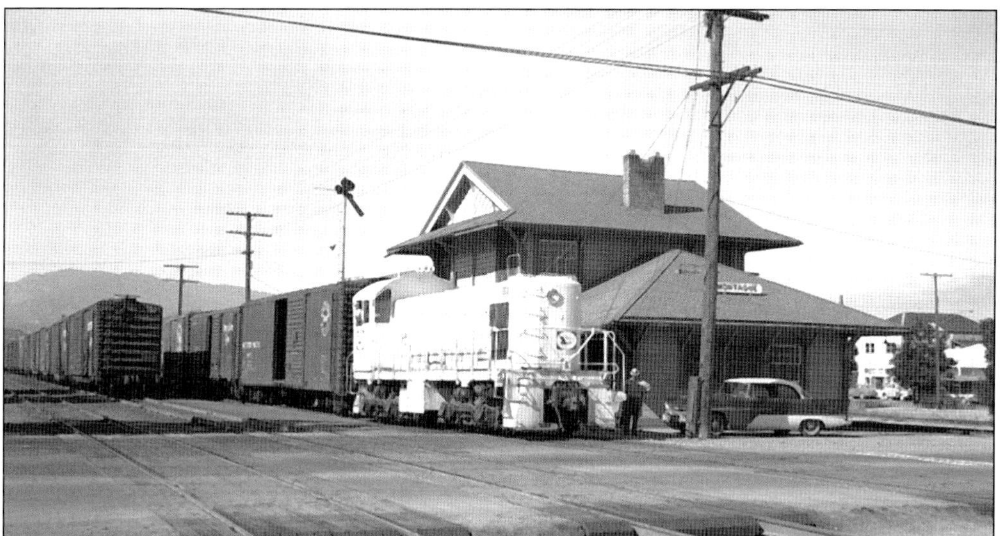

After arriving at Montague, No. 603 can begin her chores of sorting out cars in the yard in front of the depot. These cars eventually will be handed over to Southern Pacific. (Courtesy Don Hansen.)

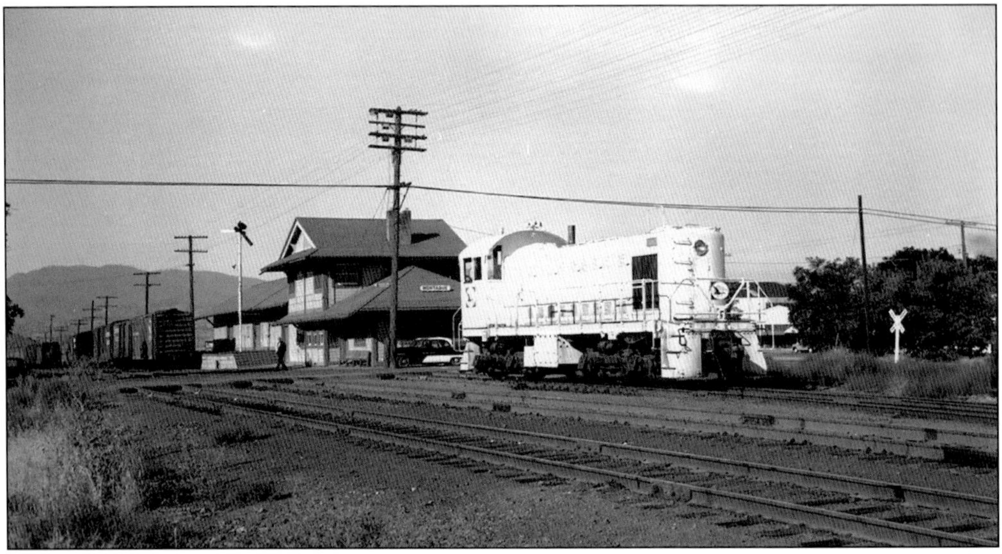

Above, No. 603 has almost finished all of her switching and needs to make room for the approaching Southern Pacific train. Shown below is a set of SP black widow SD9s from that train backing down onto the cars that the YW has set out for them. (Both photographs courtesy Don Hansen.)

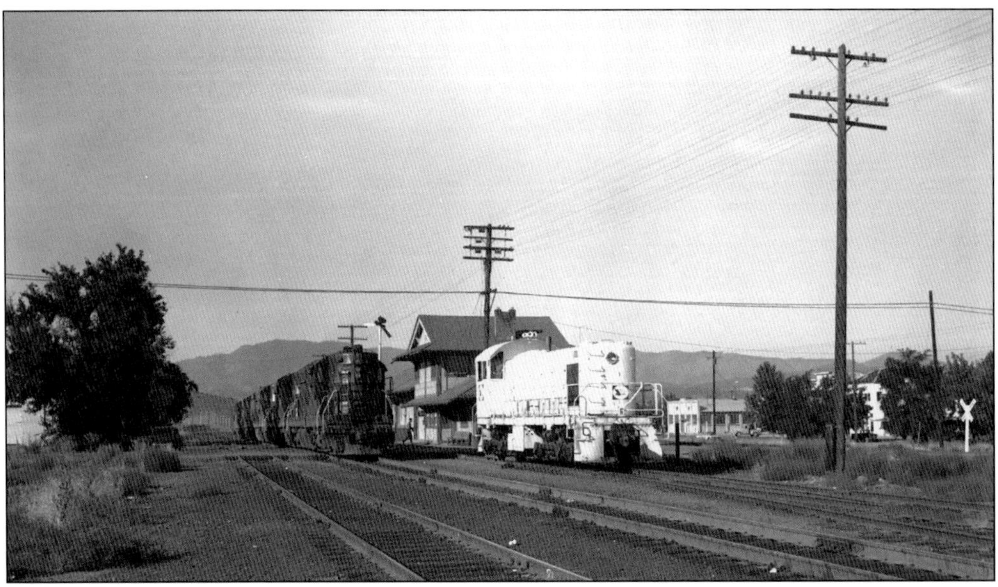

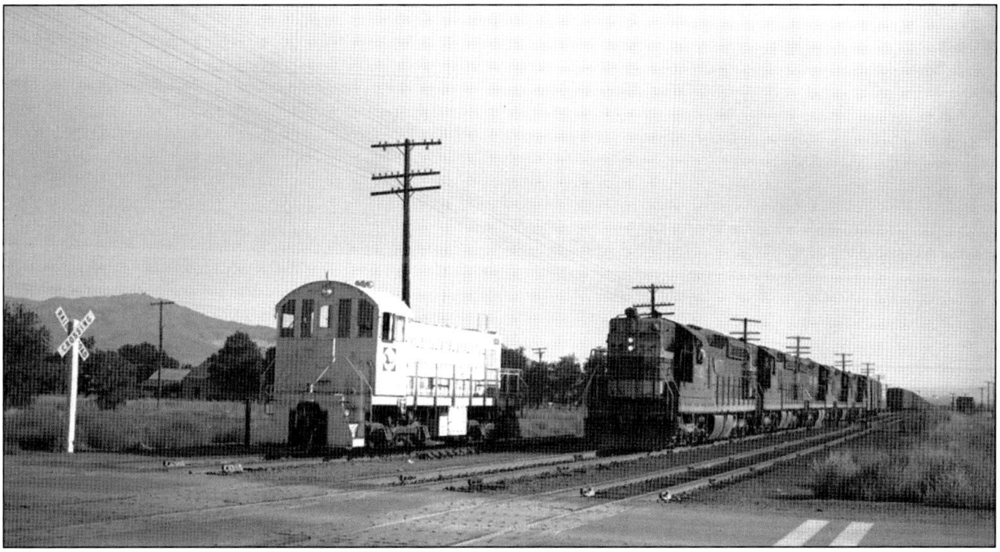

The locomotives back down onto the rest of the train. Once an air test is complete, they will continue their journey south to Weed, California. No. 603 waits patiently for the SP crews to finish their tasks so she can grab a cut of cars and return to Yreka. (Courtesy Don Hansen.)

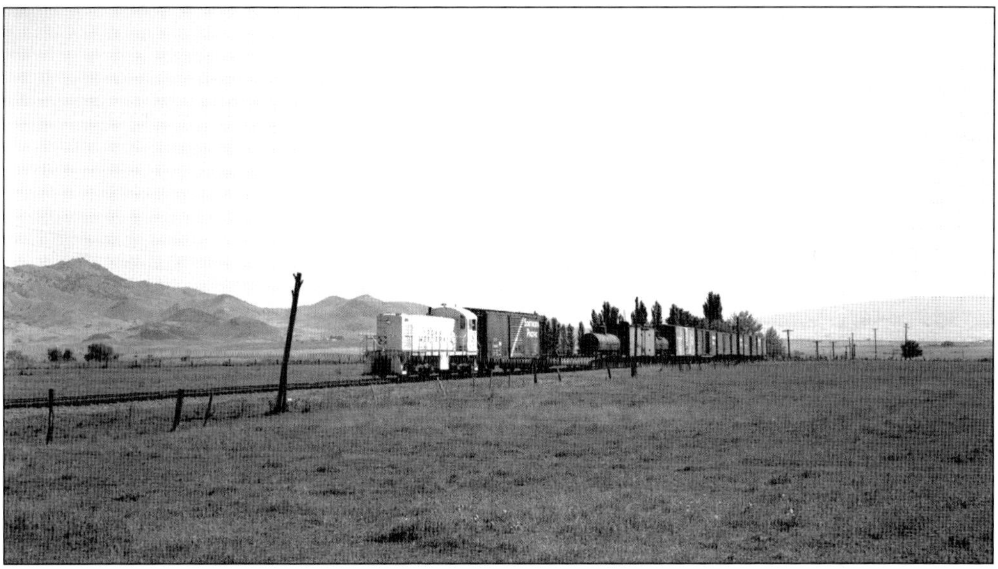

No. 603 is now on the return trip to Yreka with a cut of empty cars and two tank cars of fuel oil. The train is about cross over Highway 3 at milepost 4. (Courtesy Don Hansen.)

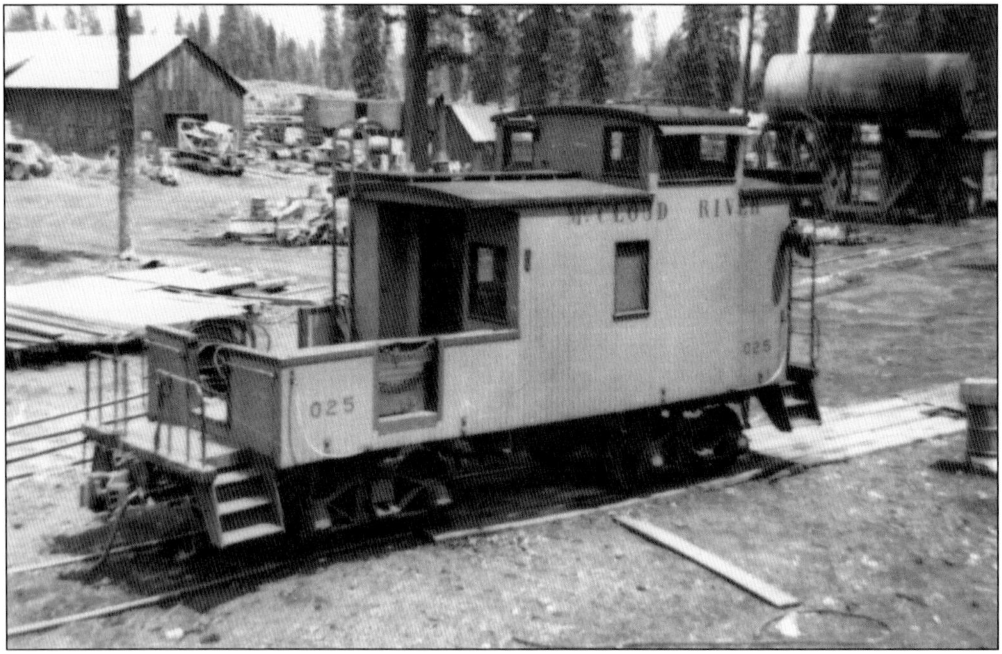

Yreka Western's sole caboose came from the McCloud River Railroad. It was originally Great Northern caboose No. X-378 until it was involved in a rear end wreck. The body of McCloud caboose No. 5 was mounted on the frame, which resulted in the open platform. It was used exclusively out of Pondosa for a number of years until a new half body was built in the McCloud shops. The caboose is pictured above on the McCloud River Railroad at Pondosa in June 1950, and below it is shown in the Yreka yards not long after its arrival on the property. (Above, courtesy of Jeff Moore.)

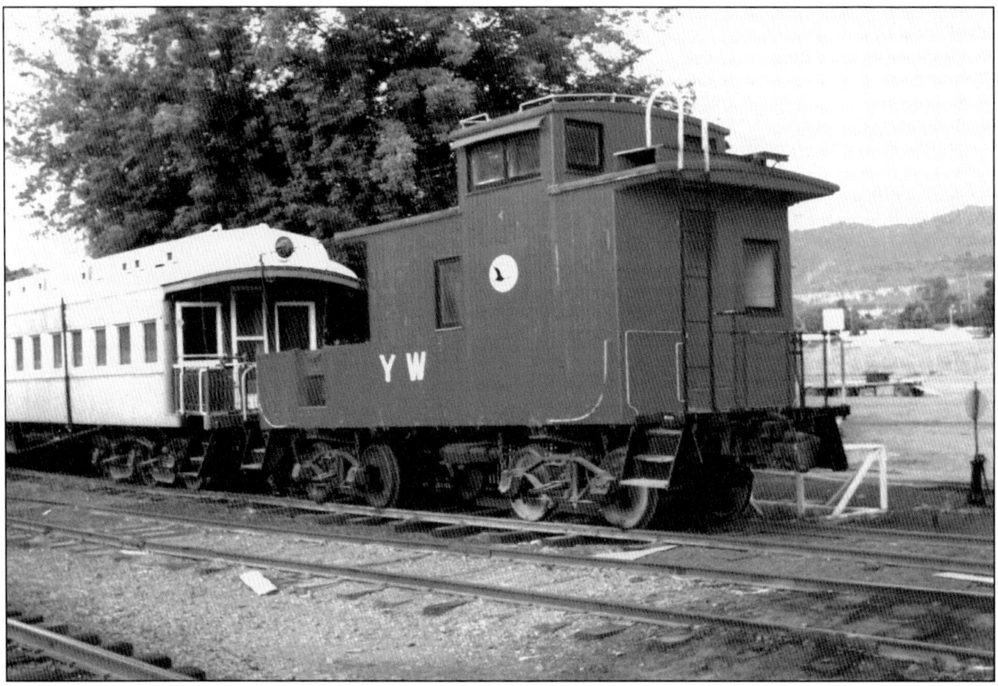

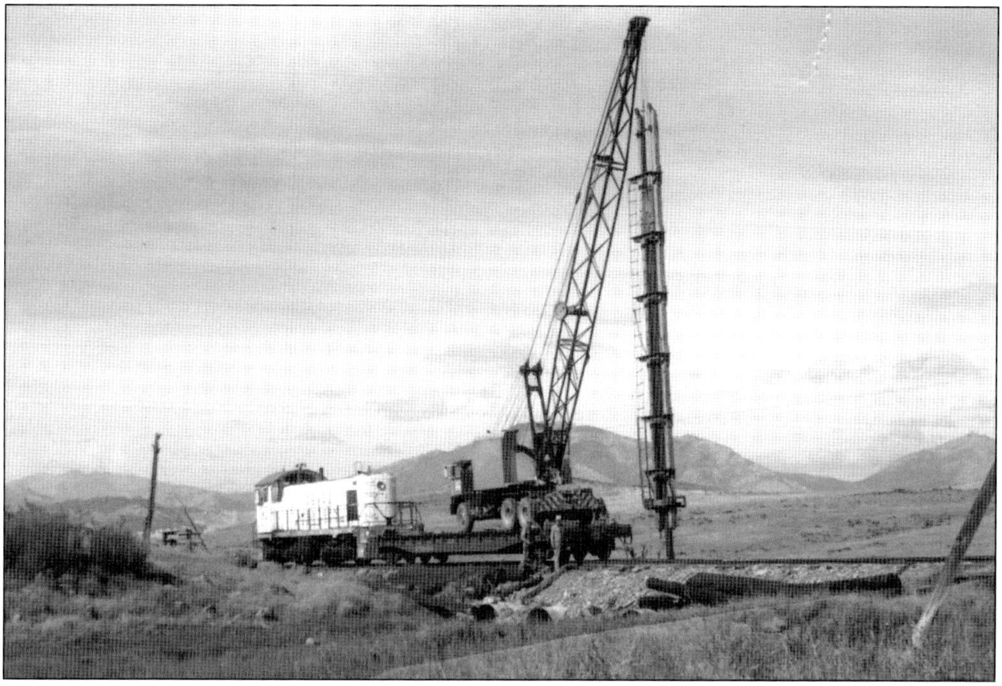

No. 604 is shown here, somewhere out in the Shasta Valley, with a pile driver mounted to the back of a flatcar.

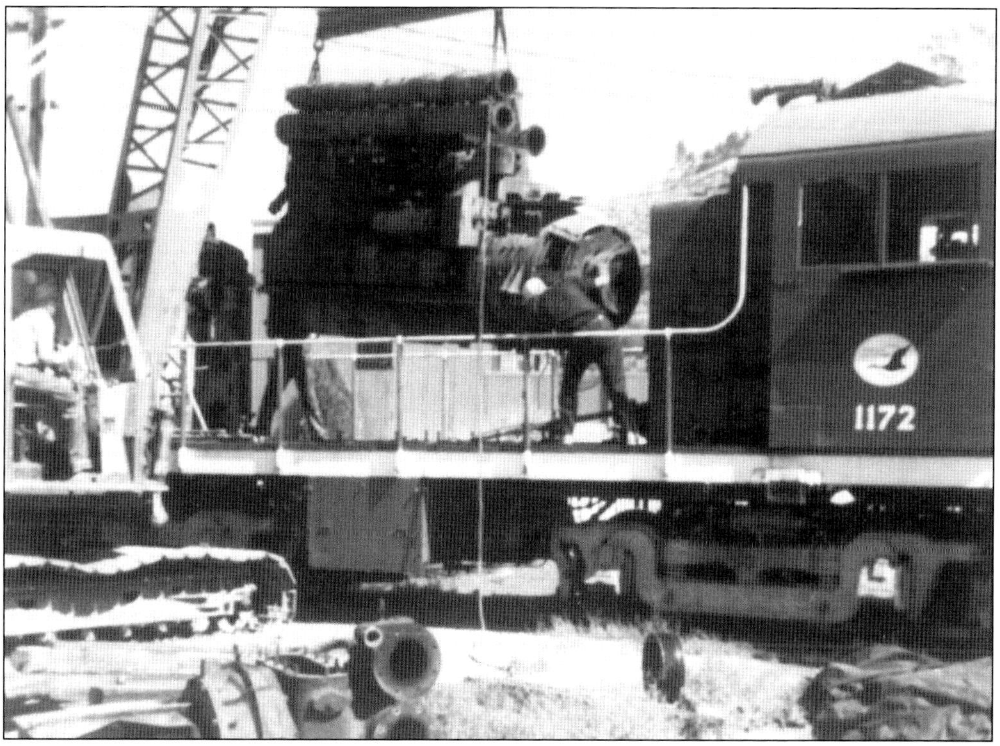

At some point in the 1970s, No. 1172 needed a new prime mover installed. Here, a crew set the new prime mover in place on the locomotive with a crane in the Yreka yards.

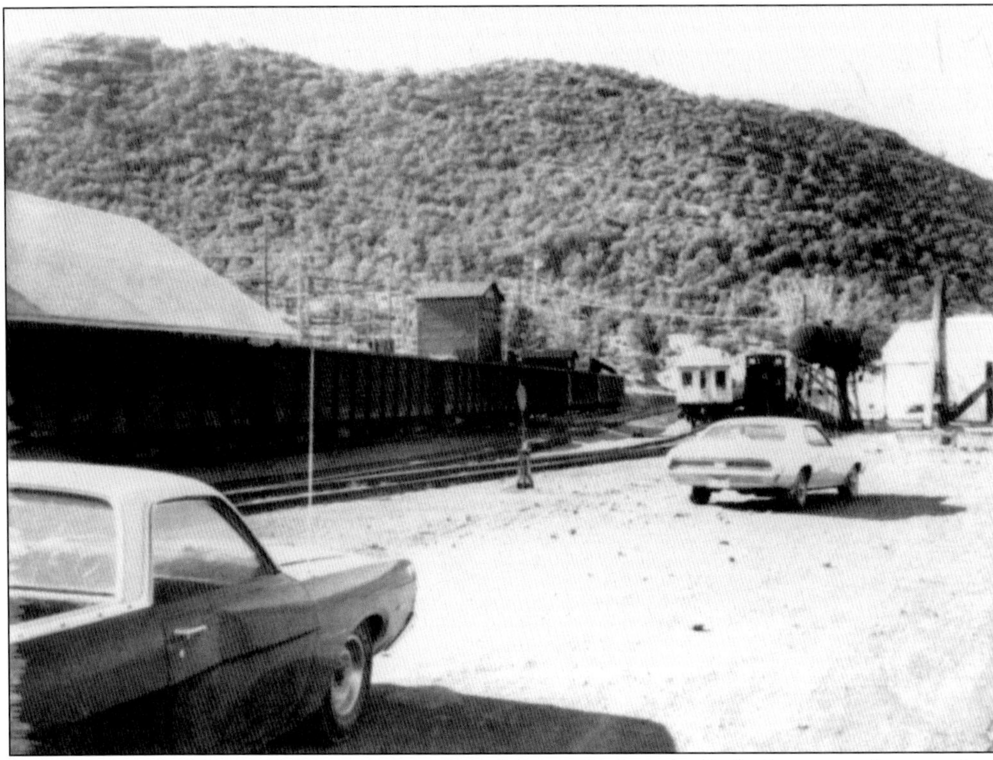

This 1975 view of the yard shows a train of gondolas parked on the Yreka house track more than likely to be loaded with ore concentrates being trucked in from mines near Happy Camp.

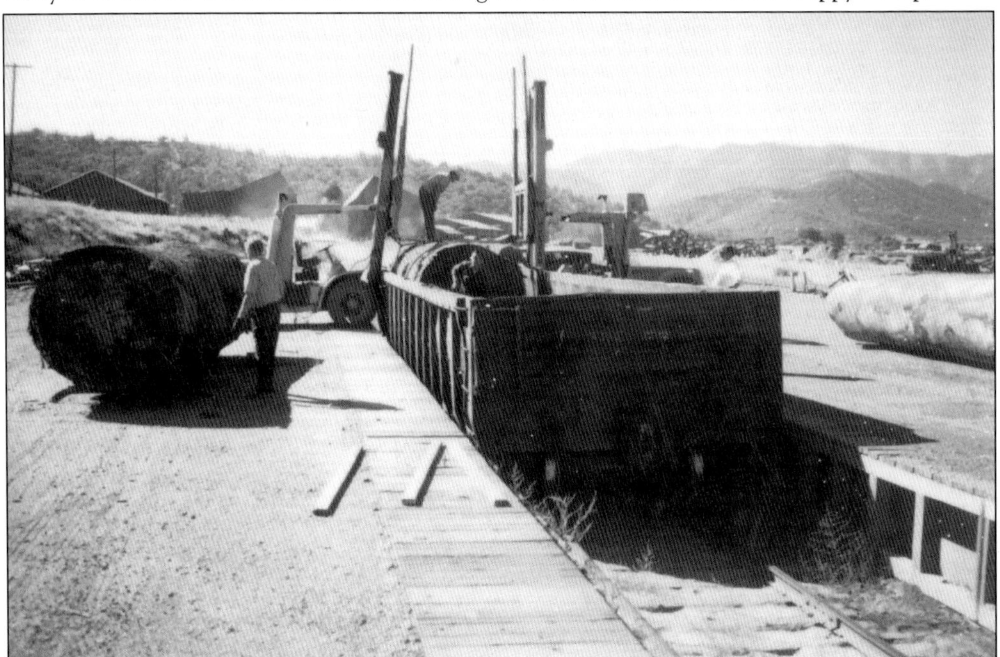

In 1976, the Pine Mountain Lumber Company of Yreka is unloading a gondola with large west fir logs imported from Africa that will be used in their timber production.

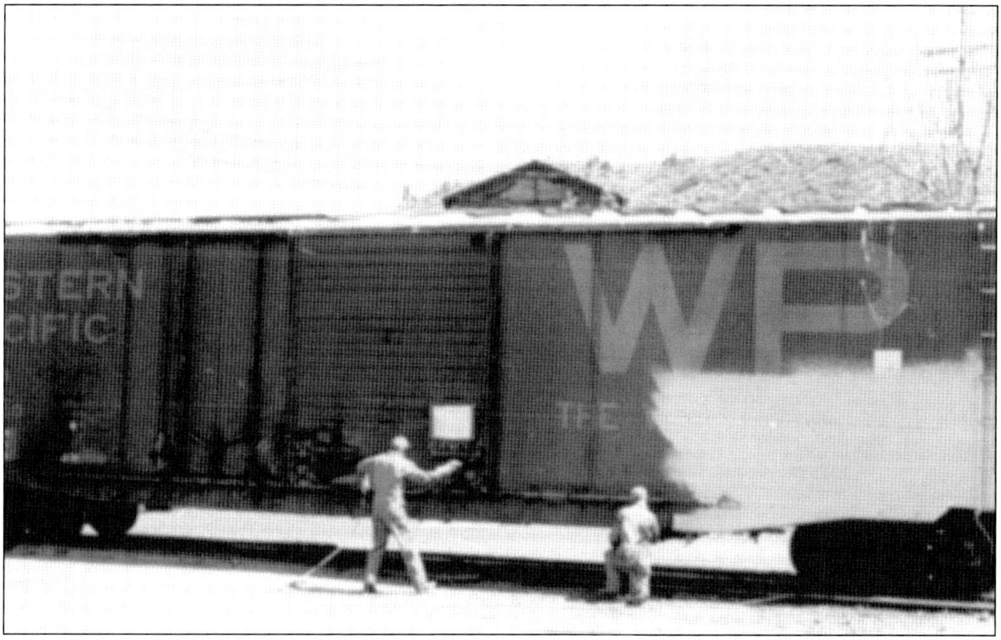

In 1976, bicentennial fever struck all across America, and many railroads painted locomotives or freight cars in a red, white, and blue scheme to honor America's 200th birthday. Yreka Western was no exception. In April of that year, crews painted a former Western Pacific boxcar with a new patriotic theme. The finished result is seen below when Yreka Western No. 35731 posed in front of the Yreka depot in March 1976.

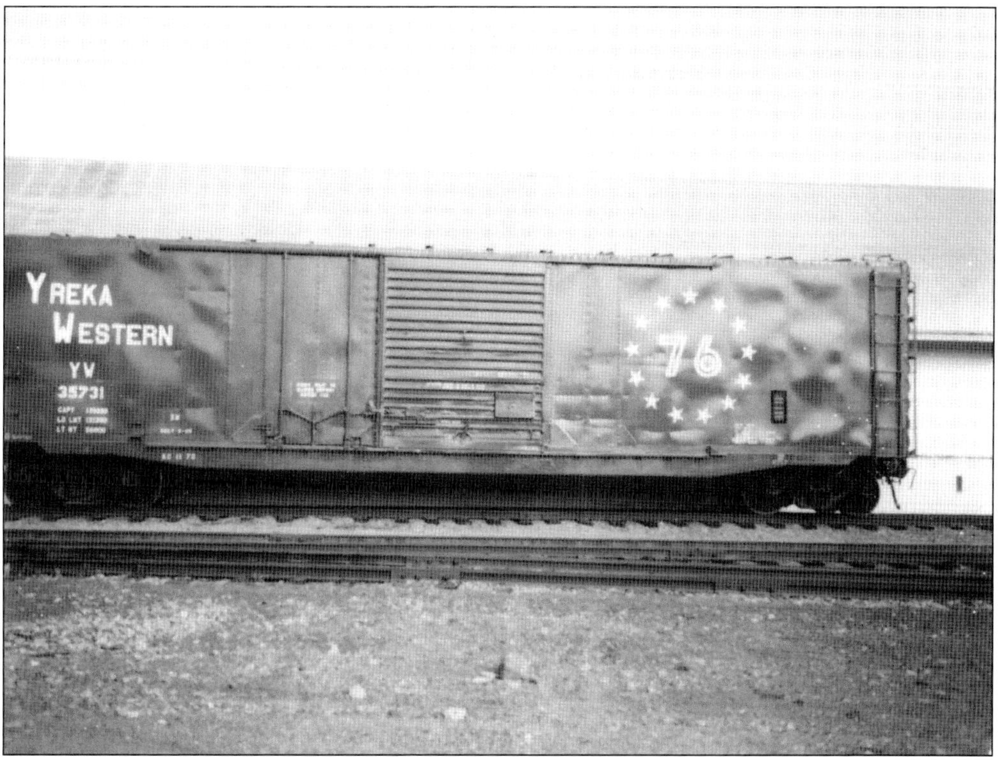

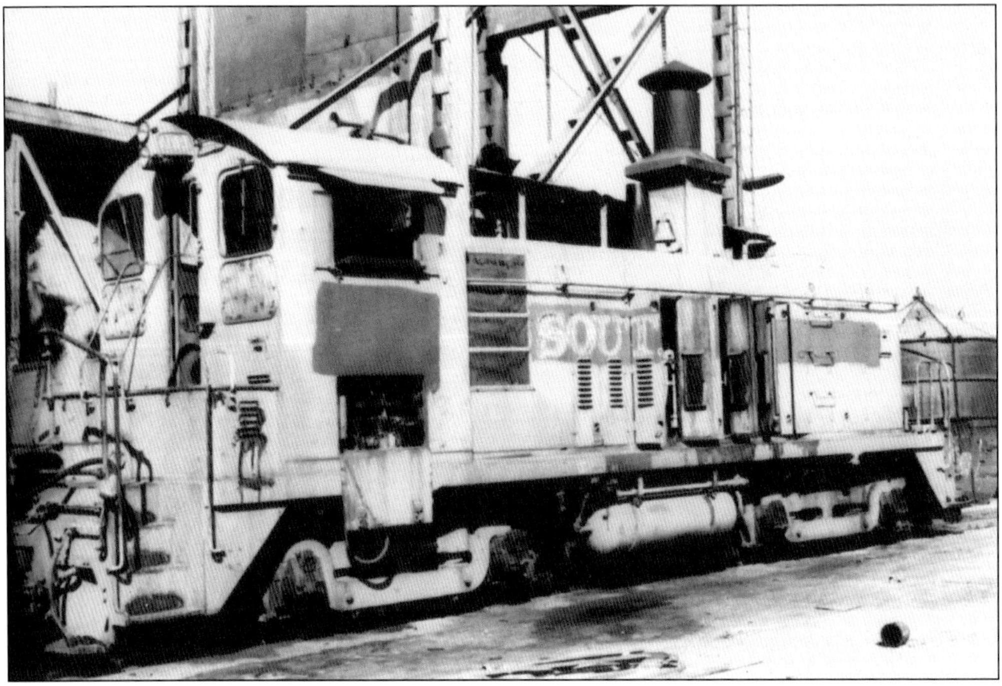

Yreka Western No. 21 is seen here in the last days of its existence as a Southern Pacific locomotive. No. 21 is former SP 1113 and arrived at the same time as No. 20, which was formerly SP 1109. Both are SW8s with dynamic brakes. Dynamics were a rarity on switching locomotives, and only 15 were ever built for the SP. This extra feature comes in handy with the Yreka Western's combination of steep grades and heavy trains.

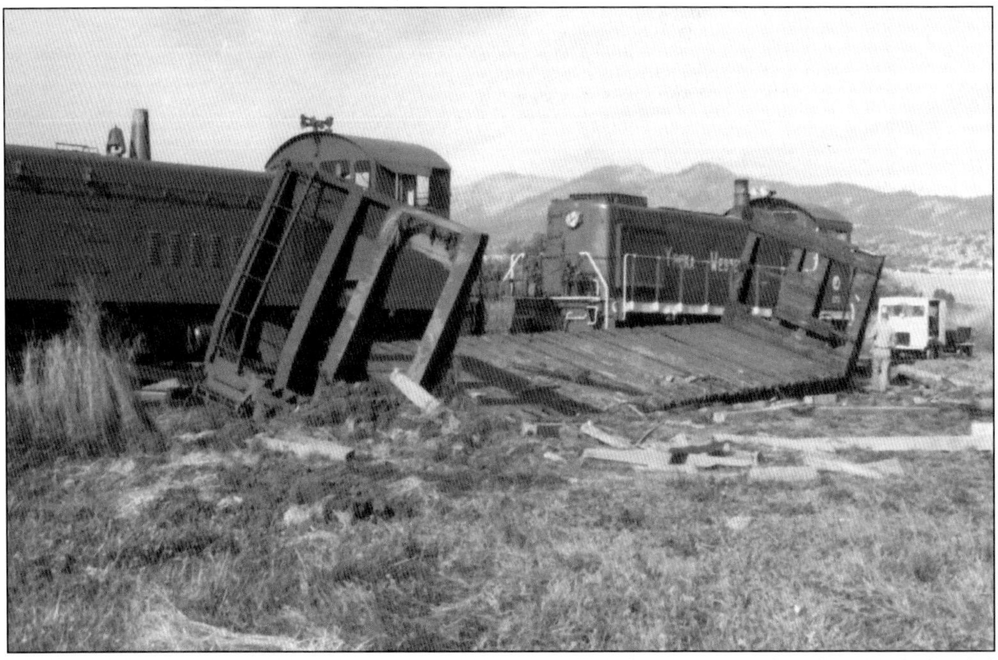

In 1978, one of the recently arrived SW8s and No. 1172 stand witness to a derailment of a loaded bulkhead at Fiock. Above is an overview of the derailment site.

During the derailment at Fiock, somehow the bulkhead got away and left the tracks, spilling the loads of lumber all over the field.

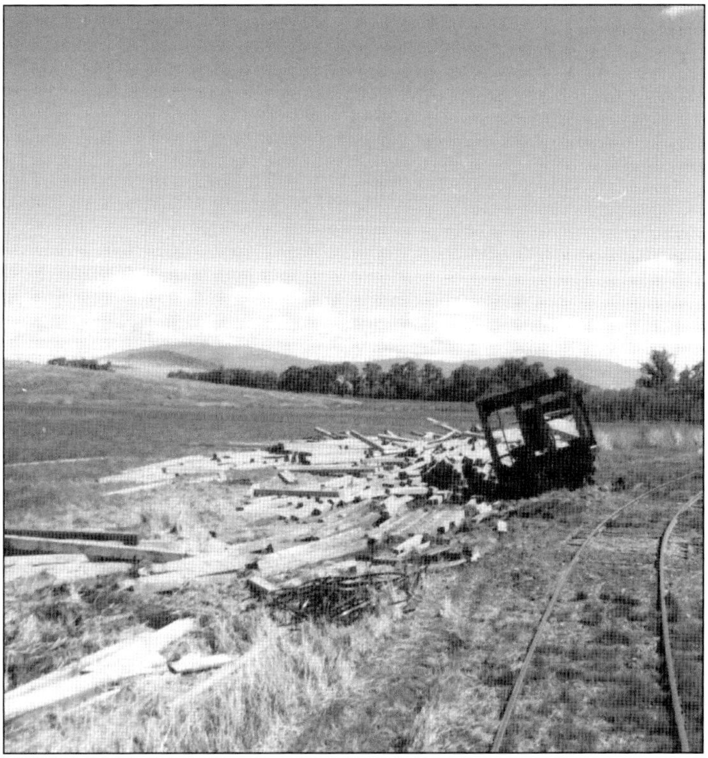

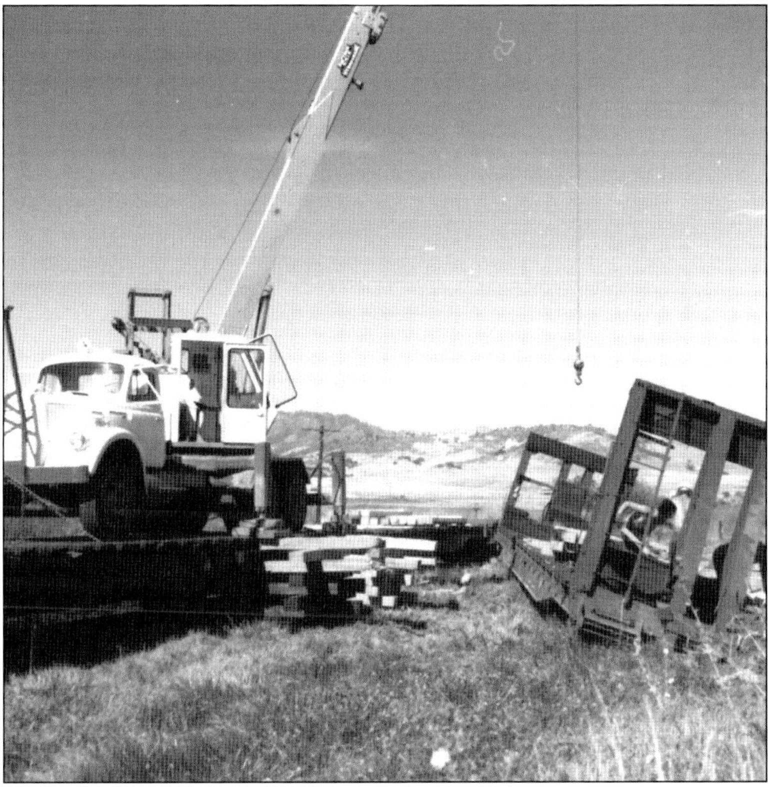

Not long after the incident at Fiock, Yreka Western brought in a pair of flatcars with a crane mounted on top of one to begin cleaning up the mess at the derailment site. The crews have begun stacking the undamaged finished lumber on one of the flatcars and will then begin the process of putting the bulkhead flatcar back on the rails.

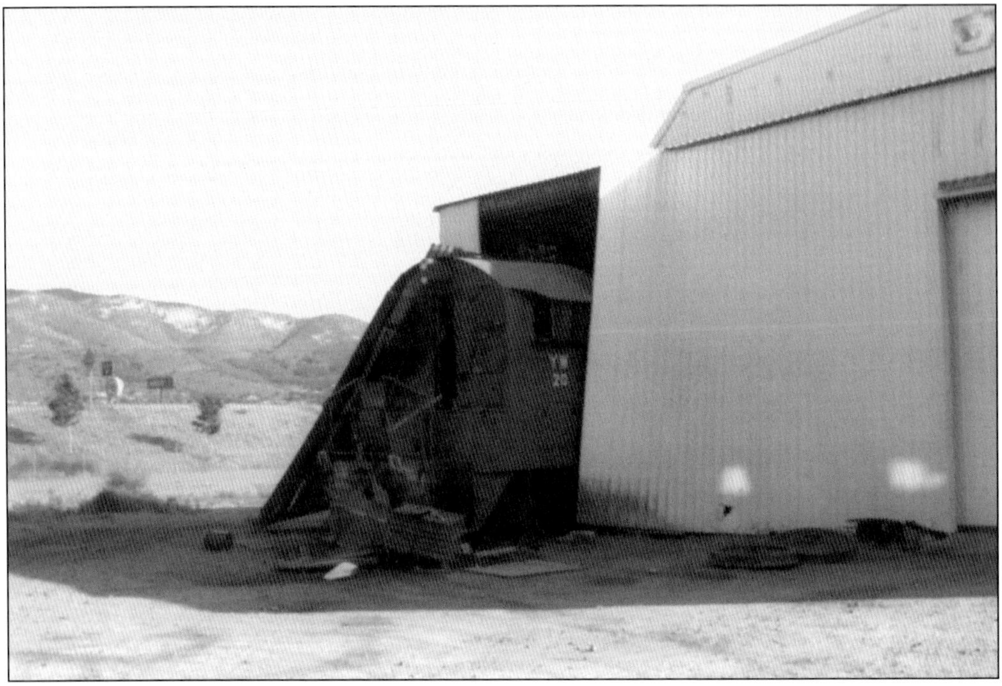

It's 1981, and a slight miscalculation has sent No. 20 through the back of the shop. No. 20 was sitting in the shop when one of the YW's business cars and caboose got away and ran down the shop lead through the doors and slammed into No. 20, sending her through the back wall of the shop.

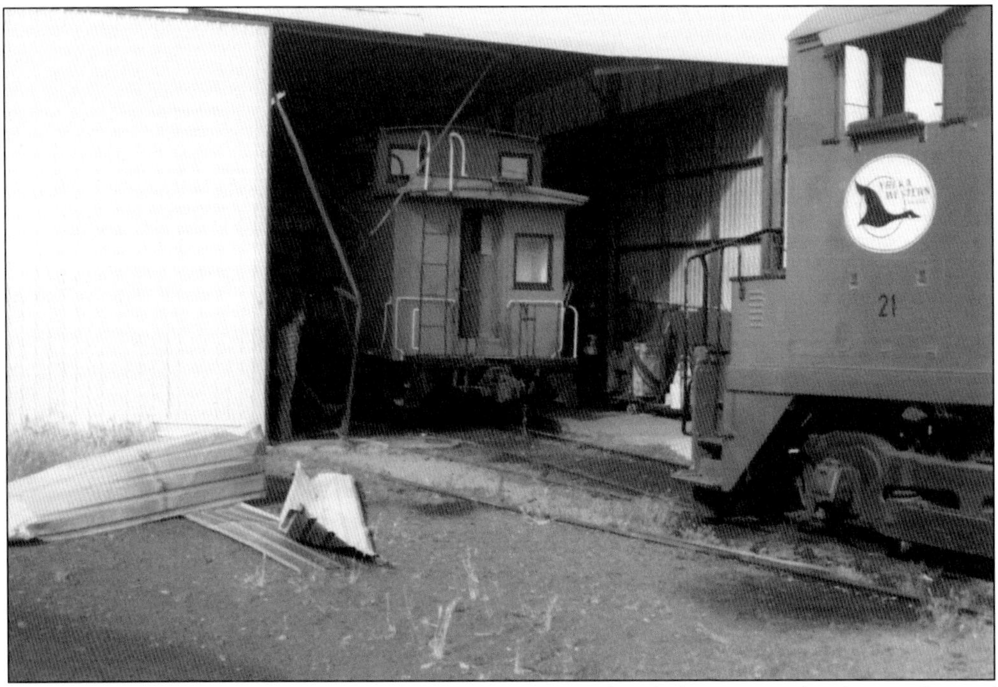

The culprits in the incident, though the business car can barely be seen in the shop in front of the caboose. Also note the bent frames for the metal shop doors to the left of the caboose.

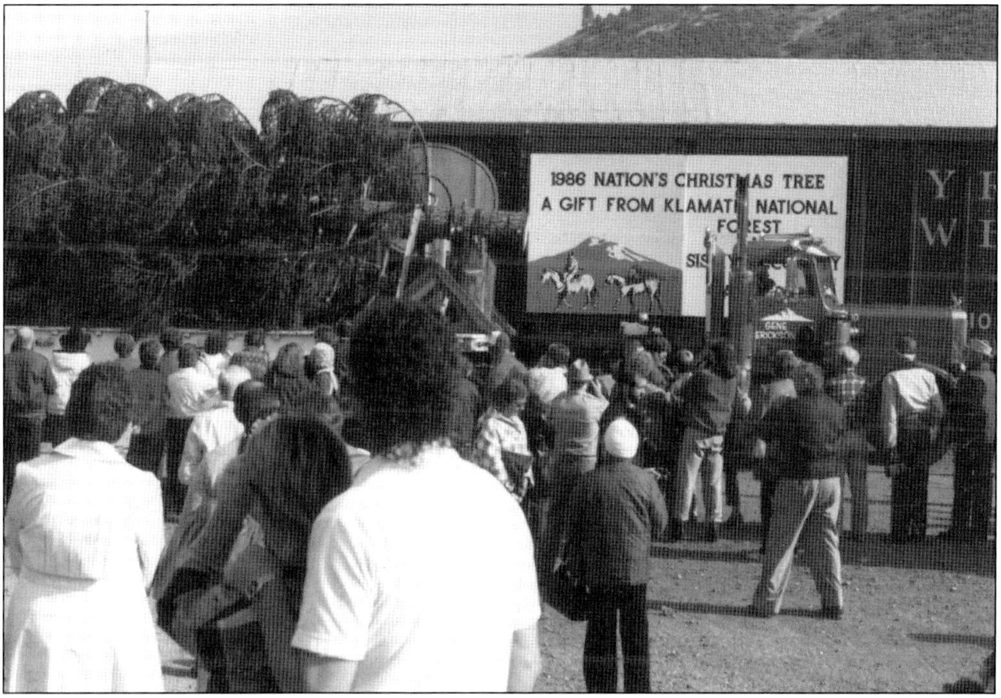

In 1986, the national Christmas tree was cut from the Klamath Forest and started its journey east on a Yreka Western freight train pulled by No. 21. Shown above is the special train at the Yreka depot, and below the train poses for a photograph at Fiocks.

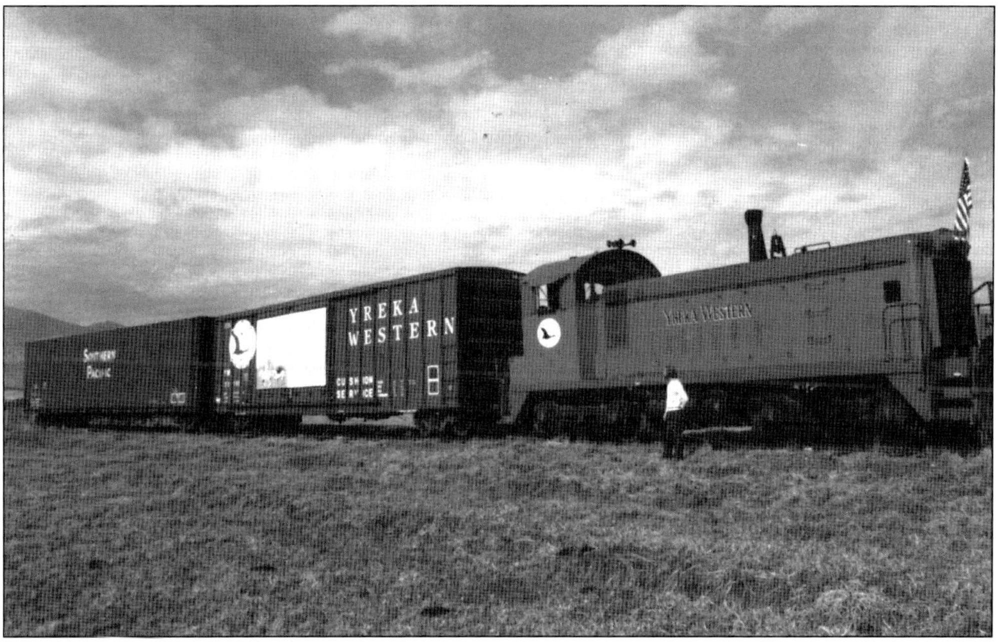

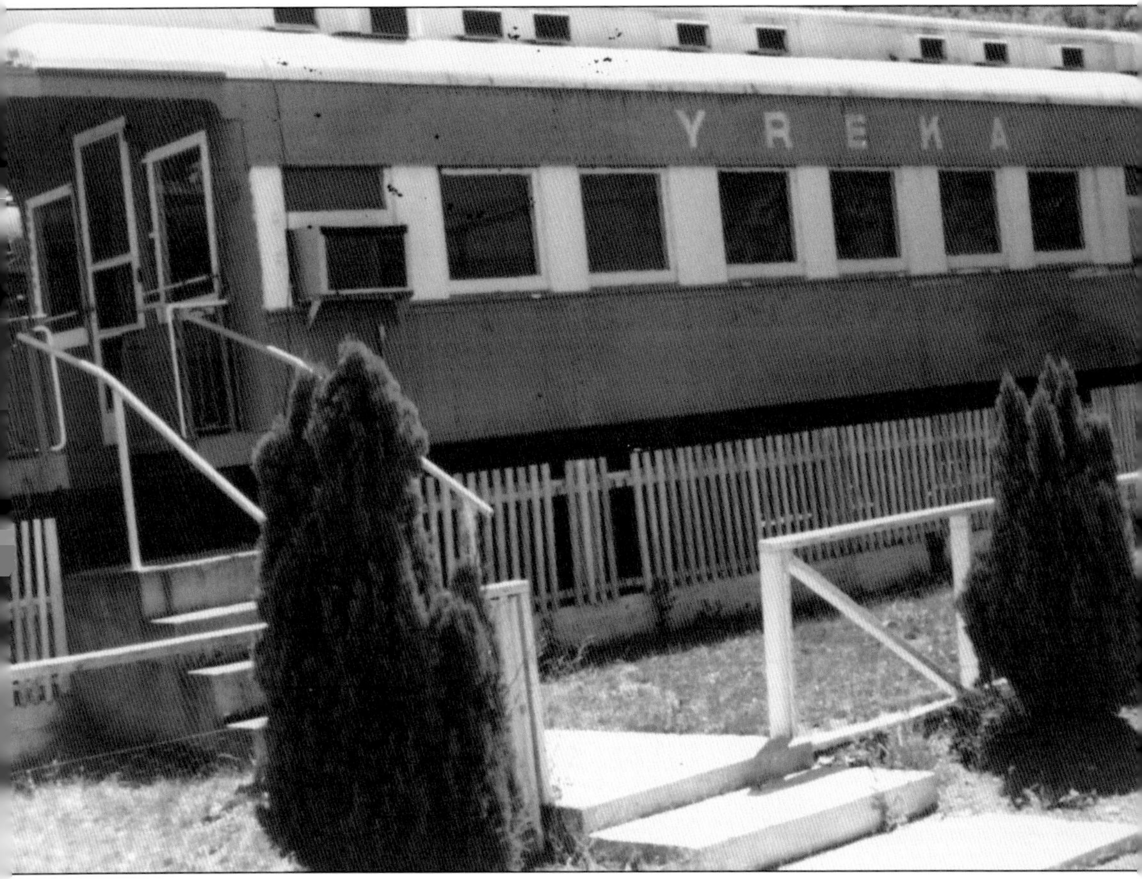

When Willis Kyle purchased the Yreka Western, he had a small spur laid next to the shop and a private business car brought in. He used this car for his accommodations when he made his trips to Yreka.

Five

The Modern Years

Yreka Western managed to hang on during the 1990s, with only two lumber mills being served by the railroad. Willis B. Kyle also passed away, leaving his short line empire to Lynn Cecil. In 1999, the Hi-Ridge Lumber Company shut down their mill in Yreka, leaving Timber Products' veneer plant and Suburban Propane as the only customers left on the line. In 1999, Cecil filed for abandonment of the YW, but Timber Products filed a motion to keep the line operating. The railroad was kept open, and Cecil put the railroad up for sale. The citizens of Yreka were fearful that they were about to lose the railroad and formed a committee known as the Committee to Save the Blue Goose. The Rocky Mountain Mining and Railroad Museum out of Denver, Colorado, noticed the movement in Yreka to save the YW. On January 14, 2000, the Rocky Mountain Mining and Railroad Museum purchased the Yreka Western. The YW then started shipping veneer along with the wood chips that they had already been shipping. That year the YW hauled over 2,000 carloads, the highest it had been in 25 years. In 2003, the summit tunnel on the Siskiyou caught fire, closing the CORP line into Oregon. This had a negative impact on the YW, and once again Yreka Western went bankrupt and was put into receivership. All operations came to a complete stop, with nothing moving on the railroad.

Also during this time, a legal battle came up. The Rocky Mountain Mining and Railroad Museum found that the general manager had embezzled money. In April 2005, the summit tunnel on the Siskiyou was reopened, and traffic once again could move north. A new general manager was hired by the railroad, and repairs began to get No. 19 back into service. Excursion trains continued to operate until the end of 2008. In May 2008, CORP mothballed the Siskiyou Line, cutting off Yreka Western from the rest of America's rail network. At the time of this writing, the railroad is surviving on car storage, though there is hope to eventually resume normal operations at a future date. Yreka Western isn't known as The Little Railroad that Refuses to Die for nothing.

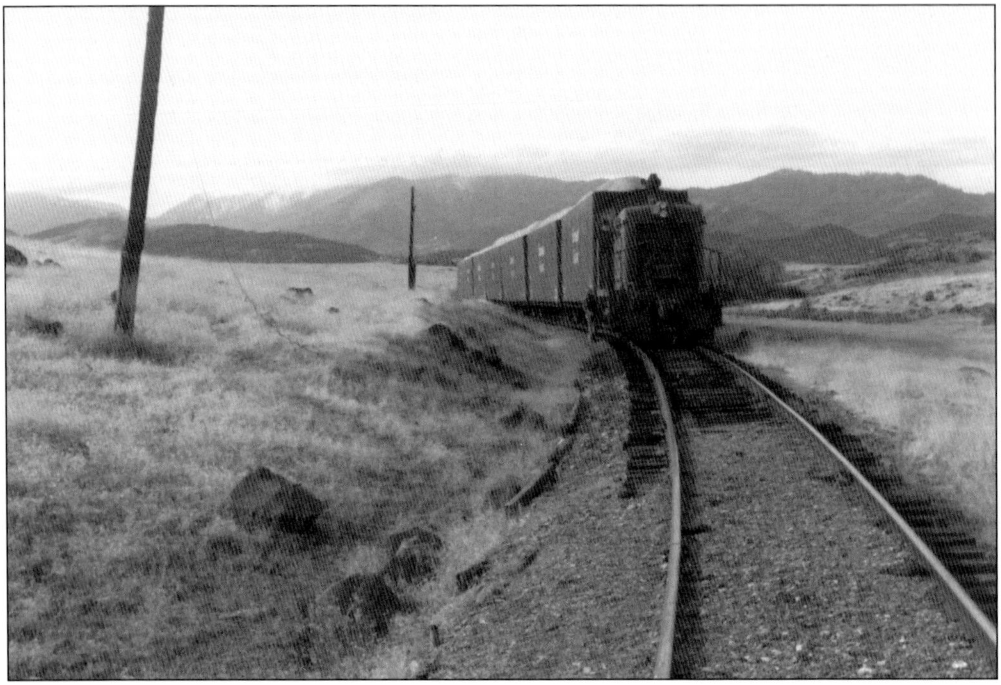

No. 20 and her train of loaded chip cars stop to pose for a photograph somewhere just outside of Montague in January 1989.

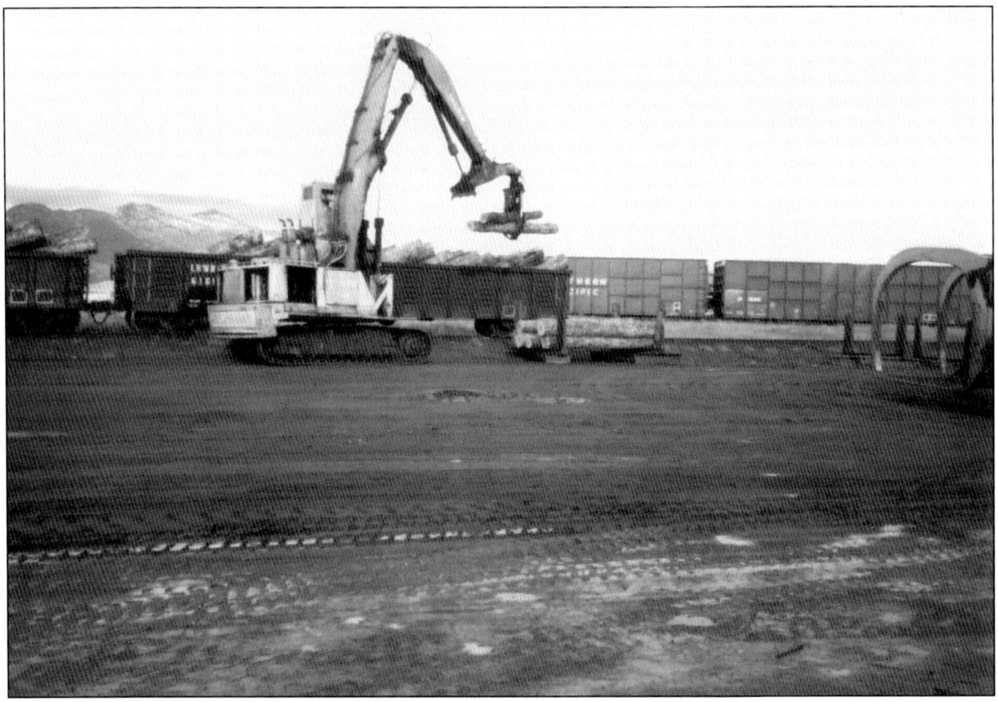

During the 1990s, Hi-Ridge Lumber Company experimented with importing logs from New Zealand. The logs were brought in by rail in gondolas to the Hi-Ridge's mill east of Yreka. The importing of logs never caught on and was only done twice.

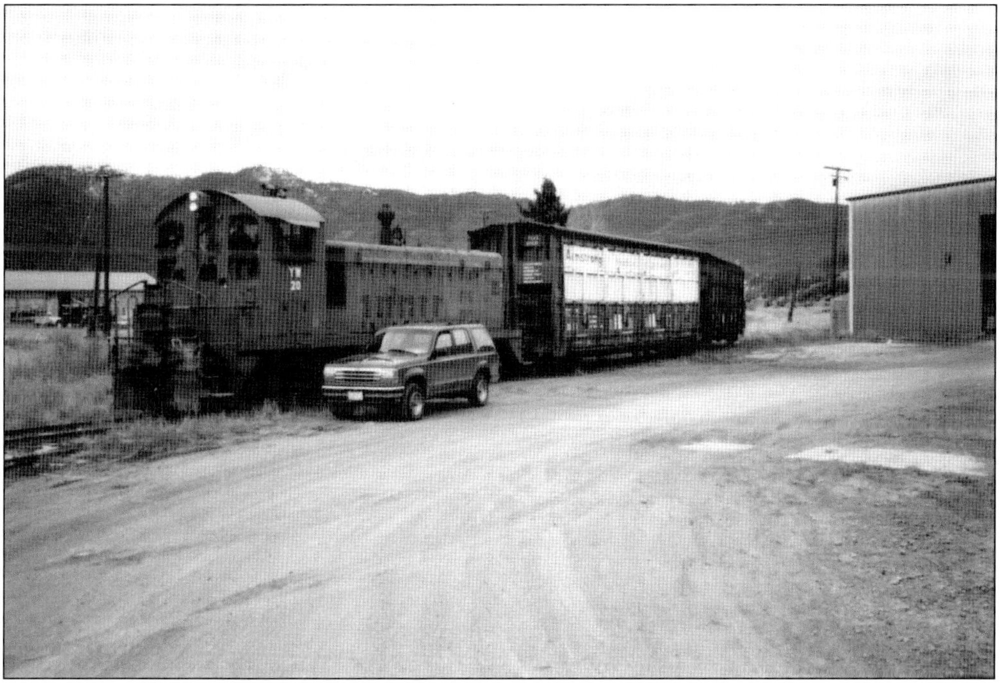

Another customer on the Yreka Western during the early 1990s was Klamath River Moulding. Their mill was the last shipper on the railroad left in the Oberlin Road area. Shipping at this time wasn't on a regular basis and was typically loads of lumber brought in to be emptied. Occasionally, chip cars would be loaded here as well.

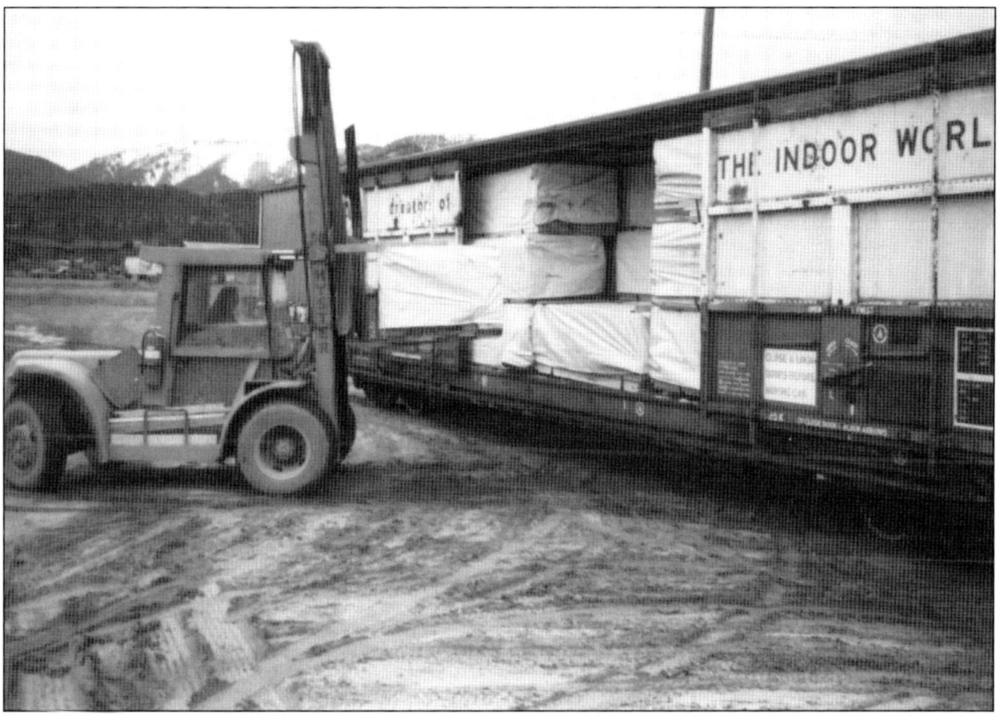

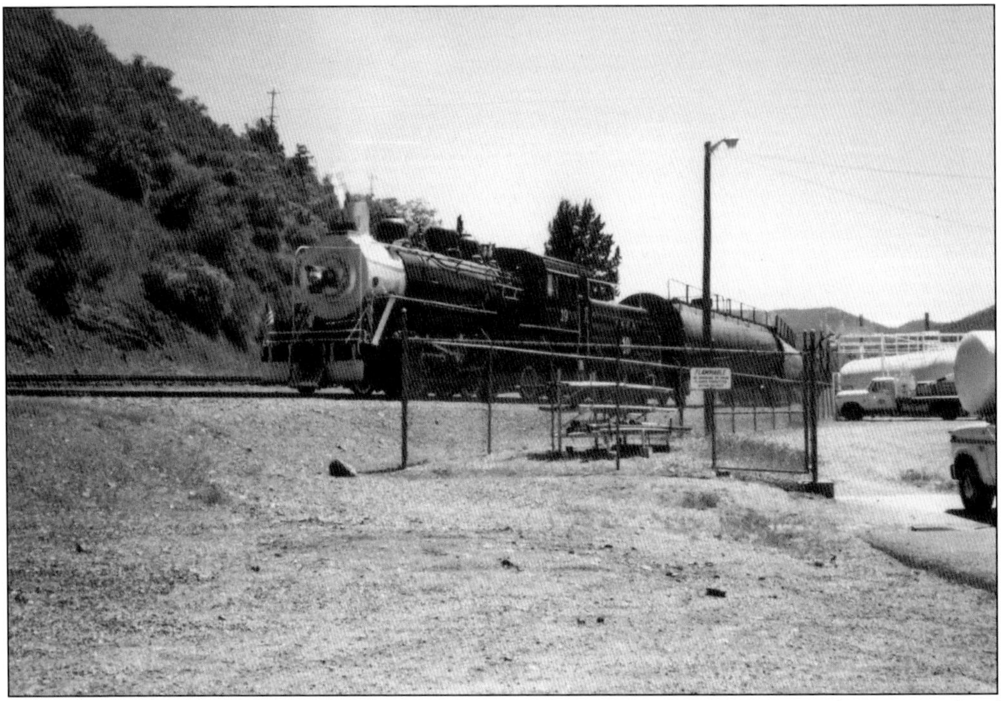

Pictured here No. 19 is switching cars into the Suburban Propane spur in Yreka just south of the depot.

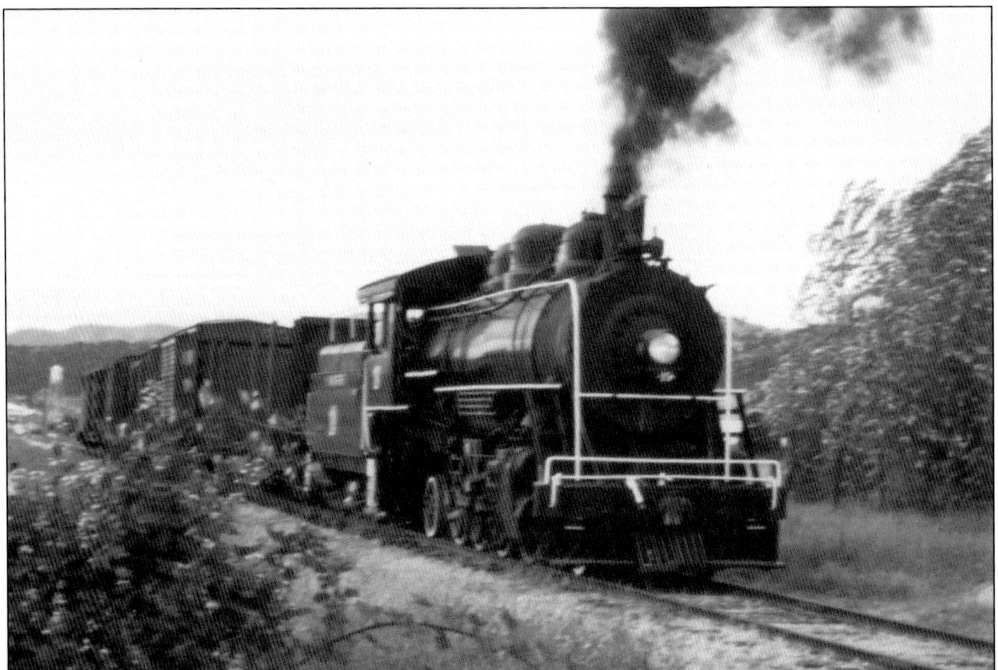

In 1995, Hollywood again came knocking at the door. No. 19 and a specially put together train were to perform a role in the television movie series *Red Shoe Diaries* in an episode titled "Slow Train." Here, No. 19 struts her stuff for the cameras at the Fiock road crossing.

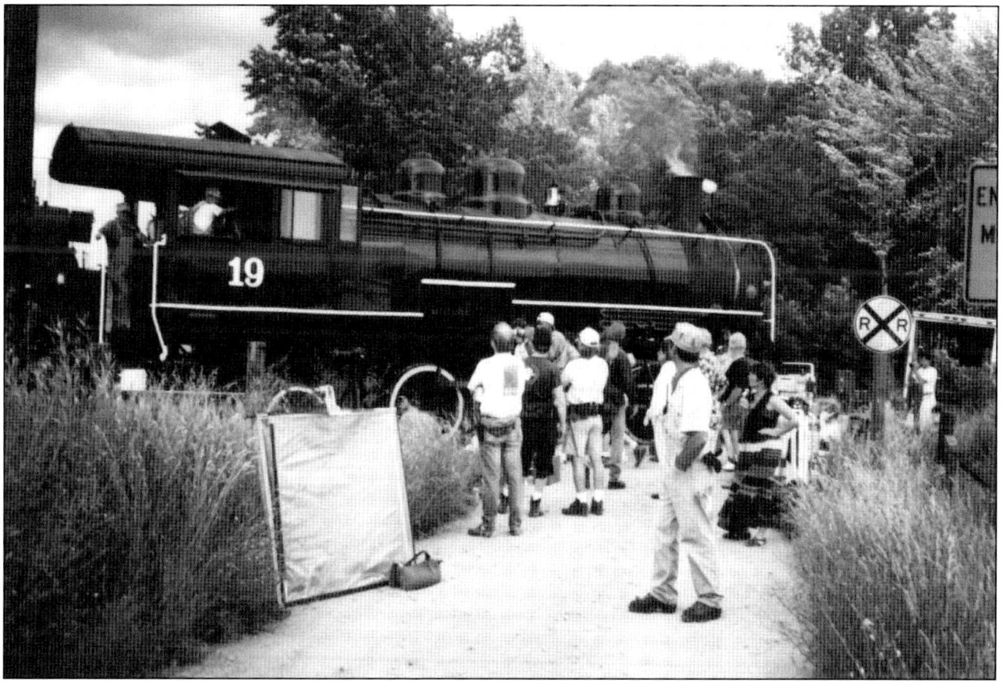

The movie and train crews discuss the next moves to be made. The same scene often required several run bys to get the shot at a variety of angles.

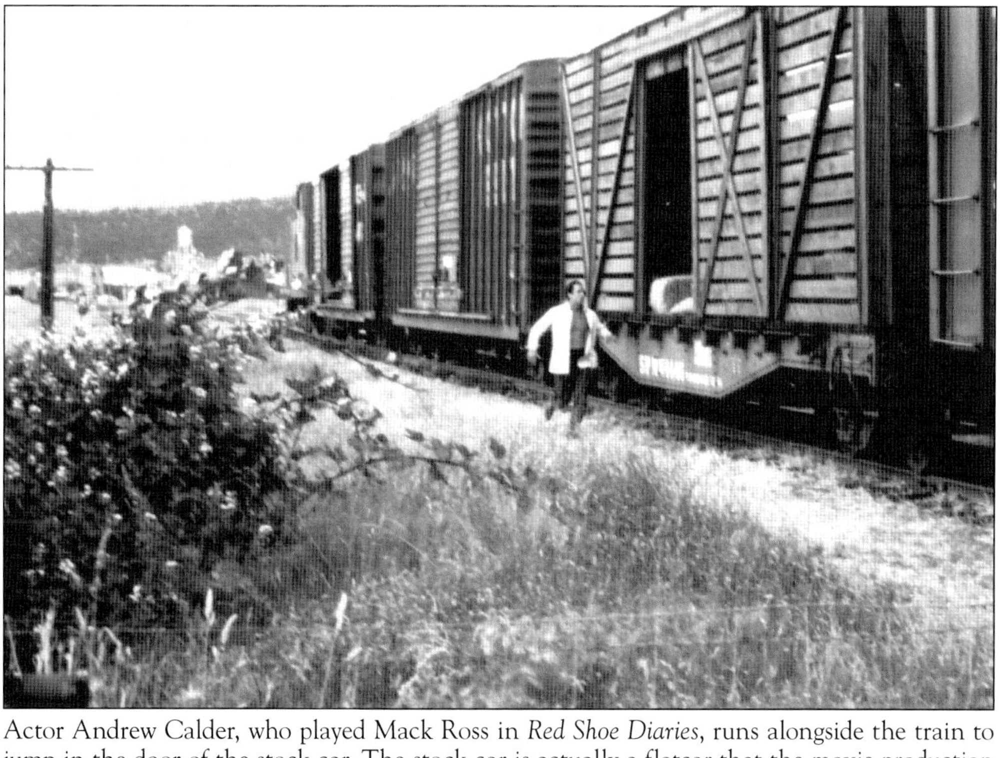

Actor Andrew Calder, who played Mack Ross in *Red Shoe Diaries*, runs alongside the train to jump in the door of the stock car. The stock car is actually a flatcar that the movie production team converted into a stock car in about a day specifically for this shot.

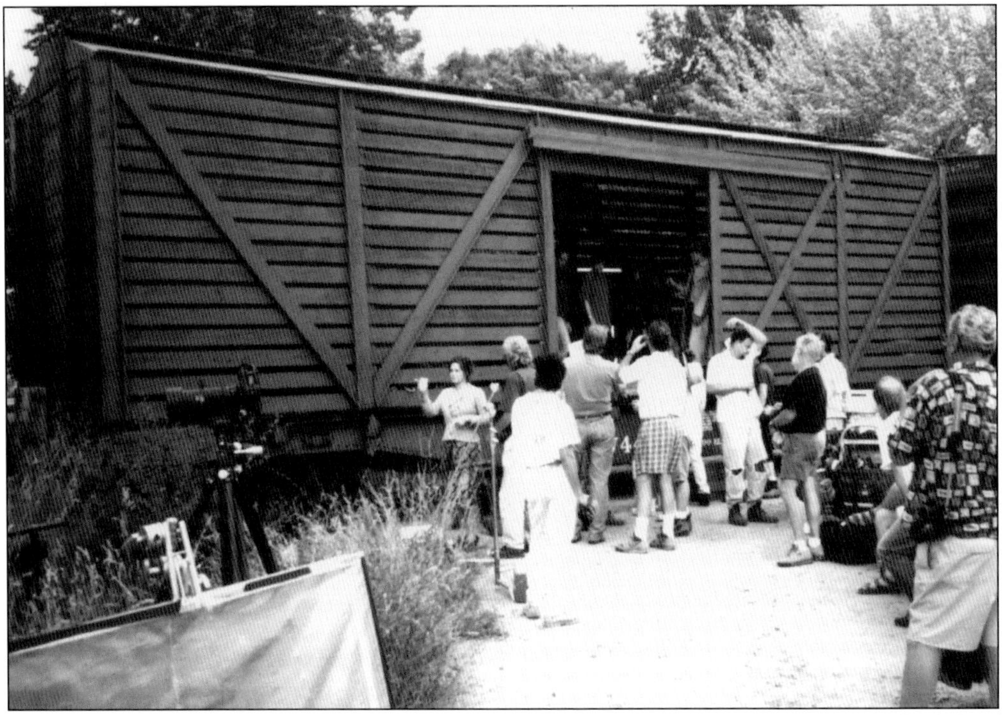

The production team sets up for the next scene to be filmed. The woman at the far left of this photograph is Athena Massey, who played the main character of Edna Gaines in *Red Shoe Diaries*.

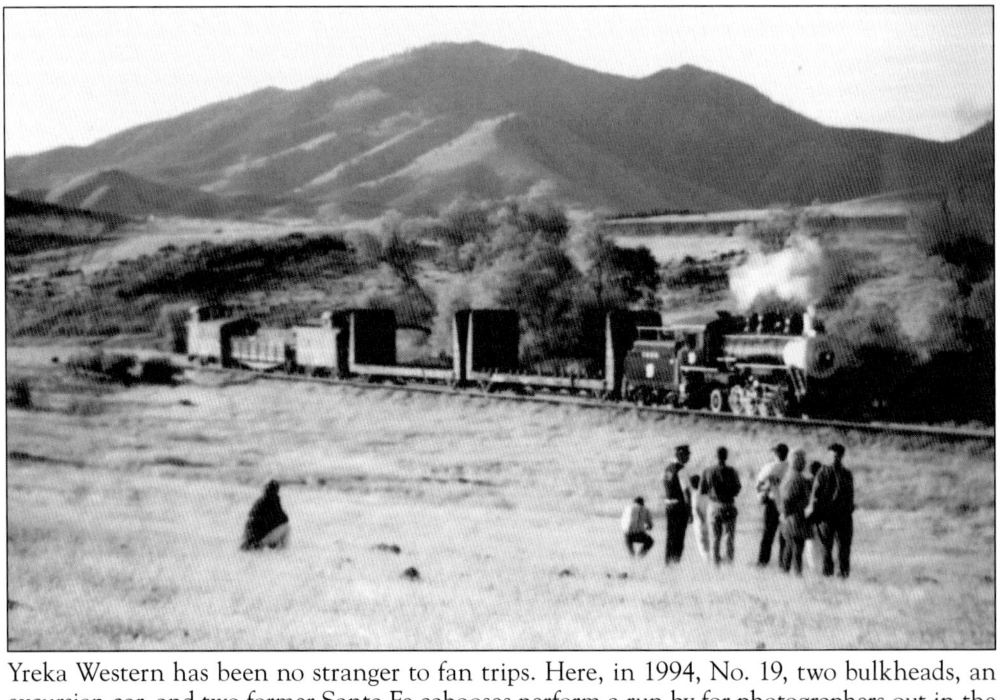

Yreka Western has been no stranger to fan trips. Here, in 1994, No. 19, two bulkheads, an excursion car, and two former Santa Fe cabooses perform a run by for photographers out in the Shasta Valley near Montague.

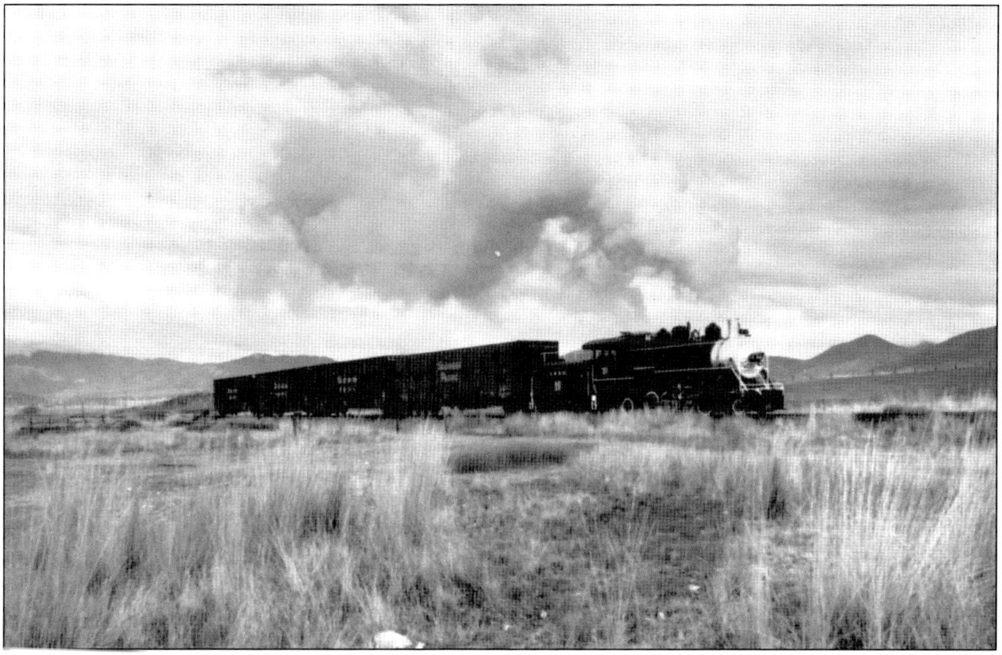

Even in today's modern times, No. 19 is still occasionally called to freight service when the diesel is unavailable due to mechanical issues. No. 19 is one of the last steam locomotives in the United States to haul revenue freight on a semi-regular basis.

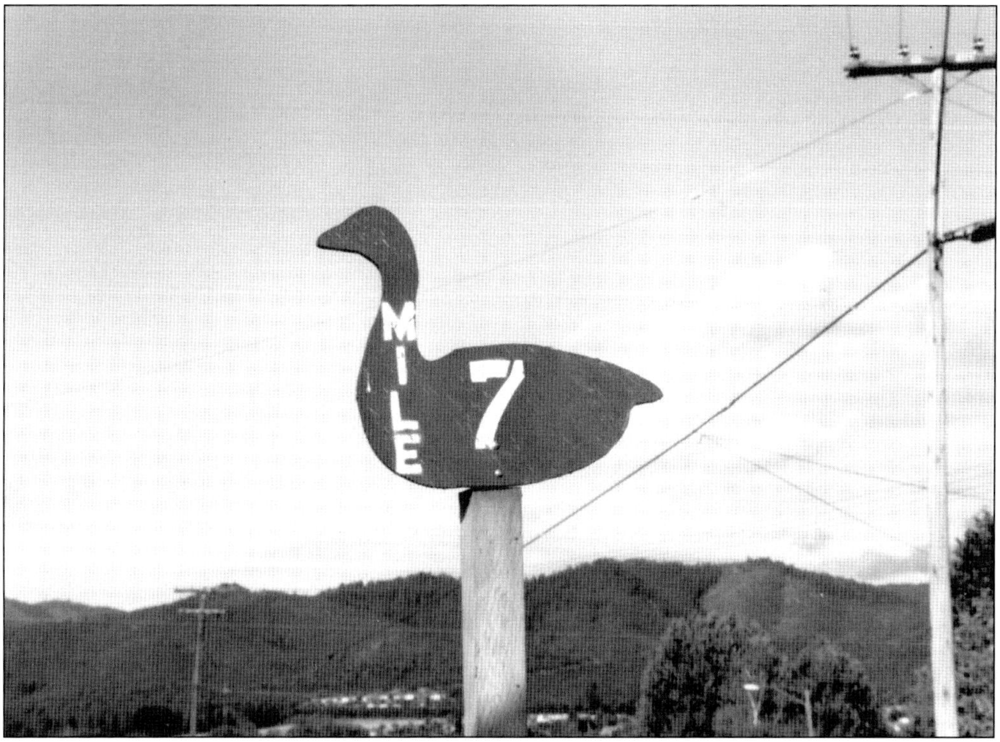

Here is one of Yreka Western's quite distinctive Blue Goose milepost markers. This particular one is located on the east side of the North Foothill Drive crossing in Yreka.

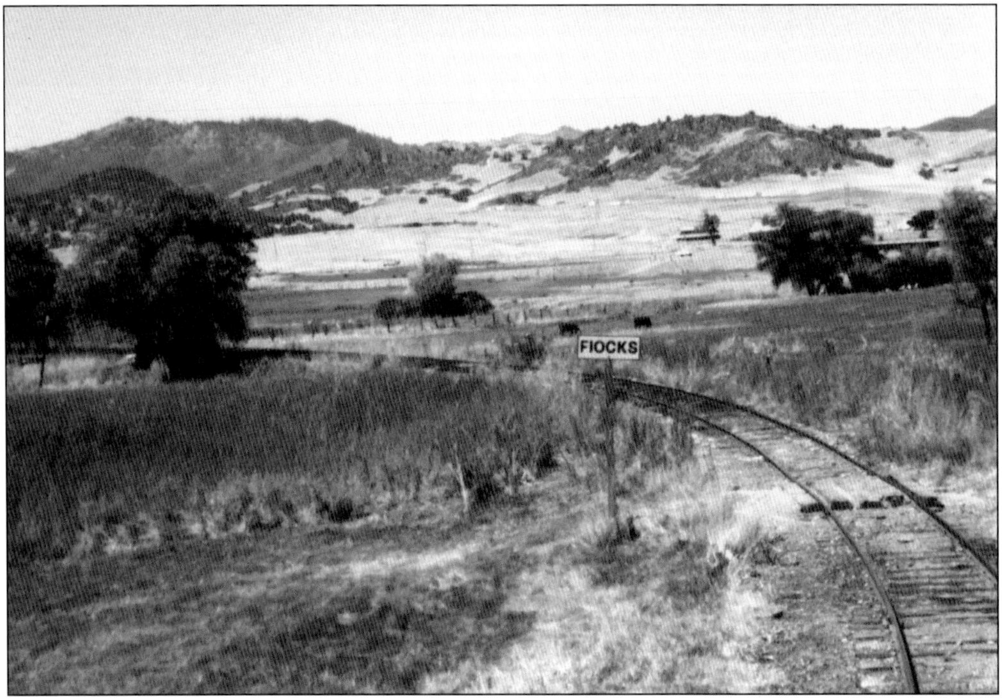

Just after the Shasta River Bridge crossing is a location on the railroad known as Fiocks, as indicated by the sign and small grade crossing. While the sign and crossing have faded away in recent years, the location is still marked on the Yreka Western timetable.

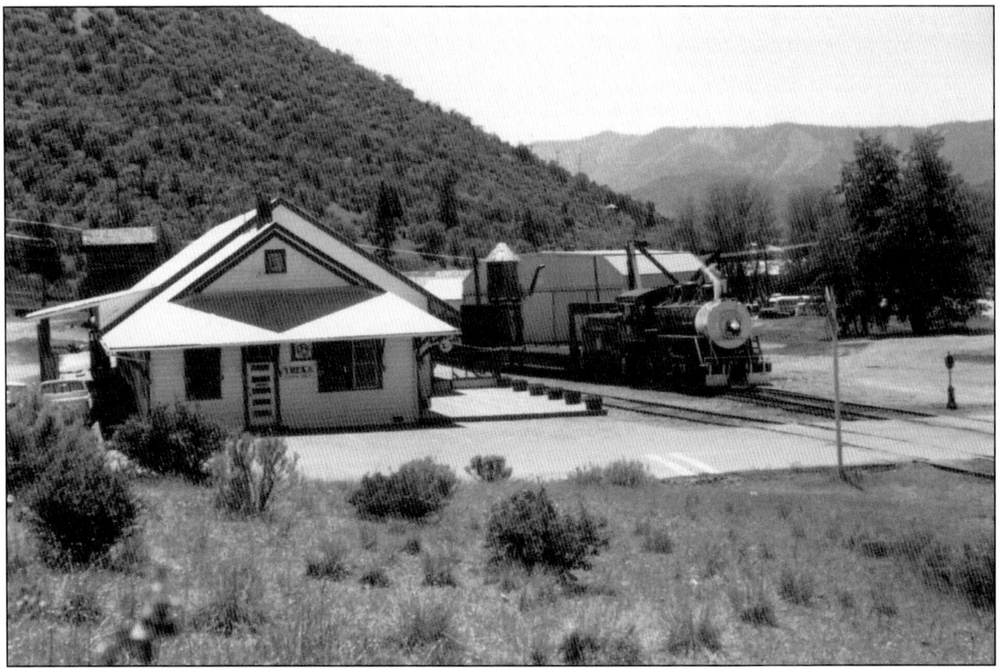

Early in 1990, No. 19 is switching freight cars in the Yreka yards. The lack of any passengers around the platform indicates this was more than likely a revenue freight run being prepared to be hauled by No. 19.

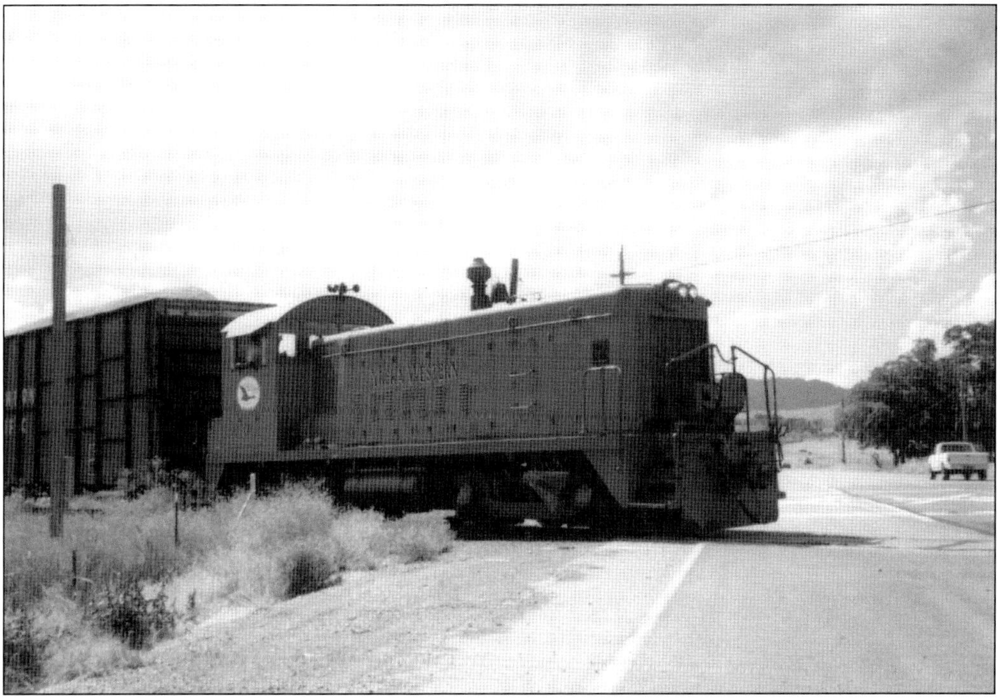

In the summer of 1996, No. 21 has finished her switching in the mill and pulls her train east towards Montague, crossing California State Highway 3. (Courtesy Jeff Moore.)

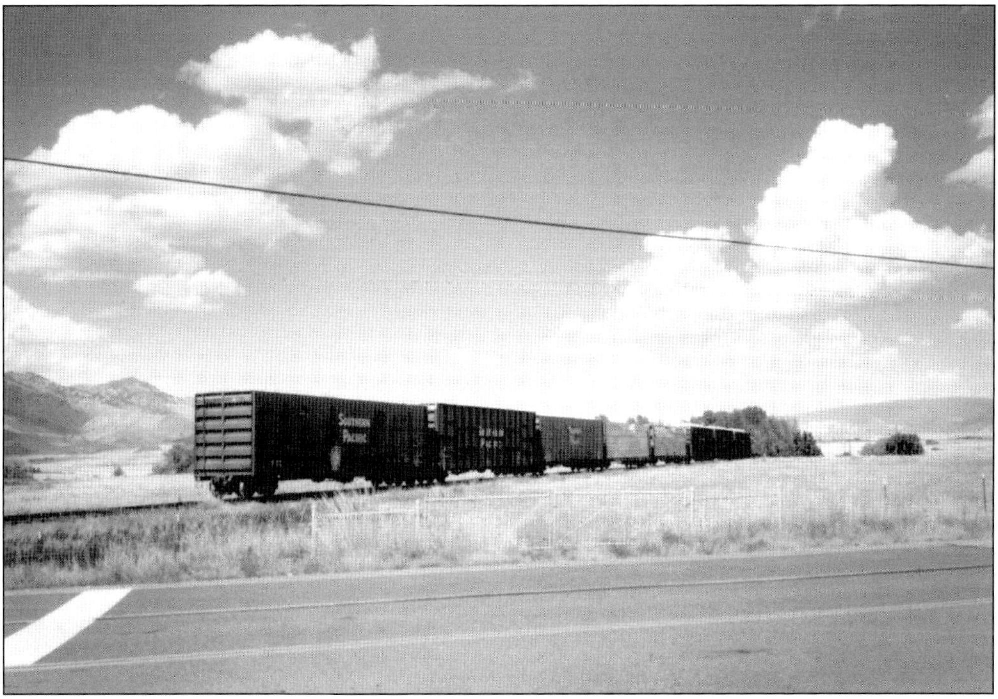

No. 21 and train headed for Montague. This photograph shows a typical train size for the Yreka Western and usually includes wood chips and veneer to head north over the Siskiyou Mountains to Oregon. (Courtesy Jeff Moore.)

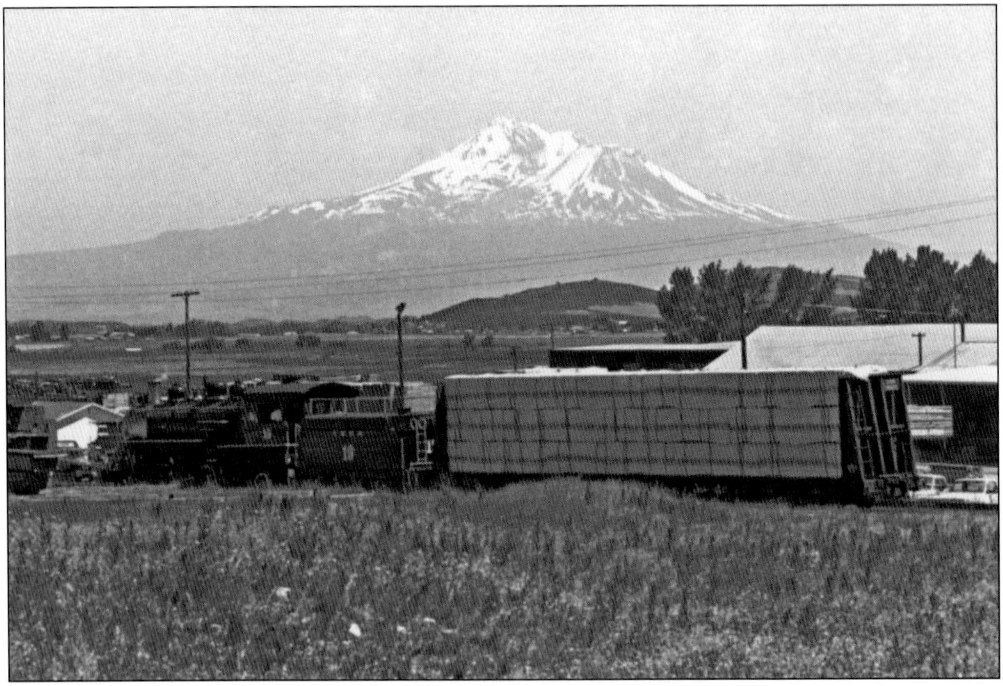

It's 1997 and No. 19 has been pressed into freight service to aid the ailing diesel. She is shown here switching the Hi-Ridge Lumber Mill. (Courtesy Bob Morris.)

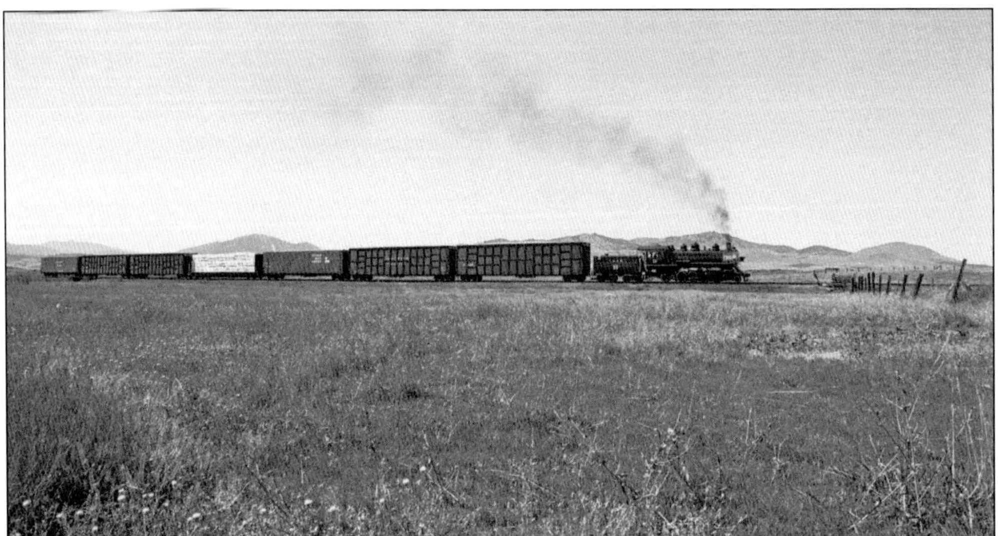

Train in tow, No. 19 has her work cut out for her with six loaded chip cars and a loaded veneer car as she approaches Montague. (Courtesy Bob Morris.)

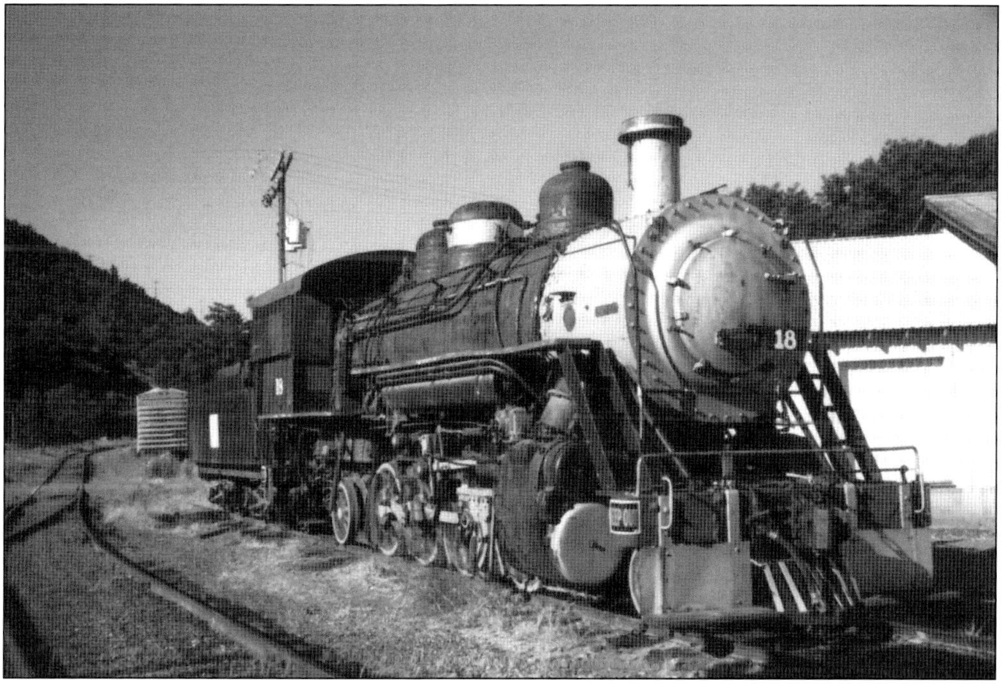

It's early morning in the Yreka yards and No. 18 is preparing to leave Yreka for her new home back on the McCloud Railway. Because she had been sitting in the yard for the past 30 years, she needed a complete rebuild, which the shops in Yreka were not capable of handling, so the McCloud, her original home, seemed like an ideal location.

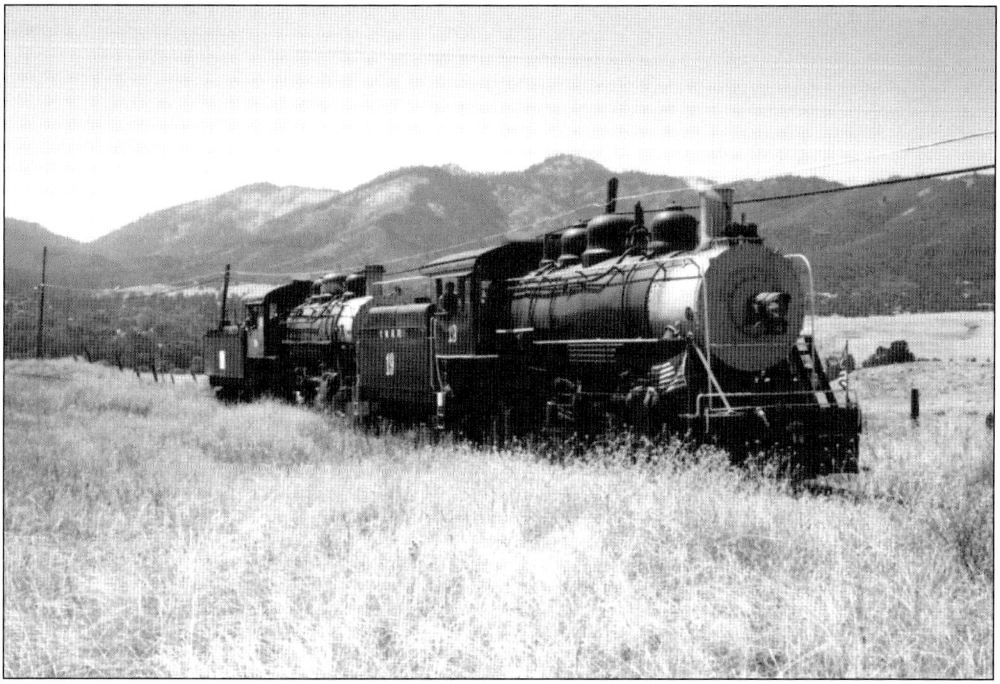

No. 18 leaves Yreka for the last time. She and No. 19 are ascending the Butcher Hill grade in Yreka.

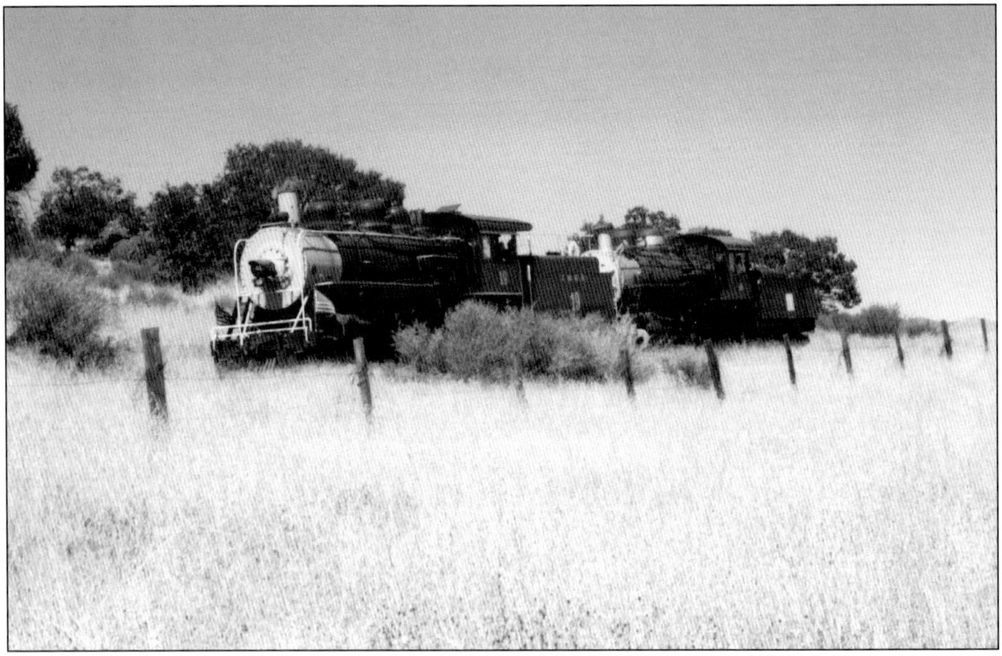

The two sisters, Nos. 18 and 19, have just passed through Dead Man's Cut and are working their way down towards Montague.

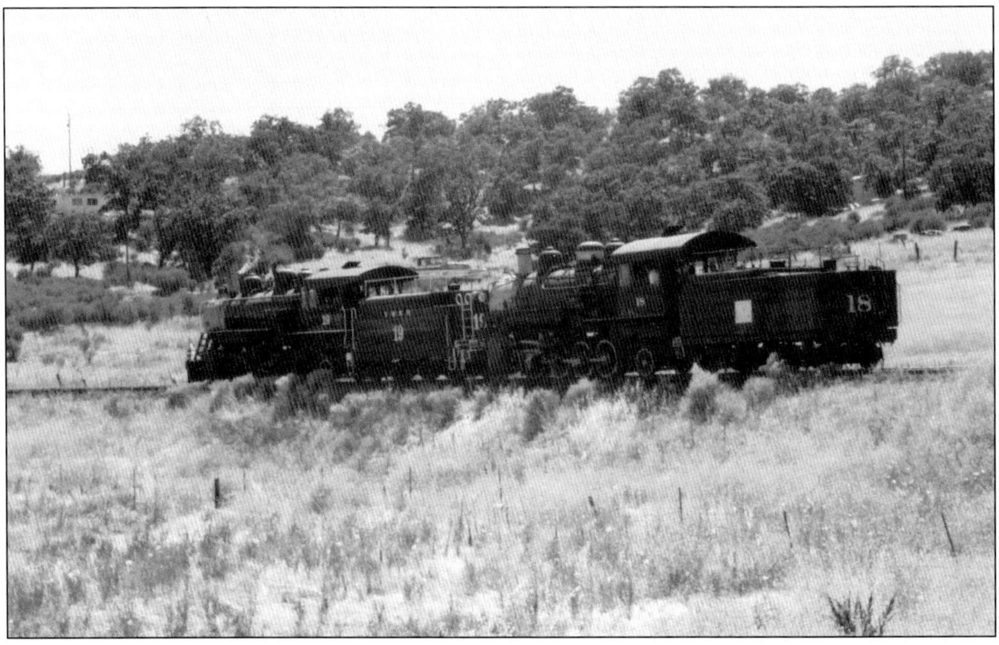

No. 19 and her sister, No. 18, descend the grade towards the mill after crossing North Foothill Drive. No. 18's time on Yreka rails is numbered.

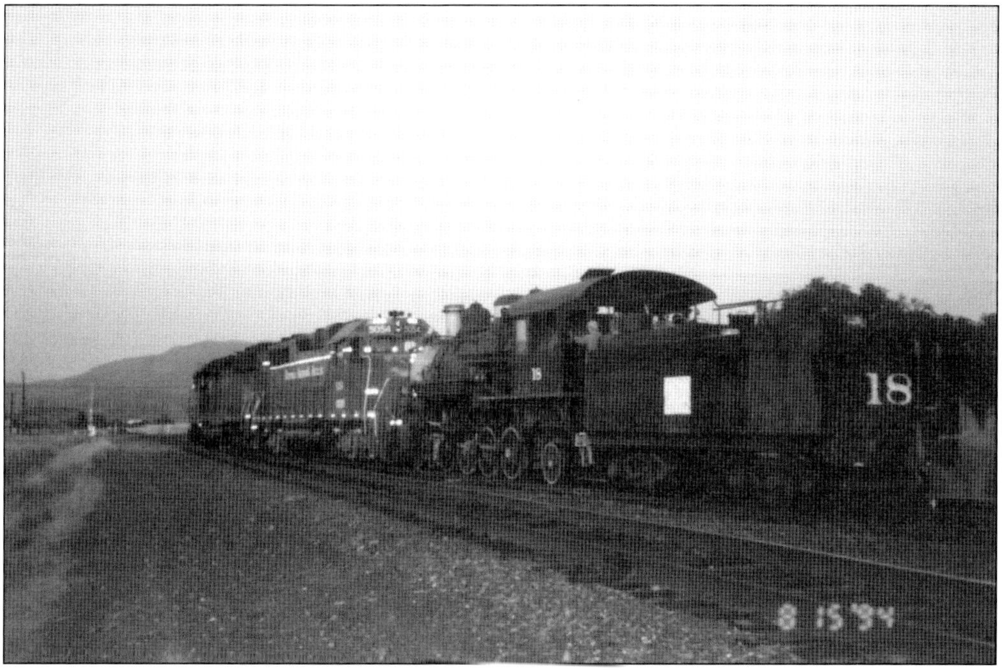

Night has fallen in Montague, and the Central Oregon and Pacific train has picked up No. 18 for the trip south to the interchange with Union Pacific at Black Butte. No. 18 has left Yreka rails for the last time, which was her home for the past 40 years.

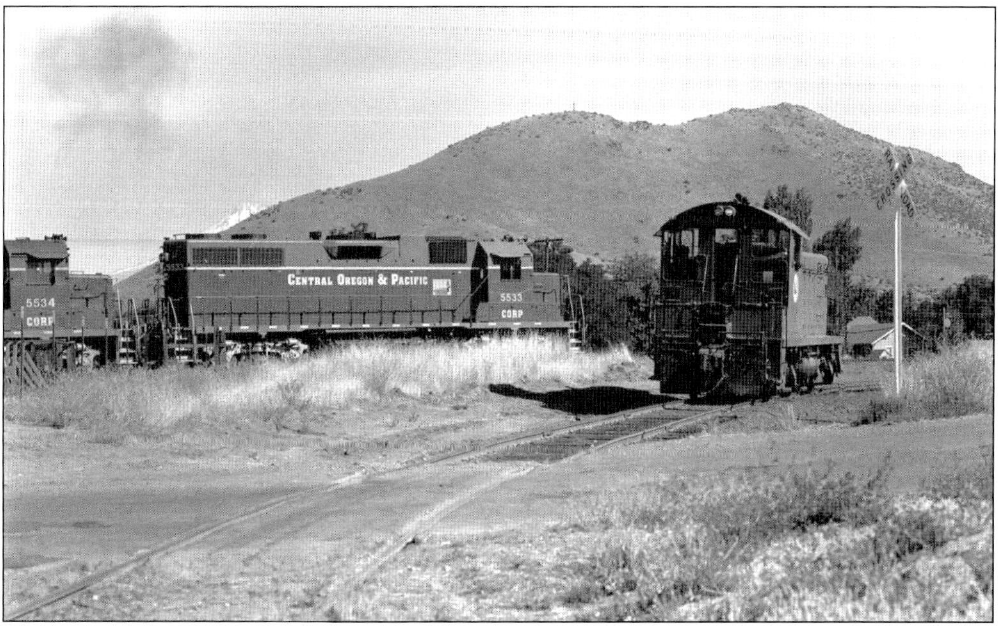

No. 21 sits on the mainline in Montague, while a southbound CORP train led by No. 5533 picks up the loaded cars set out by the YW. After the CORP train departs, No. 21 will pick up the empties set out and spot them at the mill later on in the day. (Courtesy Bob Morris.)

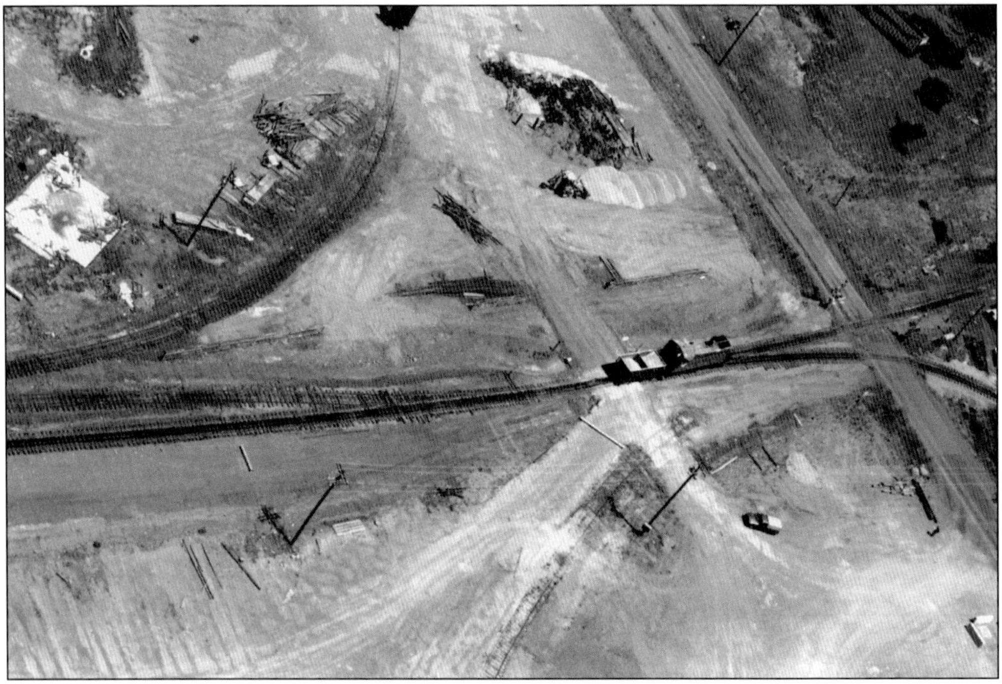

This aerial view shows No. 21 and Yreka Western's ballast car filling the new spur for Timber Products in 2002. Timber Products paid for the entire cost of this new spur to make the loading of veneer onto rail cars much more efficient. The spur at the bottom of the photograph used to serve Hi-Ridge Lumber.

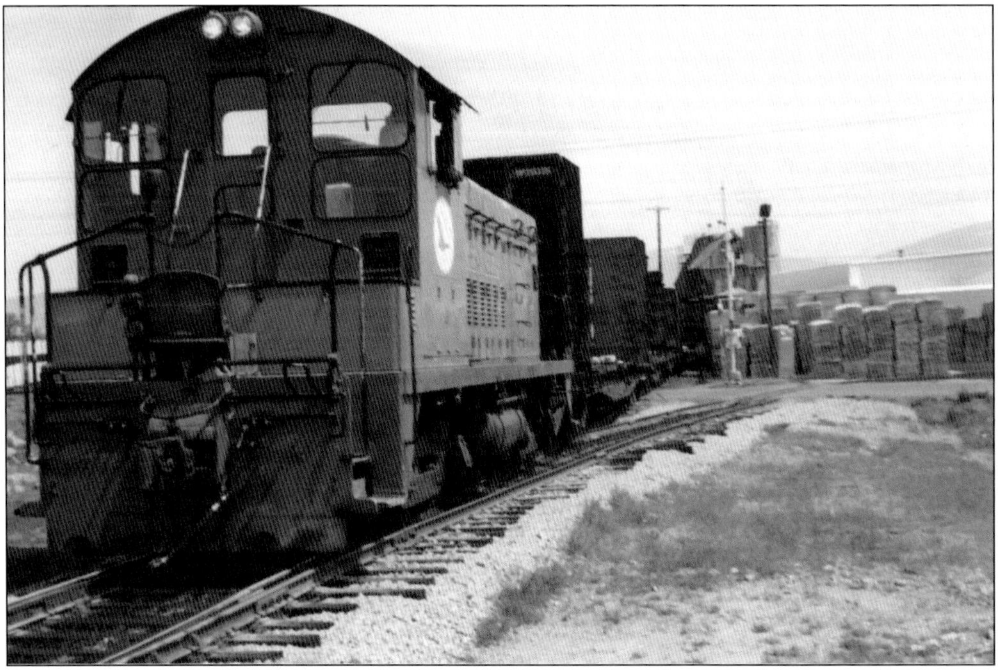

In the summer of 2002, No. 21 is switching empty bulkhead flatcars for Timber Products. By this time, the brand-new veneer spur into Timber Products was complete and put into service.

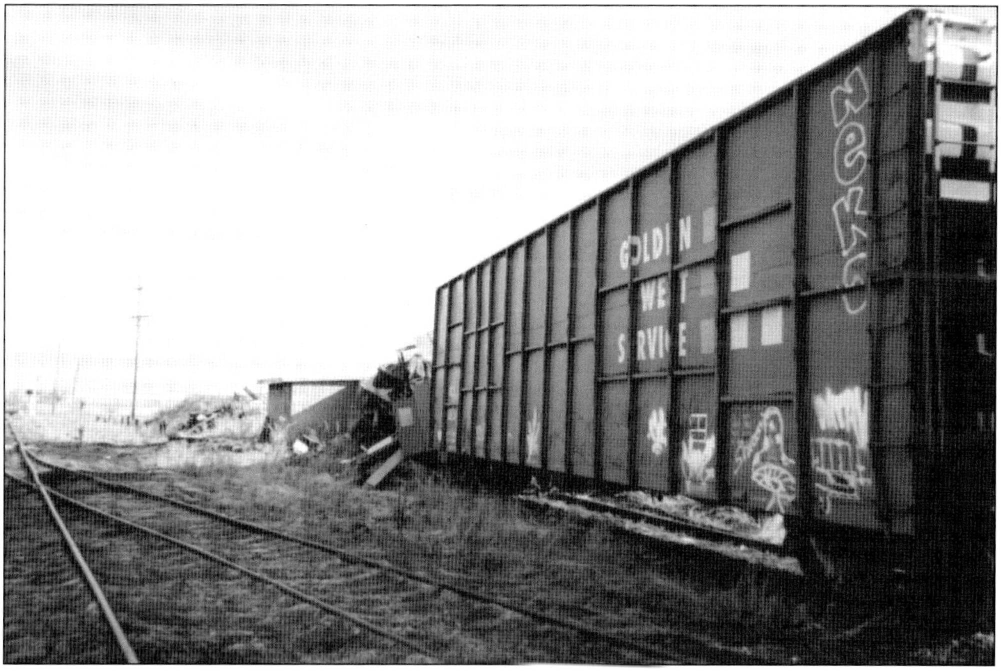

In 2003, another mishap occurred. While loading chips in the chip cars, the mill employees forgot to set the hand brakes on the cars. The cars rolled down the track into the derail spur where the maintenance-of-way employees had left a speeder and tool car. Needless to say, the small car didn't stand much of a chance against a loaded chip car. The photograph below shows the aftermath of the runaway chip cars. The speeder sitting on this track was nearly completely destroyed.

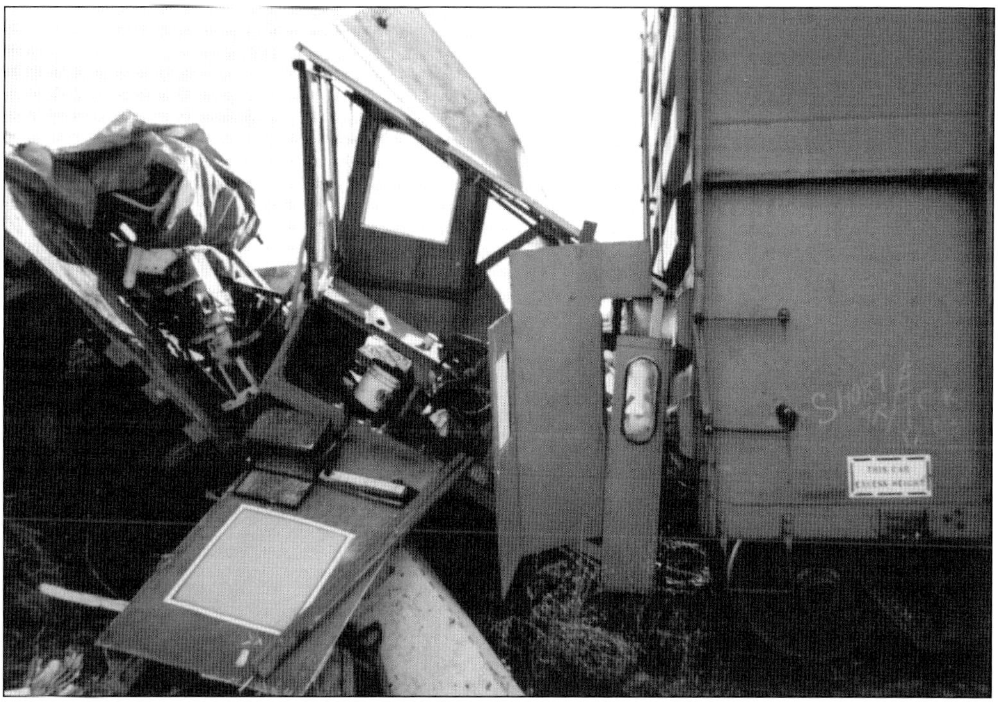

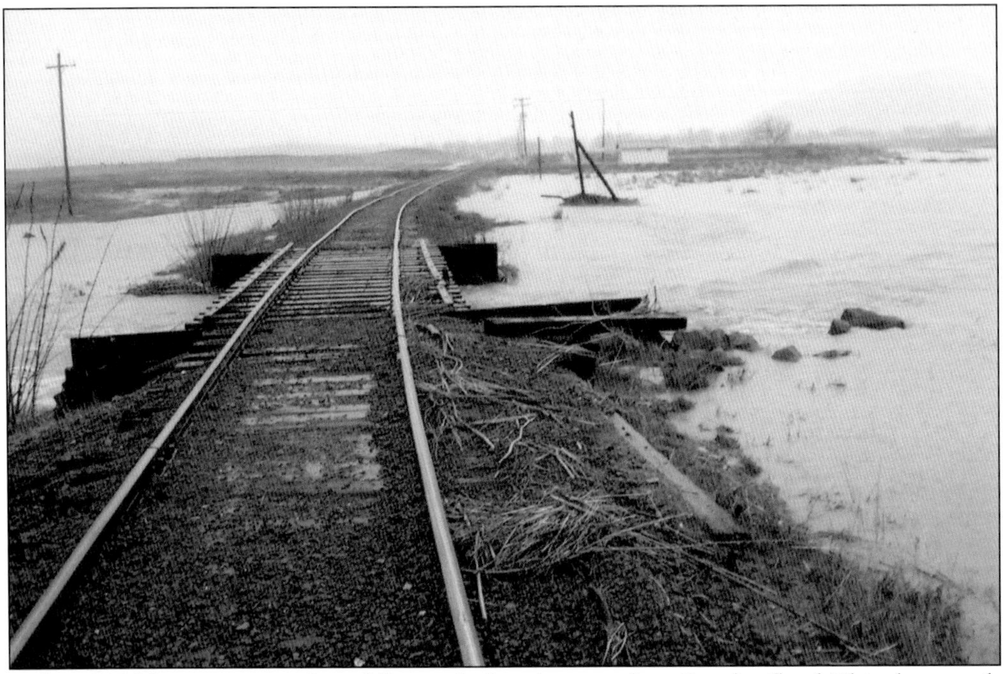

Early in 2006, large amounts of rainfall caused a few places on the railroad to flood. This photograph shows the usual tranquil Oregon Slough on a rampage near the Montague sewer ponds. The waters at this time had receded, but at one point it was above the rails in this location, as evidenced by the debris along the rails.

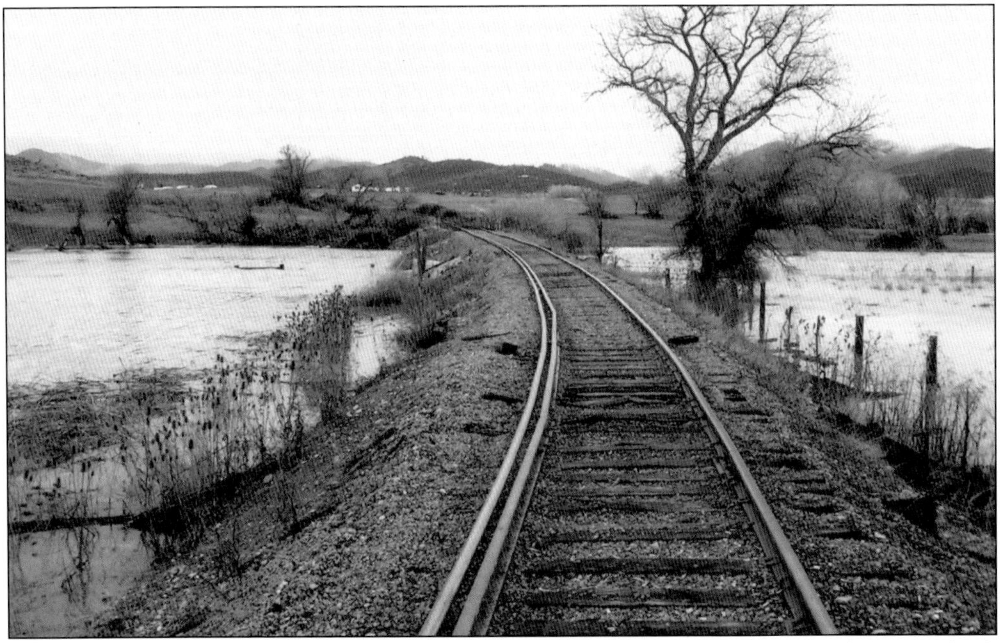

Strangely, farther down the line at the Shasta River, the water was high but didn't get high enough to clear the tops of the rails. Normally the Shasta River will flood over the tracks, and the Oregon Slough won't, but 2006 was different.

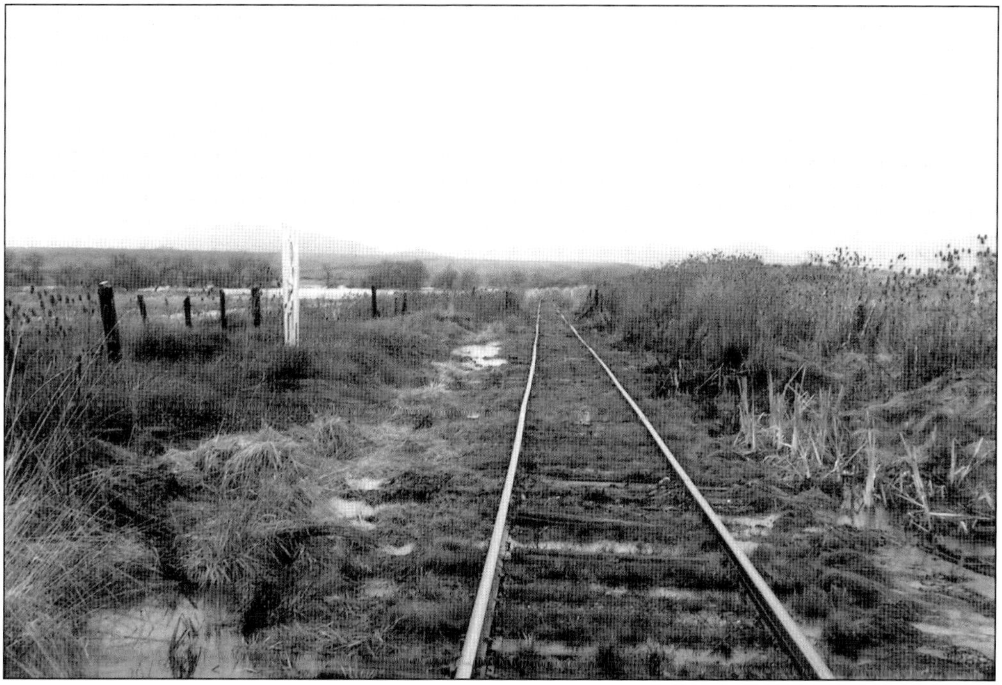

The lack of good drainage in a place known as the swamp is evident in this photograph taken after the storm of 2006, as runoff from the hillsides seeps up through the tracks.

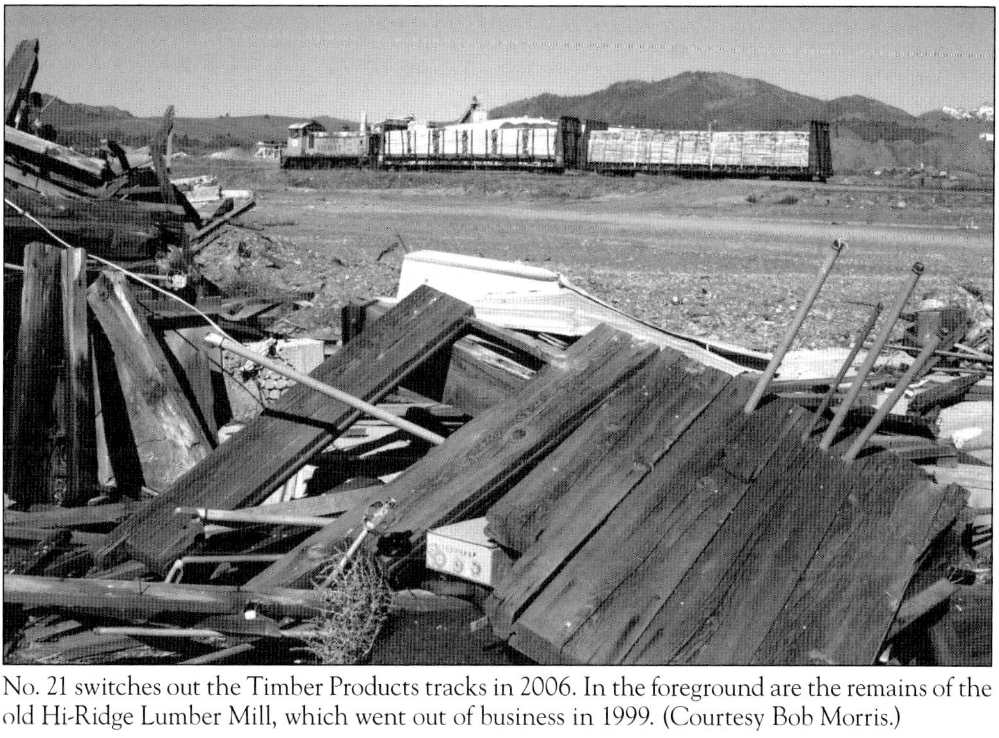

No. 21 switches out the Timber Products tracks in 2006. In the foreground are the remains of the old Hi-Ridge Lumber Mill, which went out of business in 1999. (Courtesy Bob Morris.)

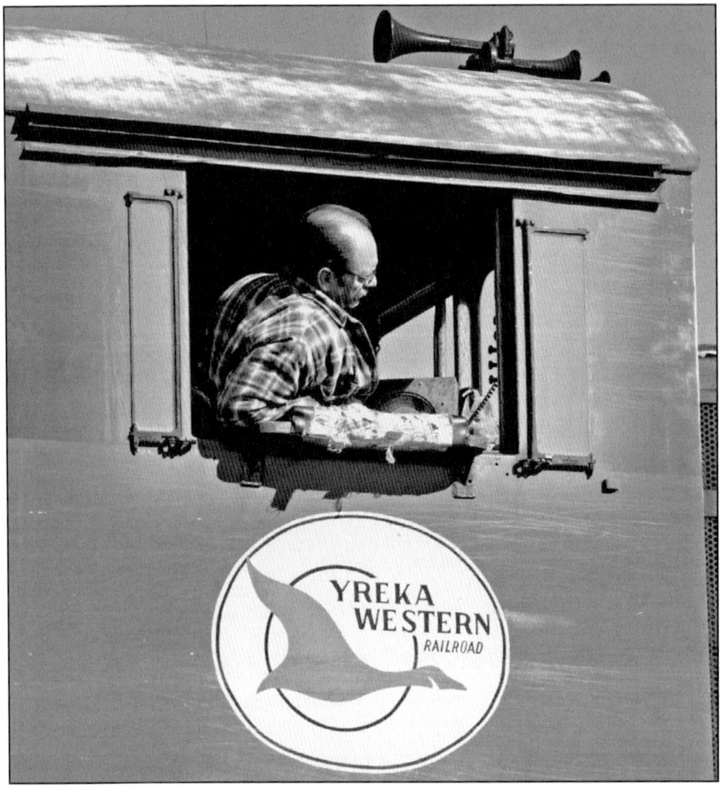

Longtime employee Dennis Woodruff is at the throttle of No. 21 during a switching move at the Timber Products mill. Dennis has been working for the Yreka Western since 1979. (Courtesy Bob Morris.)

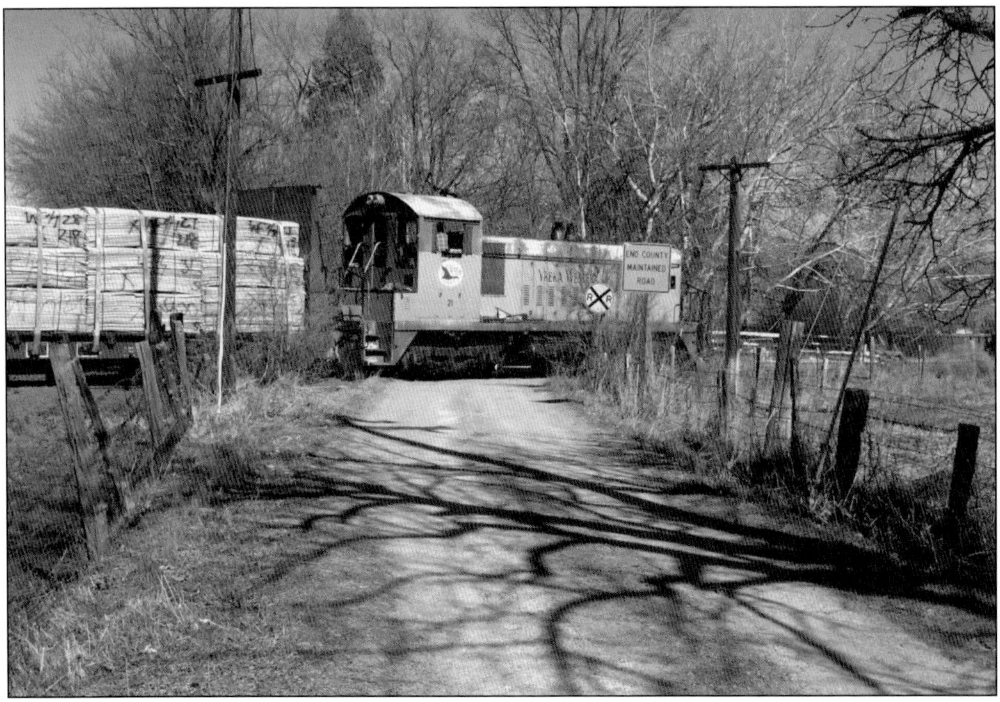

After completing all of the switching, Dennis takes No. 21 and train east towards Montague, crossing Fiock Road. (Courtesy Bob Morris.)

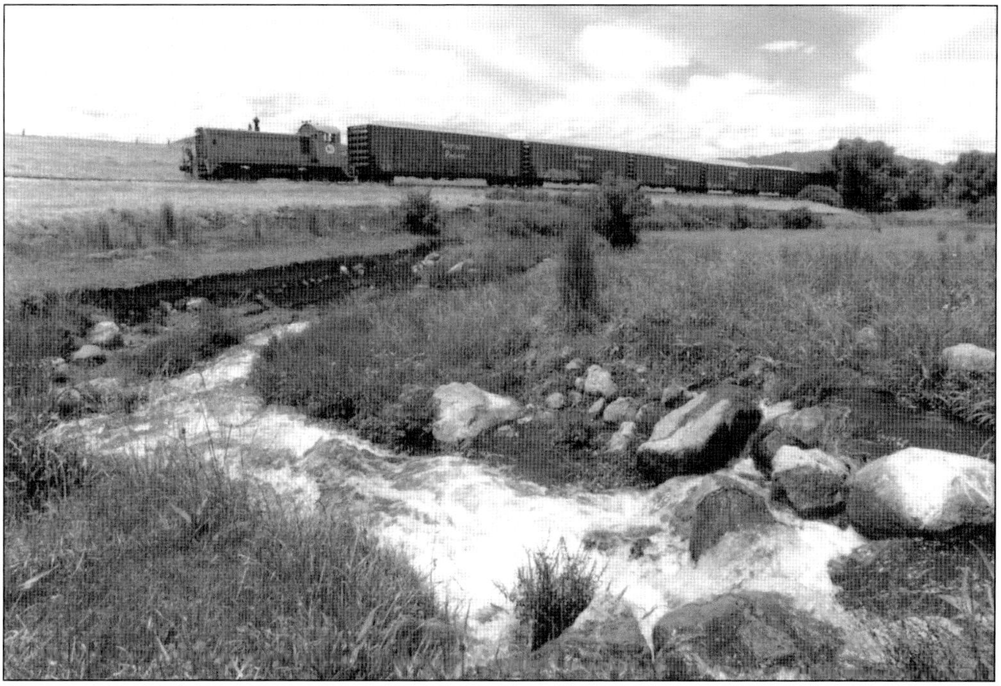

A train fully loaded with chip cars passes by Oregon Slough on its way to Montague. (Courtesy Bob Morris.)

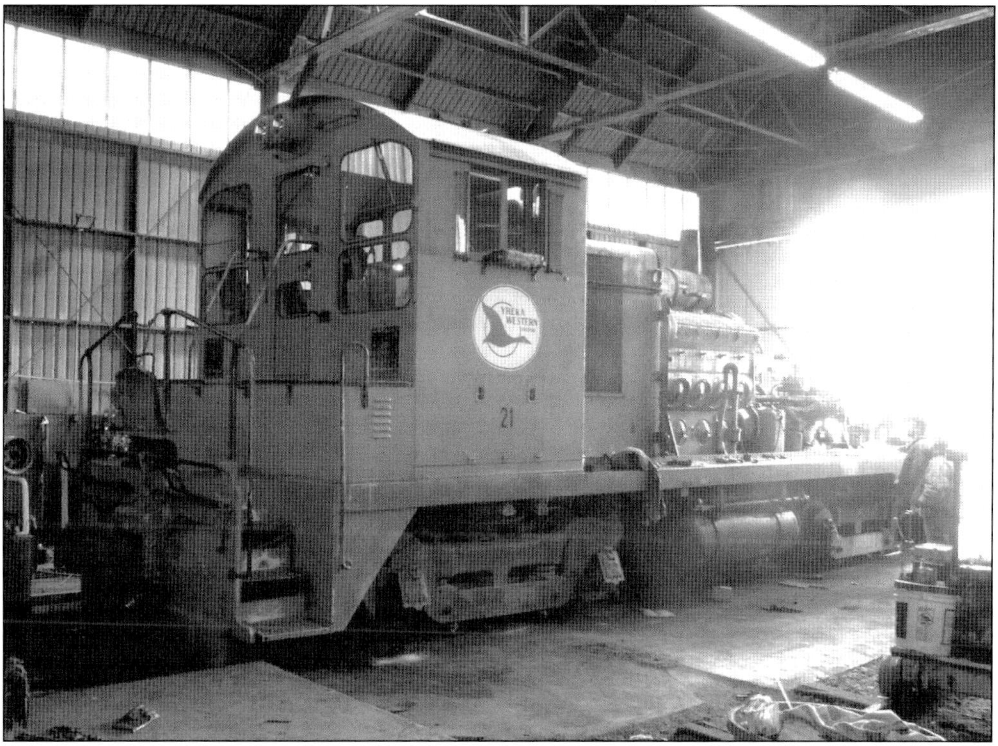

In 2007, No. 21 was in need of repair and went down for a prime mover replacement. Here, it is shown in the shop during the repair work. (Courtesy Bob Morris.)

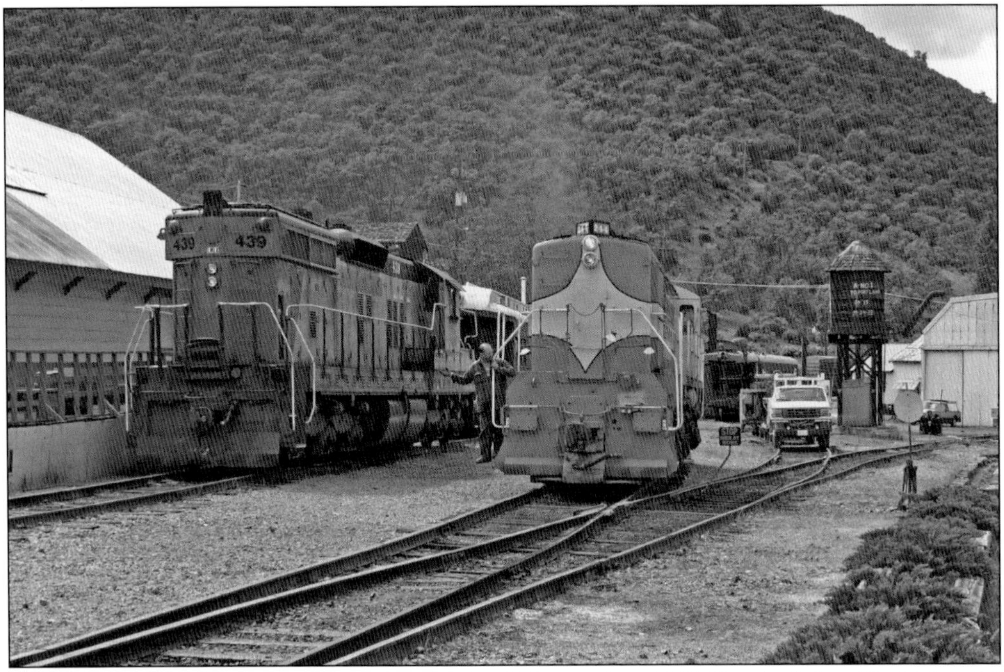

Dennis guides the Alco MRS-1 244 out of the Yreka yard in 2007. On the left is SD-9 No. 439 on lease from Livingston Locomotive Works, and on the right is Yreka Western's HY-RAIL. (Courtesy Bob Morris.)

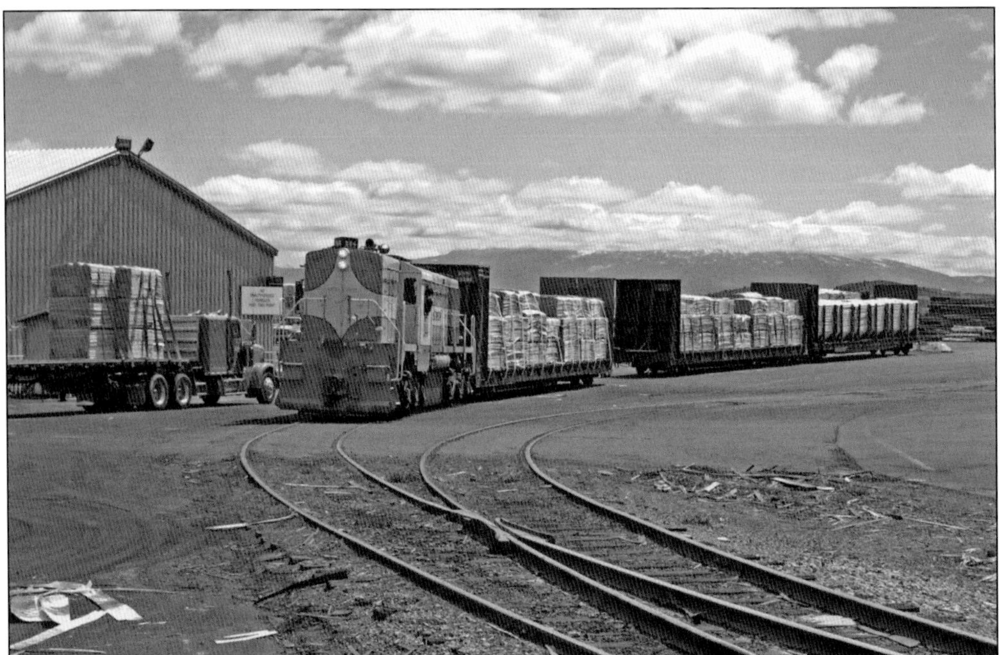

No. 244 switches out loaded veneer cars from the Timber Products mill. The peak of towering Mount Shasta is just visible above the top of the clouds. (Courtesy Bob Morris.)

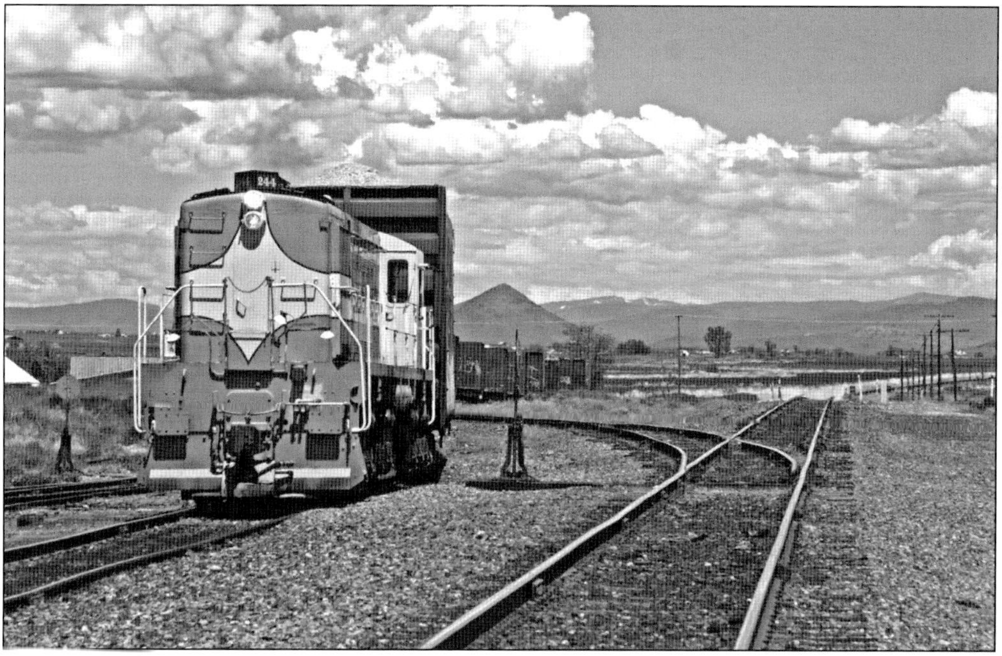

Upon arrival in Montague, No. 244 swaps out loads for empties at the interchange with the Central Oregon and Pacific Railroad. The track to the far right is the former Southern Pacific Siskiyou Line. (Courtesy Bob Morris.)

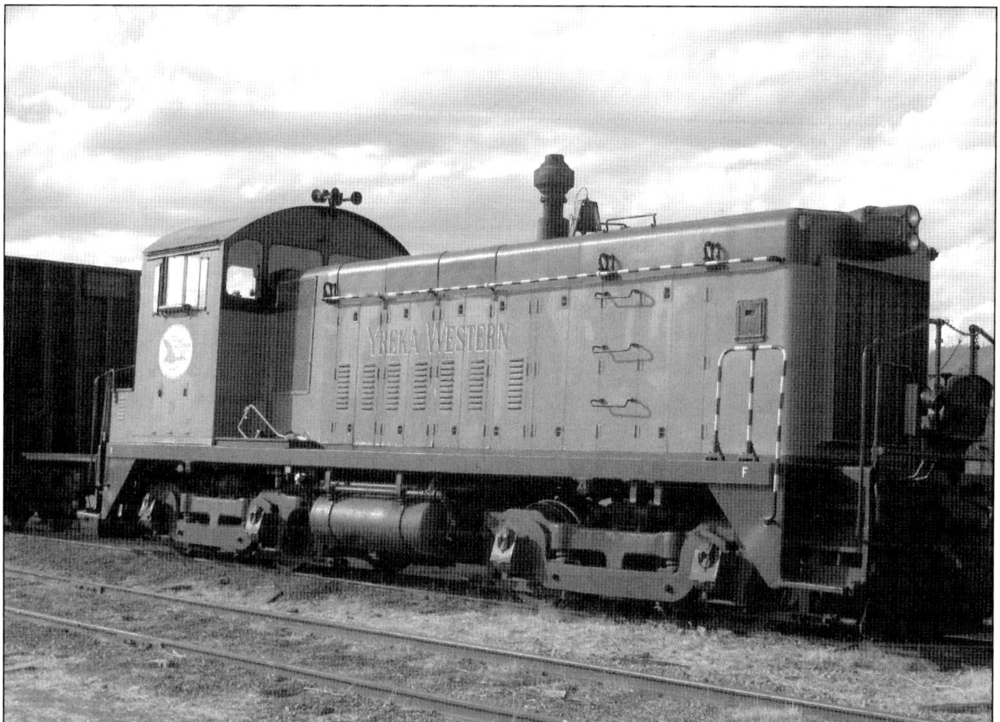

In June 2008, No. 21 received a new paint job, with the darker red paint being replaced by black and yellow stripes on the handrails. (Courtesy Tim Stricker.)

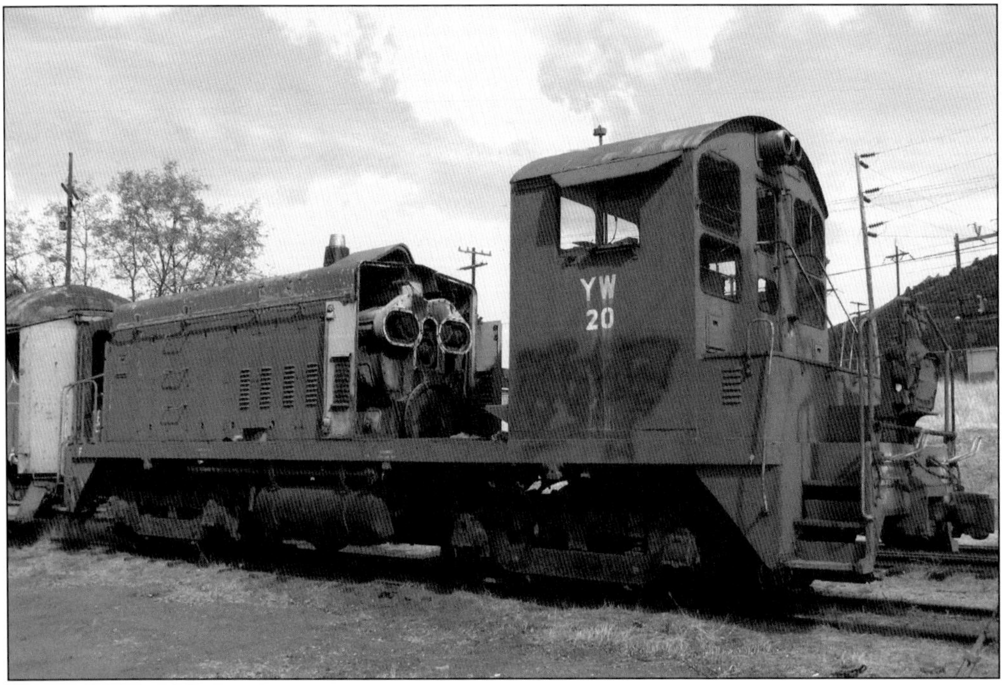

In 1995, the crankcase on No. 20 froze, resulting in the locomotive becoming a parts engine for No. 21, as shown here in this 2010 view. The locomotive no longer operates and is often moved around to various places around the Yreka yard but usually stays behind the shop. (Courtesy Matt Starman.)

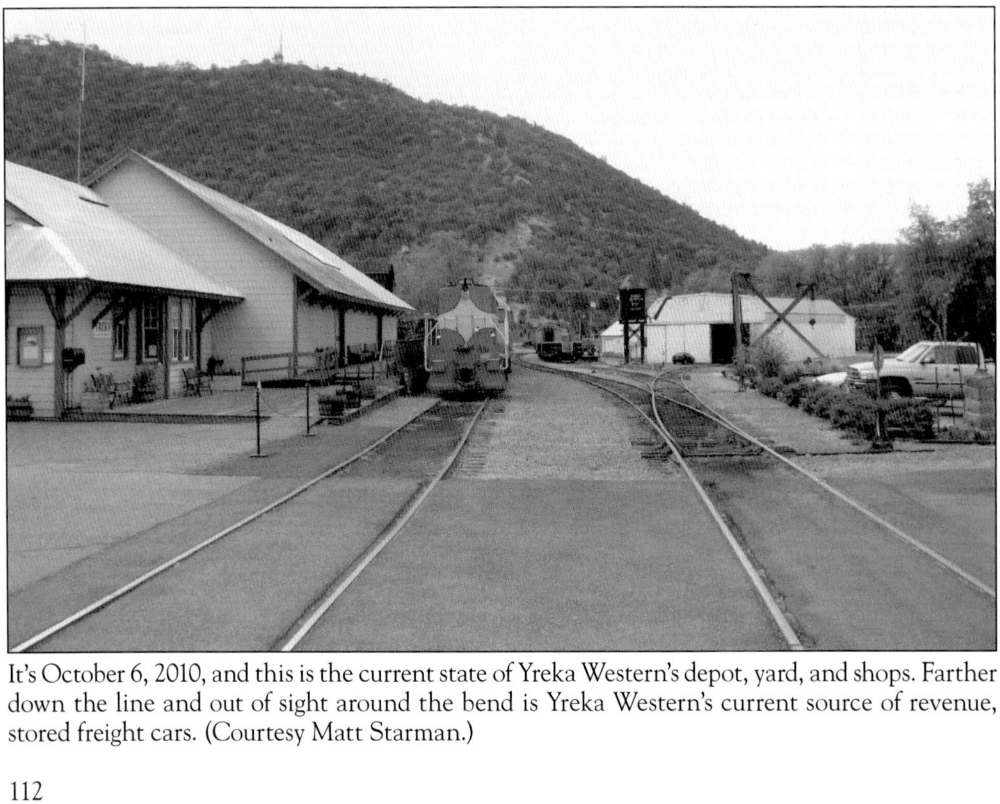

It's October 6, 2010, and this is the current state of Yreka Western's depot, yard, and shops. Farther down the line and out of sight around the bend is Yreka Western's current source of revenue, stored freight cars. (Courtesy Matt Starman.)

Six

Blue Goose Excursion Train

In June 1986, the city of Yreka and the Yreka Western Railroad filed a joint agreement to begin operation of an excursion train known as the *Blue Goose* to boost tourism in the area and save the railroad. The agreement called for the railroad to furnish a train and crew. However, since the railroad only had a two-man crew at the time, the city agreed to hire other part-time help for the train. Additionally, the city guaranteed to reimburse the railroad for any financial losses due to the operation of the excursion train. The railroad began operation of the excursion train with No. 21 and two coaches.

In 1987, an open-air car was added, and in 1988, two former Milwaukee Road *Hiawatha* cars were transferred from the California Western. Kyle Railways was encouraged by the growth in ridership and terminated the agreement with the city, taking over the entire operation. In May 1988, No. 19 returned to Yreka from Cottage Grove, where it had been on lease. However, No. 19 failed her boiler inspection and went into an extensive rebuild between 1988 and 1989. She was returned to service in July 1989, and ridership numbers increased dramatically, continuing to climb over the years, with ridership increasing every year.

No. 19 continued to pull passenger trains through the Shasta Valley until 2003, when new Federal Railroad Administration laws went into effect for all steam locomotives, which included replacing all of the flues. It was poor timing, however, because in November 2003, a fire started in tunnel 13 on the Central Oregon and Pacific and closed the line. This cut off any revenue that the Yreka Western could make from freight, and the railroad suspended excursion operations and work on No. 19, with all remaining capital going to the payroll.

In 2005, CORP reopened the Siskiyou Line, and freight was moving once again. The overhaul on No. 19 was completed, and she reentered service in 2006 to pull the *Blue Goose* once again.

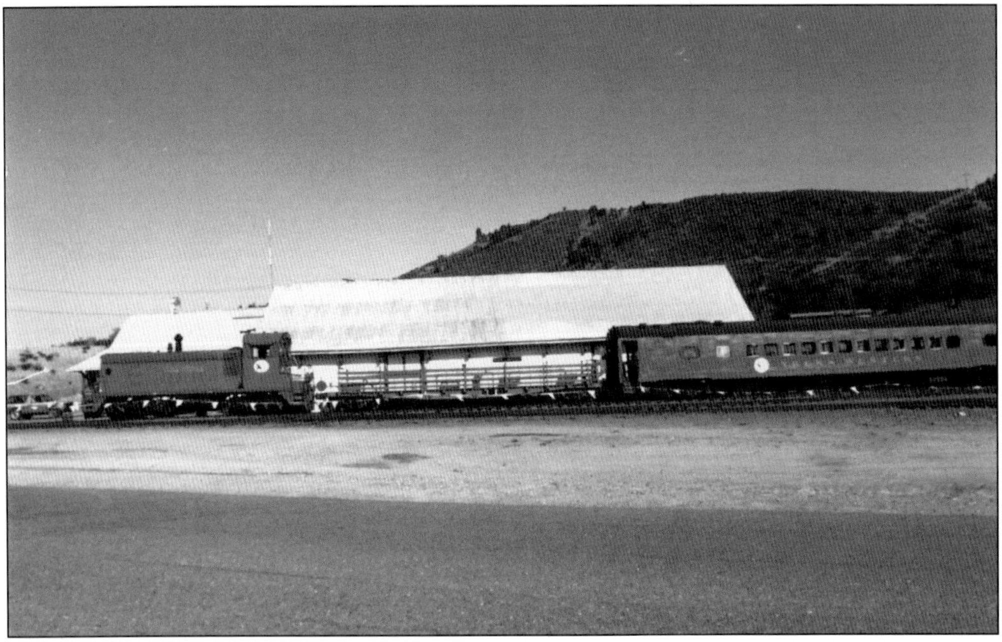

No. 21 and train sit in front of the depot prior to departure in the summer of 1988. By this time, the open-air flatcar has been added, and the *Hiawatha* cars were in service being painted in the same orange and red paint scheme as the diesel locomotive.

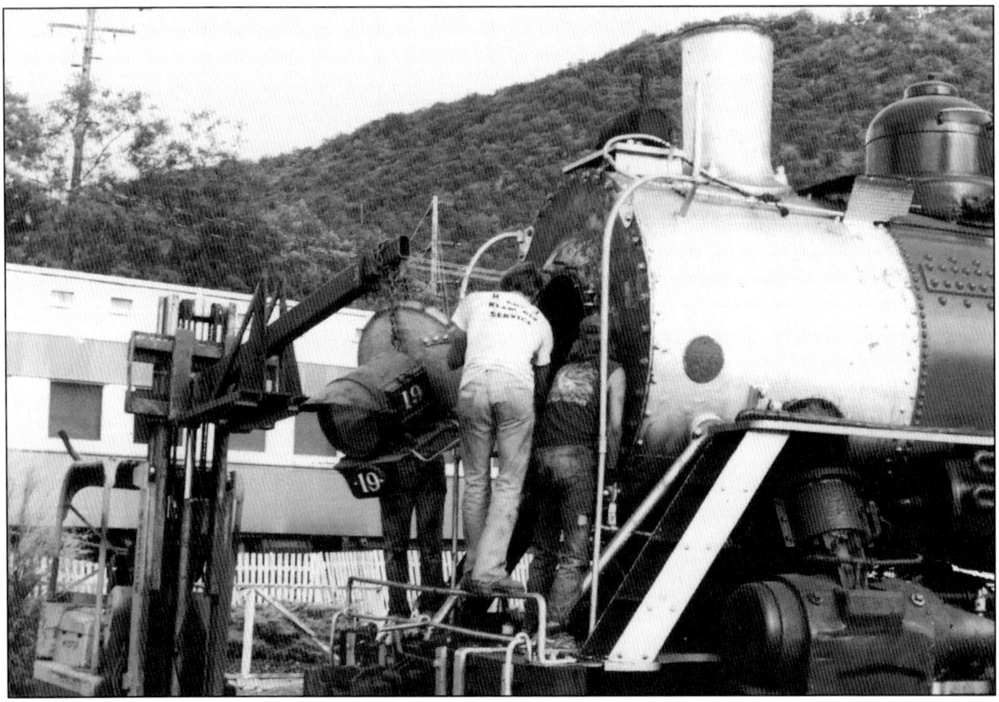

During the rebuild of No. 19 between 1988 and 1989, the smokebox door is reinstalled on the locomotive. When the 19 arrived back at Yreka, it was determined that her boiler was not up to California standards, and thus had to be rebuilt before it could operate again. This work was completed between 1988 and 1989.

In the winter of 1990, the railroad built a water tower in front of the shops to service locomotive No. 19. The tank isn't a true wood tank. It is steel tank with wood siding added to the outside to give the illusion of an actual wooden water tank.

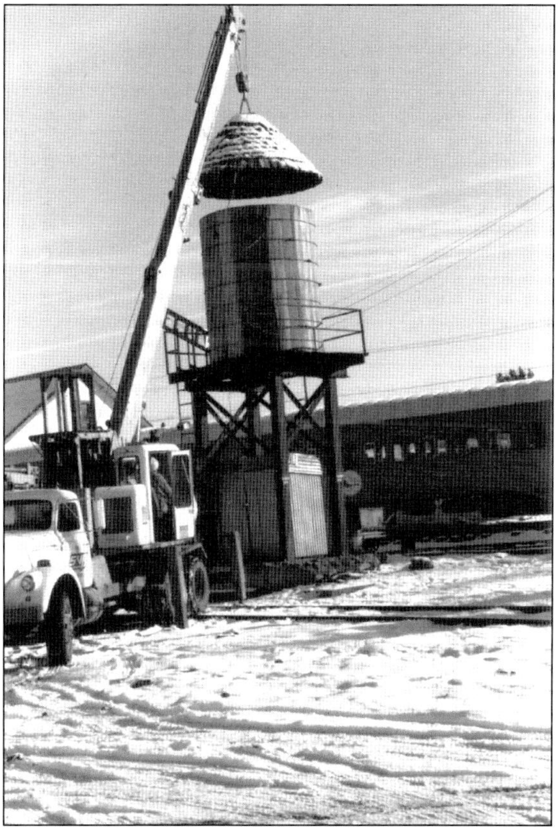

On September 22, 1990, the Siskiyou County Historical Society and the Humbug Chapter of *E Clampus Vitus* dedicated a plaque in front of the depot to commemorate the railroad's existence and huge influence on the community. The community members, from left to right, are unidentified, Dan Weimers, Mary Lou Smith, Patti Jackson, Larry Bacon (YWRR general manager), and unidentified.

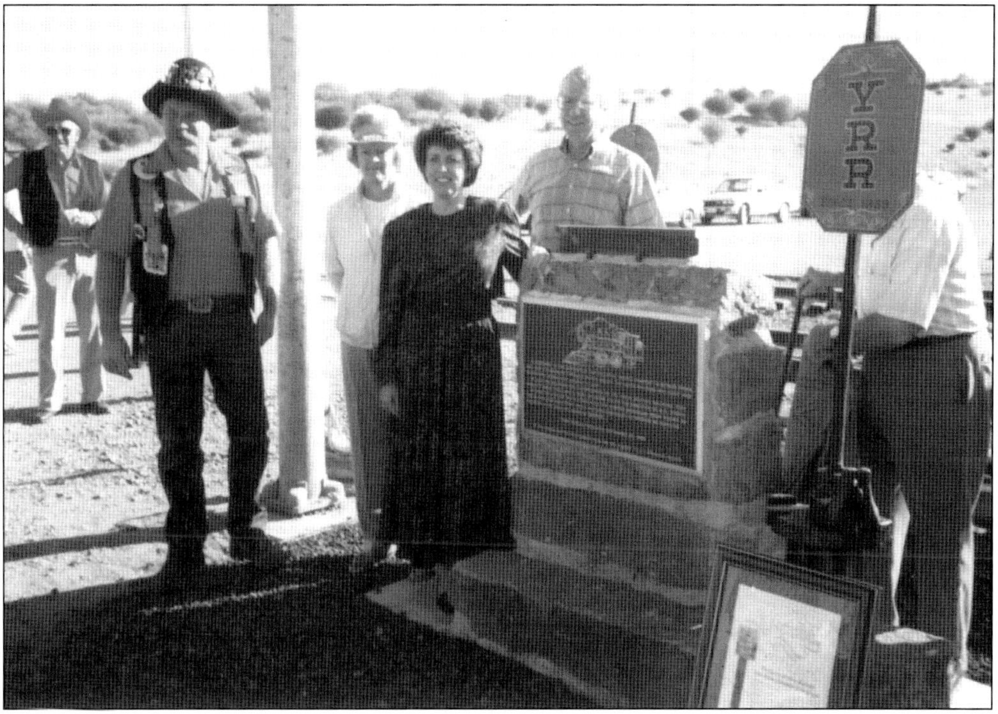

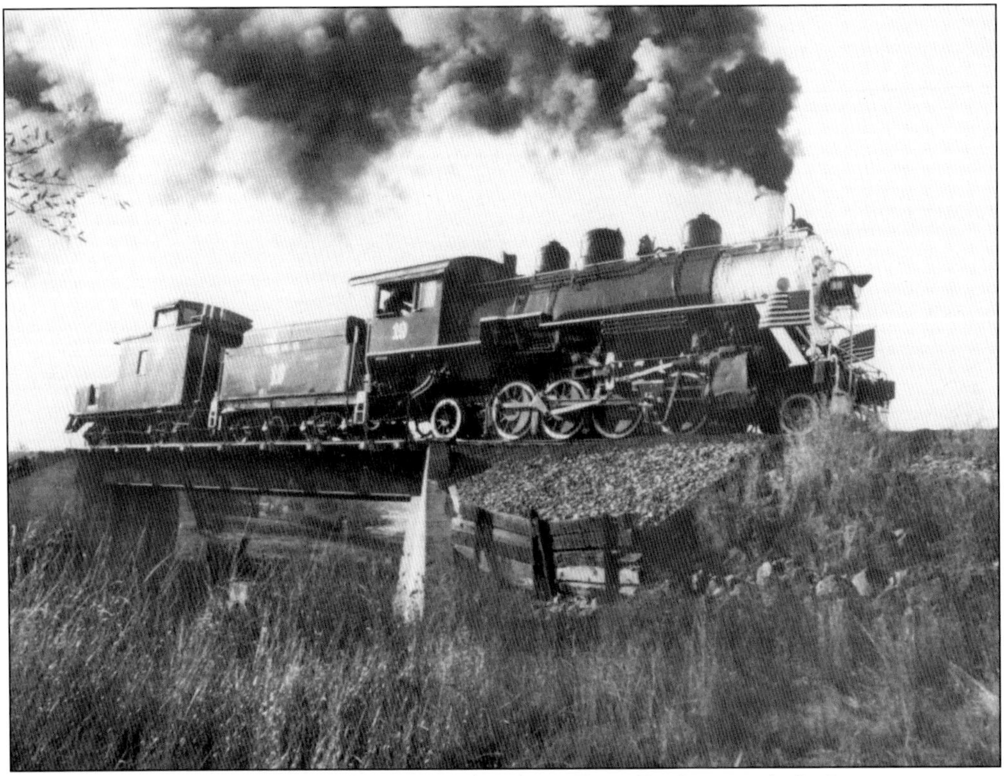

The crew takes No. 19 and the caboose over the Shasta River Bridge on a shakedown run prior to the beginning of the 1990 season. The locomotive is fresh out of the shop from winter maintenance and is being tested to work out any last minute quirks and to make adjustments.

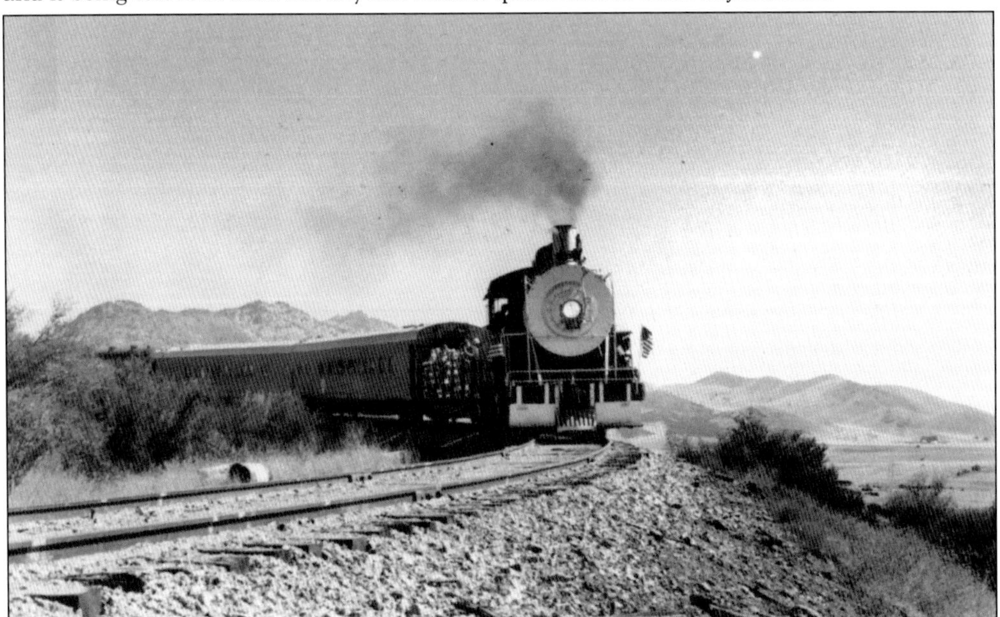

No. 19 rounds the curve out of Dead Man's Cut in the summer of 1990, pulling one of the first steam-powered excursion trains the Yreka Western had seen in quite some time.

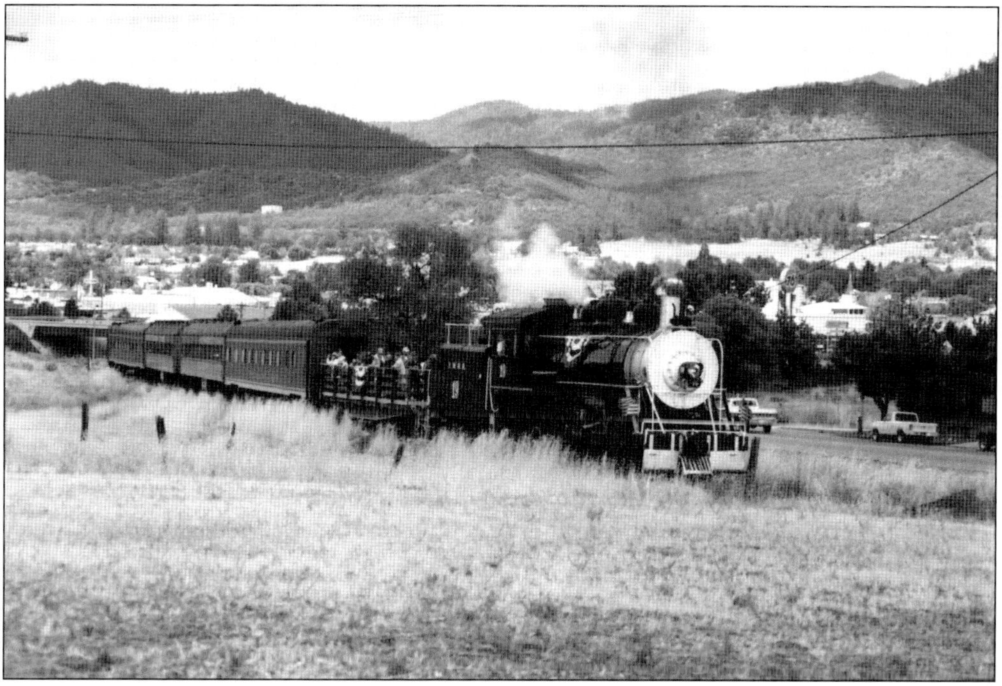

It's 1992 and No. 19 has just begun the trip out of Yreka on her way to Montague, working her way up Butcher Hill. Also by this time, the two *Hiawatha* cars had been repainted blue to match the rest of the *Blue Goose* consist.

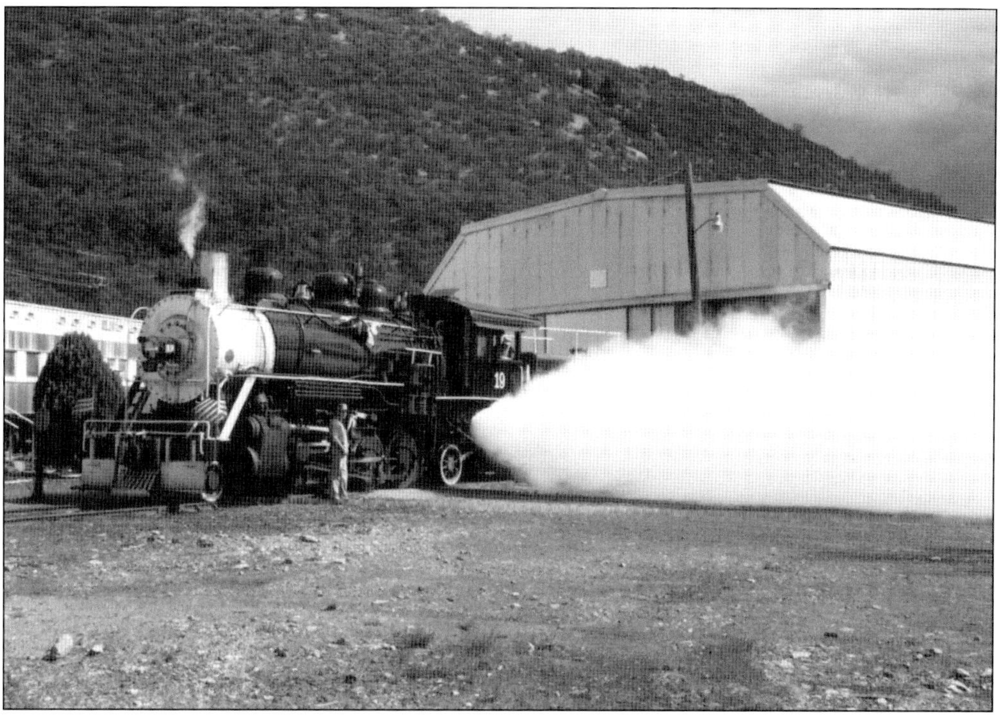

Down in front of the shops, the crew blows down the boiler before moving No. 19 up to her train. Blowing down the boiler gets rid of the sediment and scale that settles in the boiler.

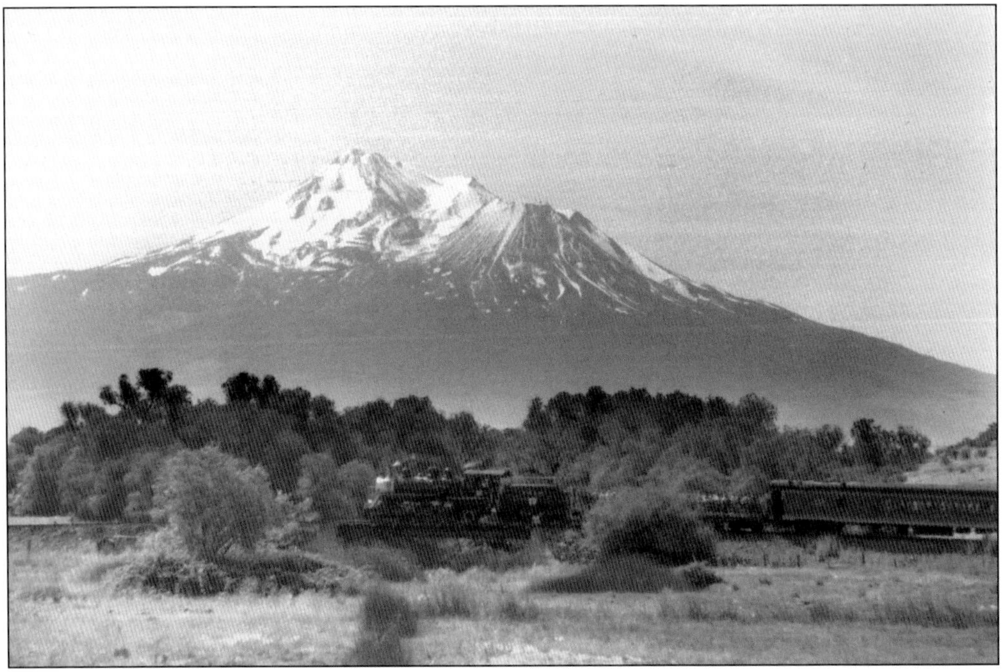

The dominant 14,162-foot Mount Shasta dwarfs No. 19 as she crosses the Shasta River Bridge.

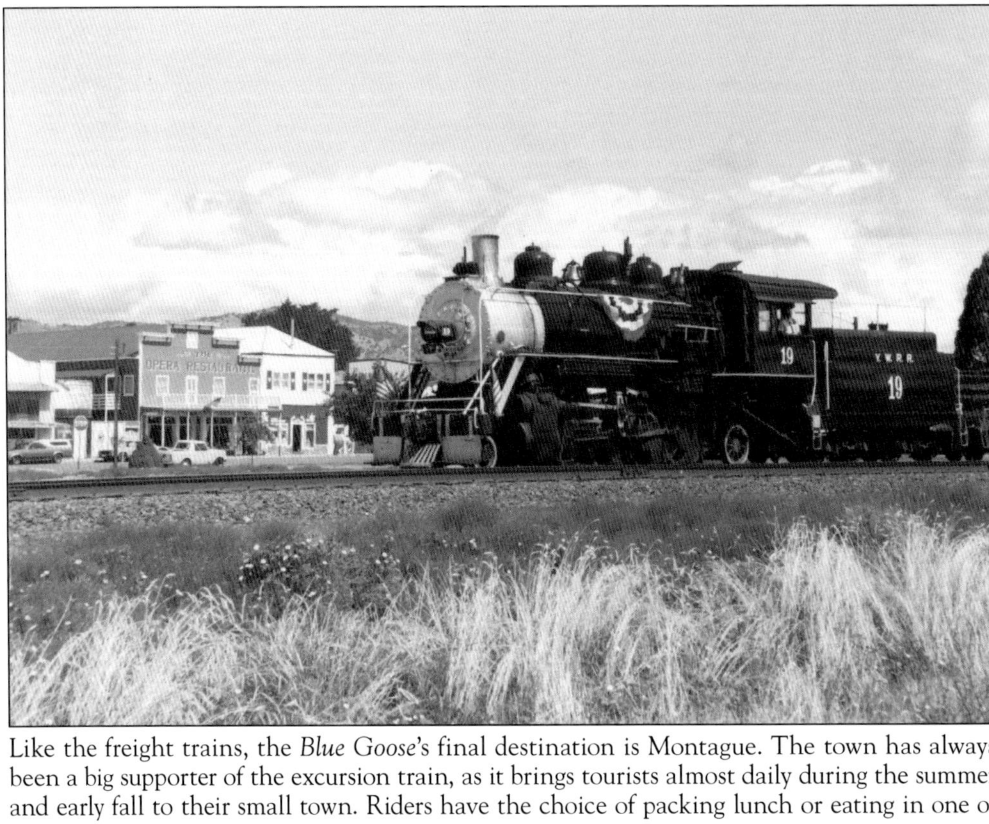

Like the freight trains, the *Blue Goose*'s final destination is Montague. The town has always been a big supporter of the excursion train, as it brings tourists almost daily during the summer and early fall to their small town. Riders have the choice of packing lunch or eating in one of Montague's restaurants.

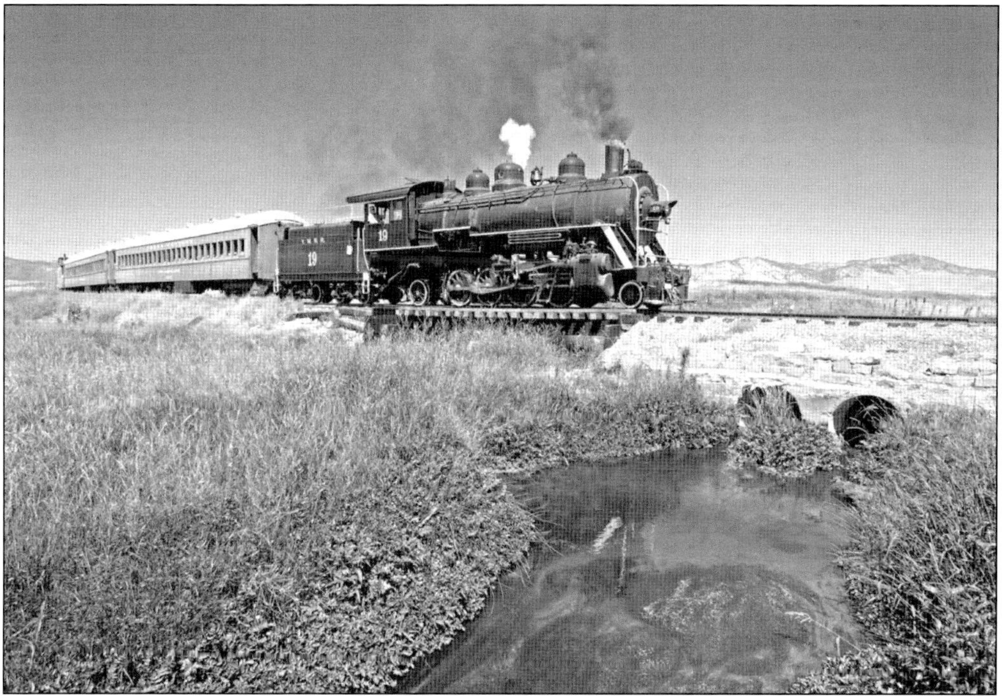

In 2006, the Blue Goose returned after a three-year absence due to complications caused by a tunnel fire and collapse on the Central Oregon and Pacific Railroad that drastically affected the freight business on the Yreka Western. Here, No. 19 rolls across Oregon Slough about a mile outside of Montague during the 2006 season. No. 19 also returned to service in 2006 after an extensive overhaul of the boiler, as required every 15 years. (Courtesy Bob Morris.)

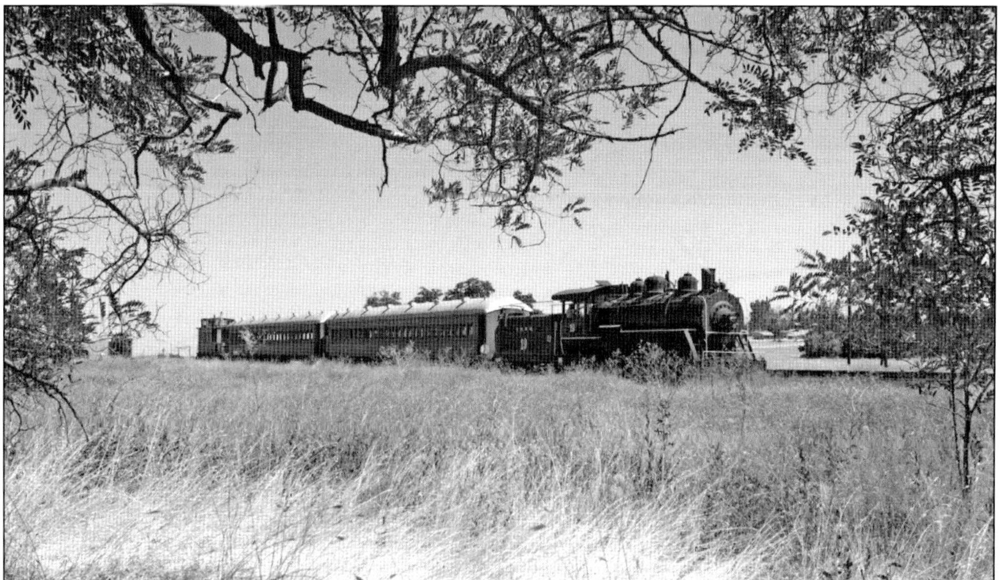

The *Blue Goose* is being backed onto the runaround track in Montague after off-loading passengers. There has never been a turning facility built in Montague, so all trains return to Yreka tender first. (Courtesy Bob Morris.)

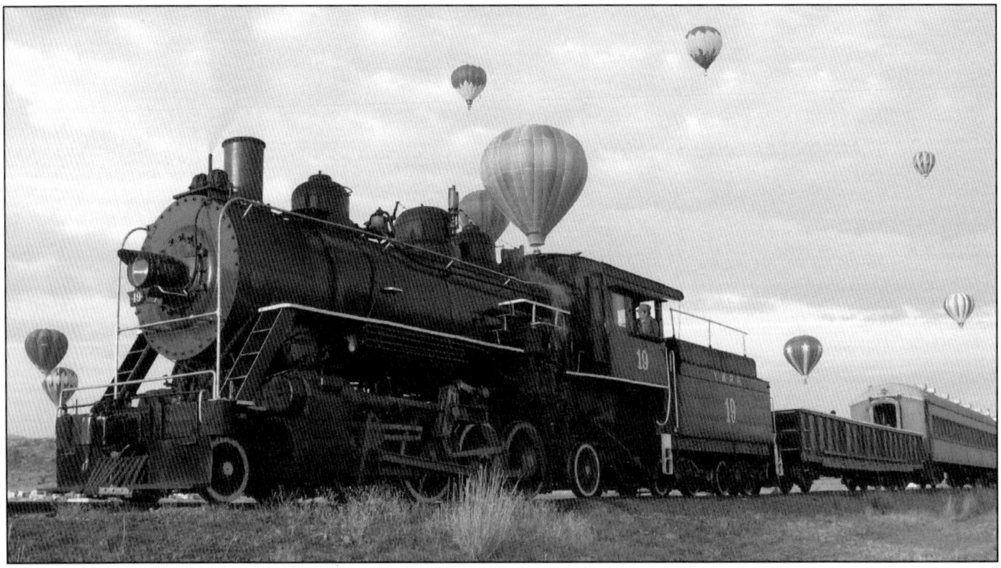

Pictured here is No. 19 on a special train known as the *Dawn Express* on September 20, 2008. The train departs Yreka at 5:30 a.m. to reach the outskirts of Montague by sunrise to watch the hundreds of hot air balloons take off for the yearly Montague Hot Air Balloon Festival. (Courtesy Tim Stricker.)

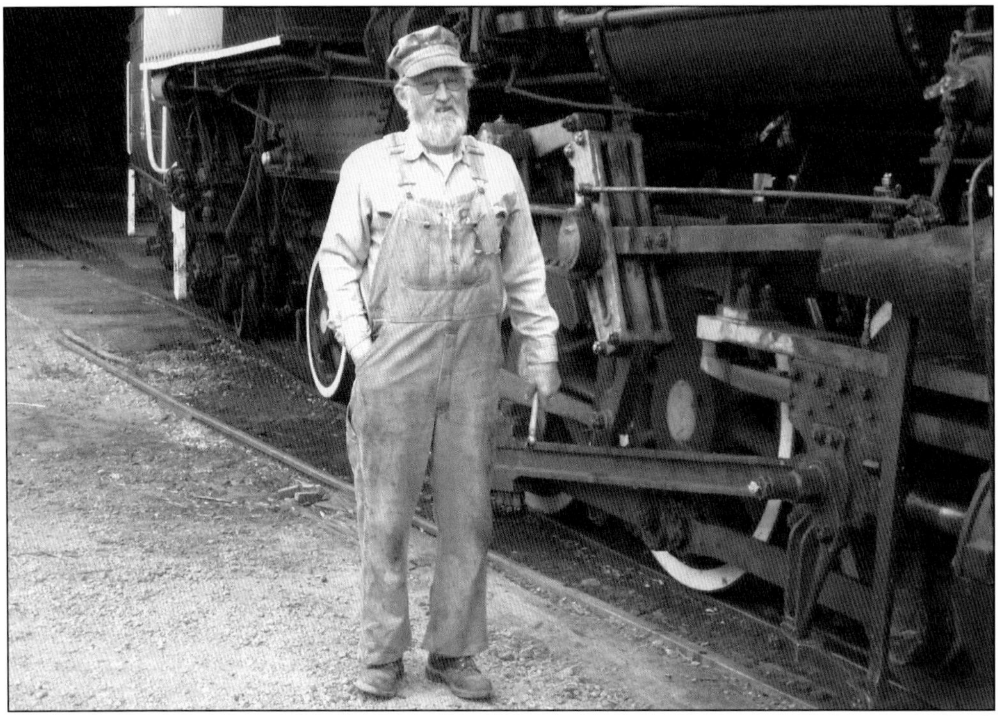

Part of the magic associated with steam locomotives today is the ability to send someone back in time to another era. Here, Yreka Western's steam mechanic, locomotive fireman, and hostler, Bill Ainsworth, helps to do just that as he pauses from his duties of prepping No. 19 for the run to Montague to pose for a photograph that may just as well have been taken in the 1930s instead of 2008. (Courtesy Sharon Biswell.)

Seven

No. 19

Yreka Western's No. 19 is the railroad's much celebrated steam locomotive. The Baldwin Locomotive Works of Philadelphia, Pennsylvania, built her in April 1915 for the Caddo River Lumber Company and their Caddo and Choctaw Railroad that operated out of Rosboro, Arkansas. It was given the roster number 4 and named *R. L. Rowan*, which refers to Rufus Lee Rowan of Rosboro, Arkansas, who was an engineer on the railroad. Around 1920, the locomotive was sold and moved to Mexico. She was acquired by the *Cia de Real del Monte y Pachuca* Railroad, which was owned by the United States Refining Mining and Smelting Company and renumbered 105. This railroad operated between Pachuca (capital of the Mexican state of Hidalgo) and the town of Real de Monte (now Monte de Mineral), which lays about 8 miles to the east in Mexico's rich silver mining region.

In 1923, it was purchased by the McCloud River Railroad and arrived there in April of that year and was given the roster number 19. When it arrived, it is rumored that shop hands found bullet holes in the side of the cab and tender, beginning the story that she had come into a bit of a squabble with Pancho Villa while in Mexico, thus earning the engine the permanent nickname of *Pancho*. *Pancho* served on the McCloud pulling freight trains until 1953, when it was sold to Yreka Western—which was looking for larger motive power—with her sister, No. 18, arriving three years later. The two were put on standby status with the advent of diesels and began pulling railfan excursion trains, often doubleheaders, until No. 18 blew a cylinder head. No. 18 was eventually sold and now resides at the Virginia and Truckee Railroad. In 1970, No. 19 was leased to the Oregon Pacific and Eastern and starred in two movies during her time there: *Emperor of the North* in 1973 and *Stand By Me* in 1986. When the OP&E discontinued steam excursion operations, No. 19 returned to California in 1988 and began pulling the *Blue Goose* Excursion Train and the occasional freight train, as she still does to this day.

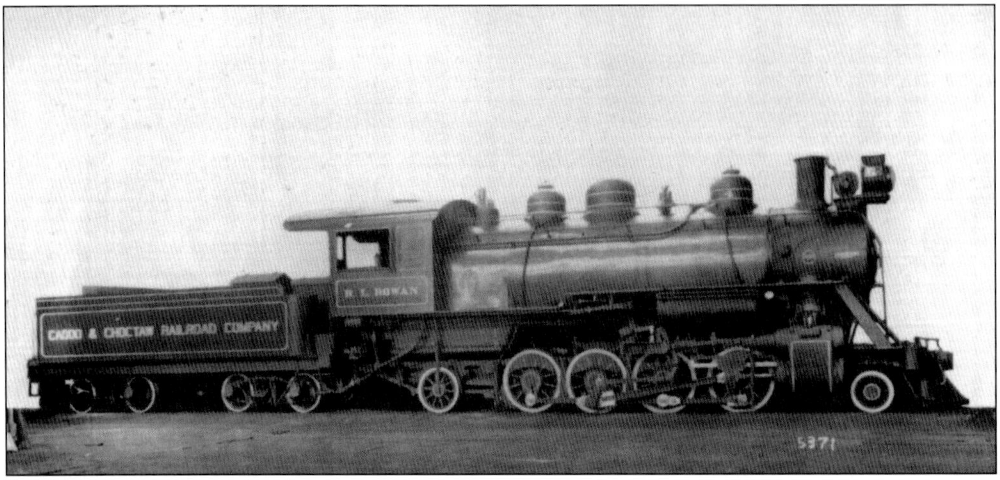

Pictured here is No. 19's Baldwin Locomotive Works builder's photograph in April 1915, showing how she looked when built as Caddo River No. 4. She was Baldwin's 42,000th locomotive and is known as a 90-ton logging 2-8-2. (A 2-8-2 is also known as a *Mikado*). She features 48-inch drivers, 20-by-28-inch cylinders, weighs 140,000 pounds on the drivers, has around 34,000 pounds of tractive effort, is equipped with super heaters, and was originally built as a coal burner.

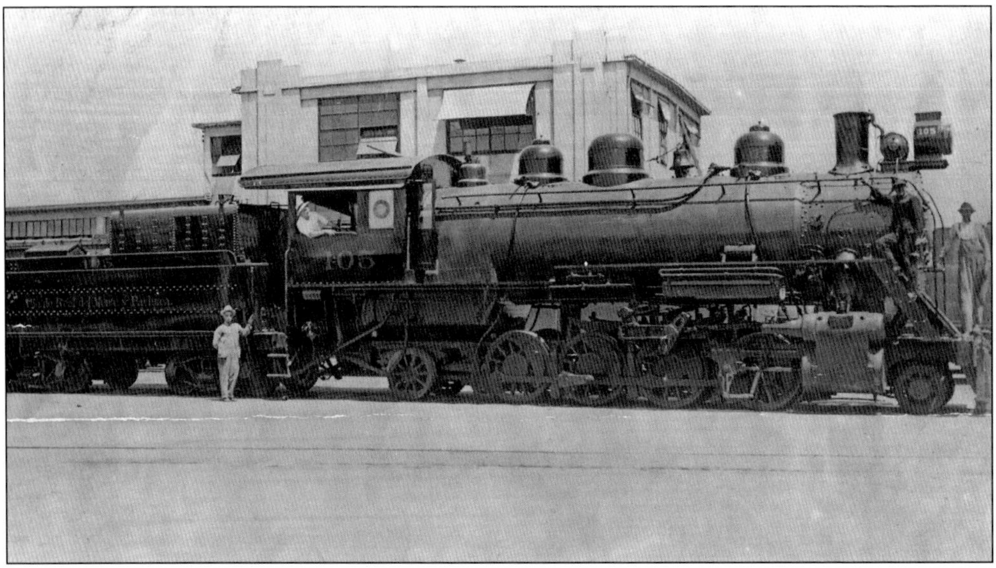

This photograph is the only known image in existence of No. 19's time in Mexico on the *Cia de Real del Monte y Pachuca* Railroad. Also notice that by the time this photograph was taken in the early 1920s, the locomotive had been converted to burn oil instead of coal, noticeable by the large oil tank in the tender.

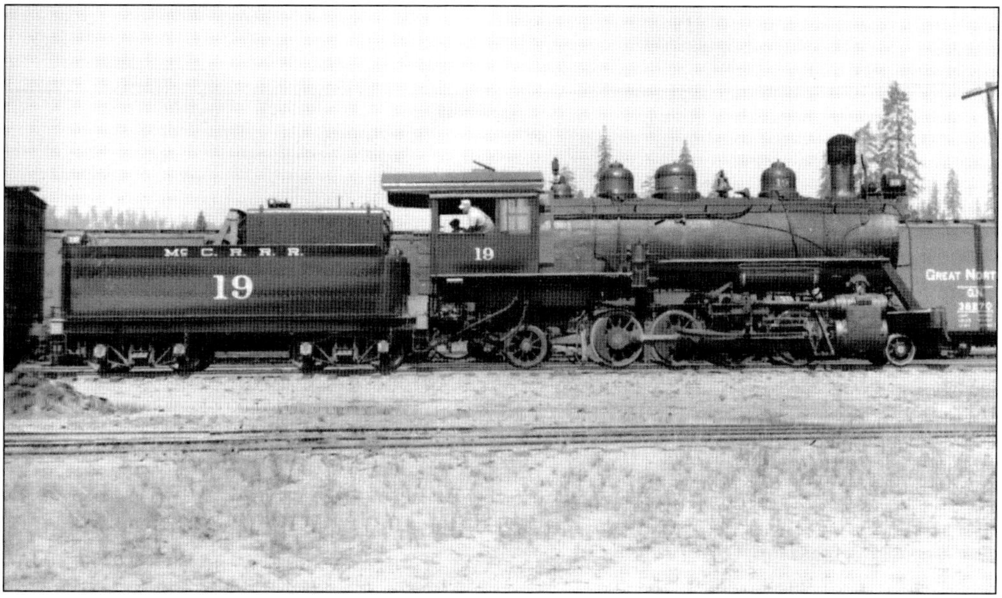

In July 1939, No. 19 is switching around the yard in McCloud, California, on the McCloud River Railroad. The McCloud would be the locomotive's home for the next several decades and would go through many modern changes in the process.

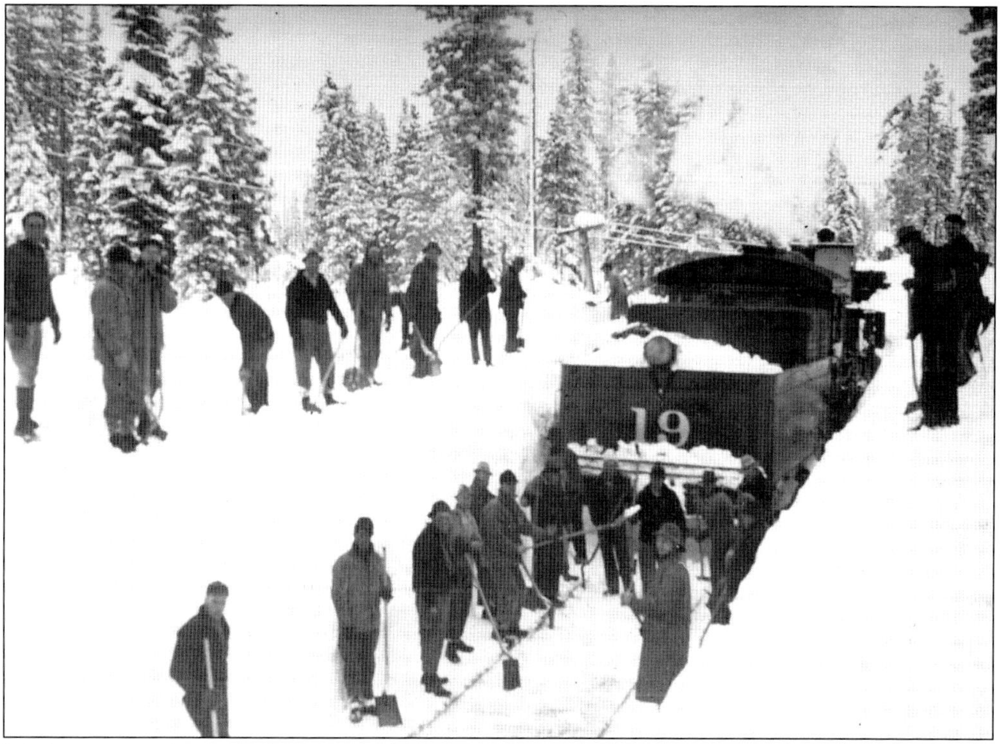

It's the winter of 1938 and No. 19 and crew are out removing snow somewhere on the McCloud River Railroad. Snow was always a constant battle on this railroad during the winter, and No. 19 is pushing one of the railroad's box plow flanges, attempting to clear the railroad. (Courtesy Siskiyou County Historical Society.)

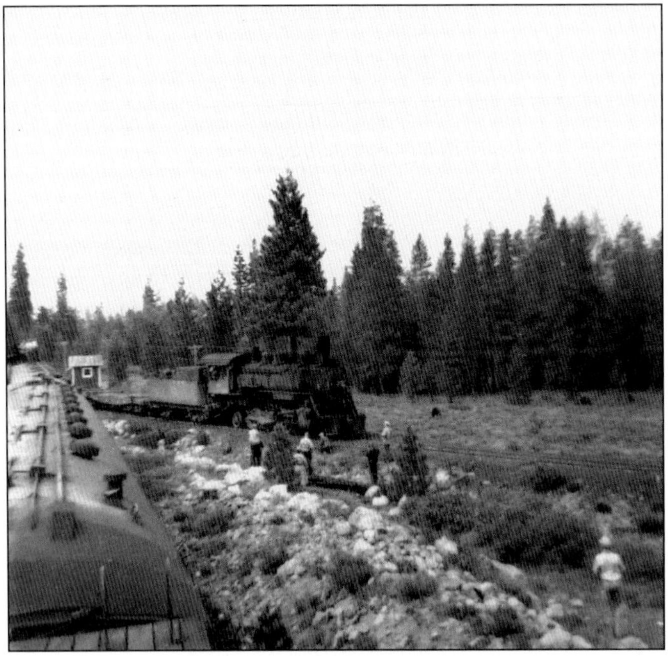

In June 1950, No. 19 is pulling an empty log train at Car A, California, on the McCloud River. The photograph is shot from atop a passenger car that was on a railfan excursion this day. However, in this photograph, No. 19 is just another *Mikado* making a profit for the railroad. (Courtesy Jeff Moore.)

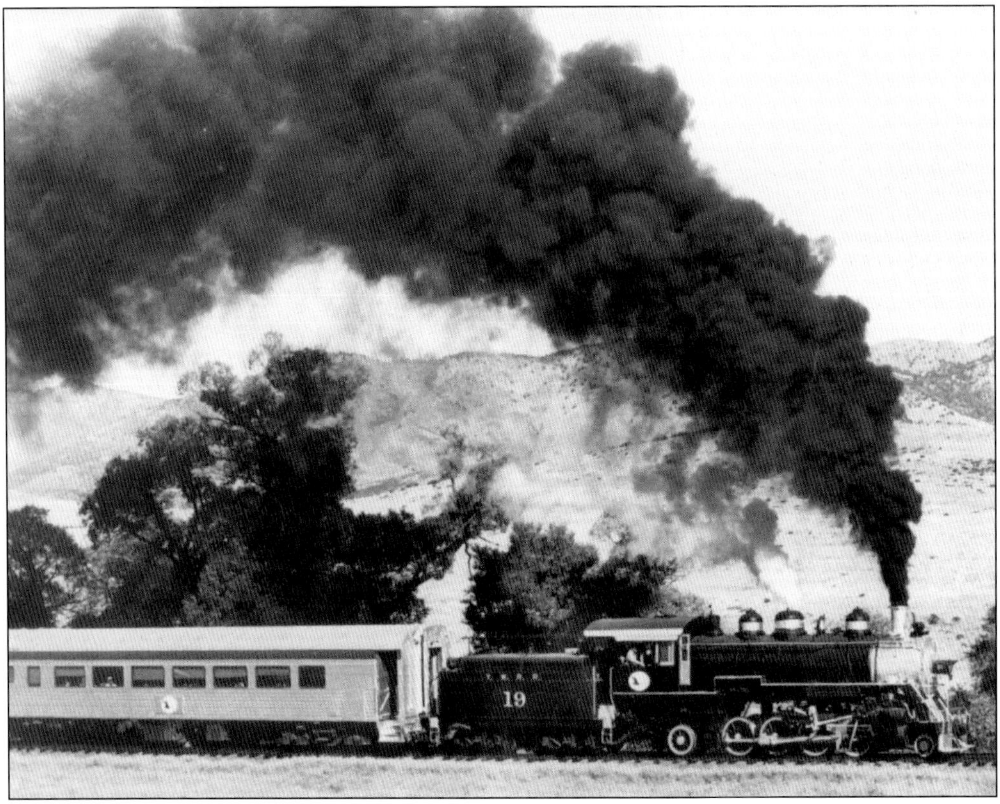

In the early 1960s, No. 19 began pulling railfan excursion trains on the Yreka Western after being displaced by diesels. Here she is shown making her way towards Montague, passing a spot known as the Hobo Camp.

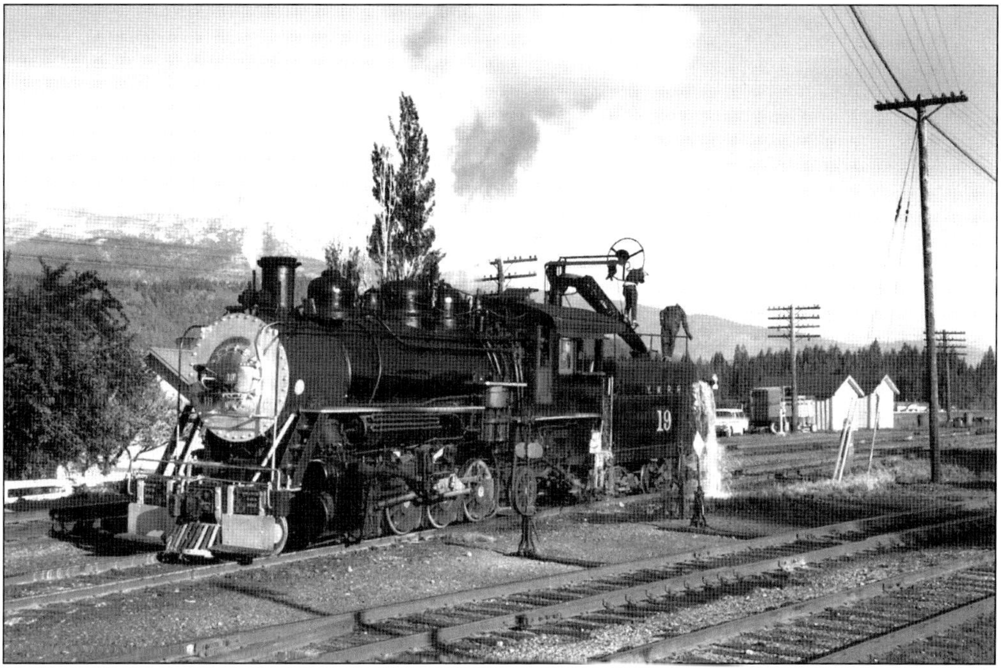

In June 1962, No. 19 briefly returned to the McCloud River Railroad as a doubleheader with McCloud River's No. 25 on an excursion out to Pondosa and back. Here, No. 19 takes on water at the interchange with the Southern Pacific and the McCloud River at Mount Shasta.

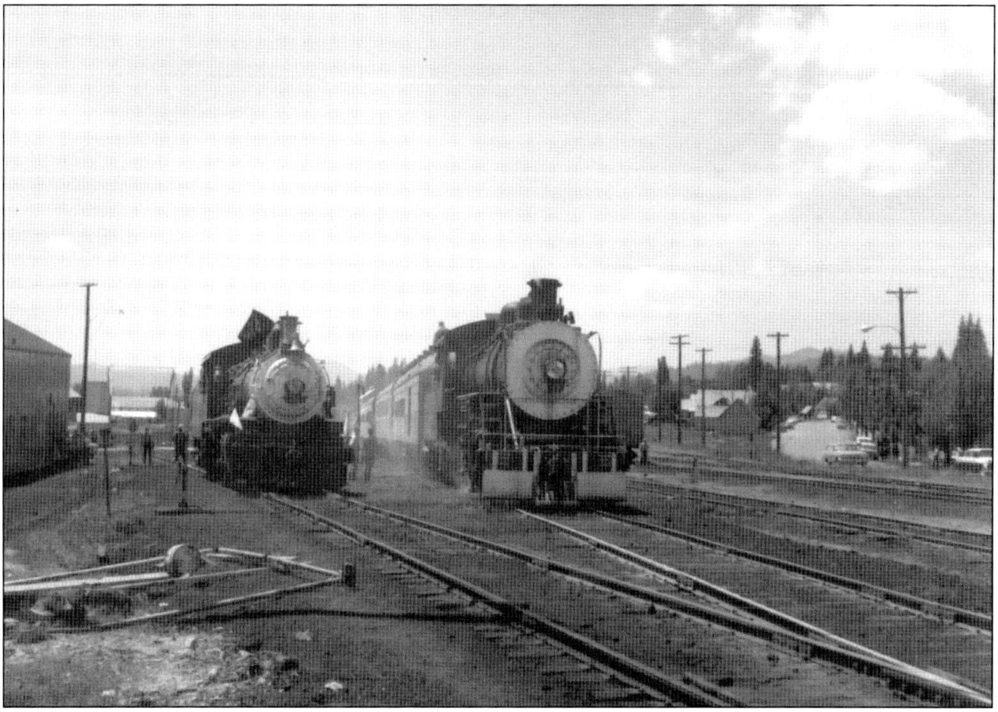

No. 19 and consist have arrived in the McCloud, California, yards. No. 25 sits on the engine house lead next to No. 19, preparing for the excursion up to Pondosa. (Courtesy Tim Stricker.)

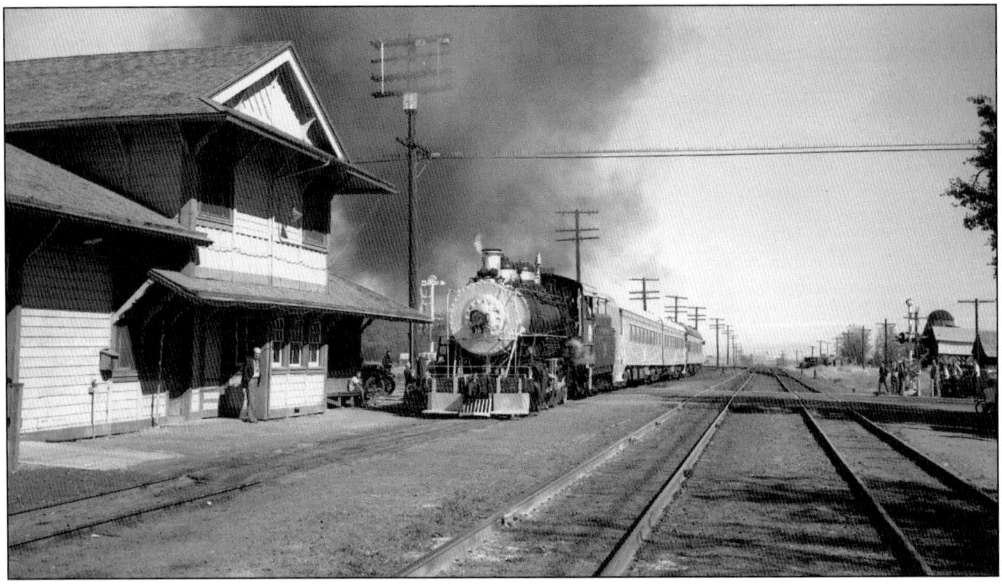

No. 19 continued to pull the occasional excursion on the Yreka Western until 1970. Here she pulls into the depot at Montague on an excursion in October 1970, not long before being sent to the Oregon Pacific and Eastern. (Courtesy Don Hansen.)

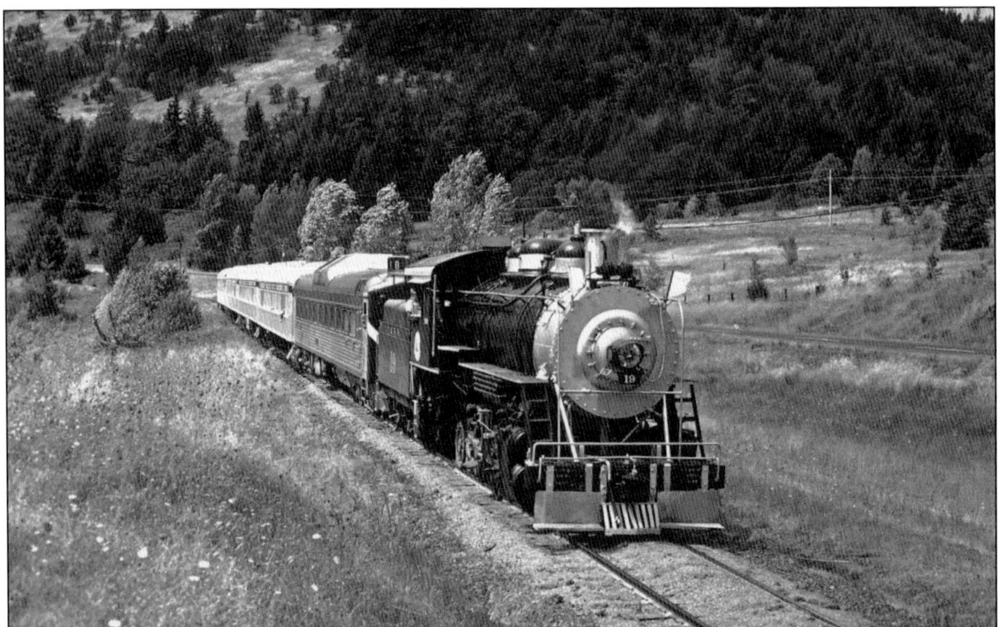

In 1970, No. 19 was transferred to Oregon Pacific and Eastern under a lease agreement to pull excursion trains between Cottage Grove, Oregon, and Culp Creek, Oregon. This lasted until excursion trains ended in 1988 and No. 19 was returned to Yreka. Here she runs along Row River Road, west of Dorena, Oregon. (Courtesy Drew Jacksich.)

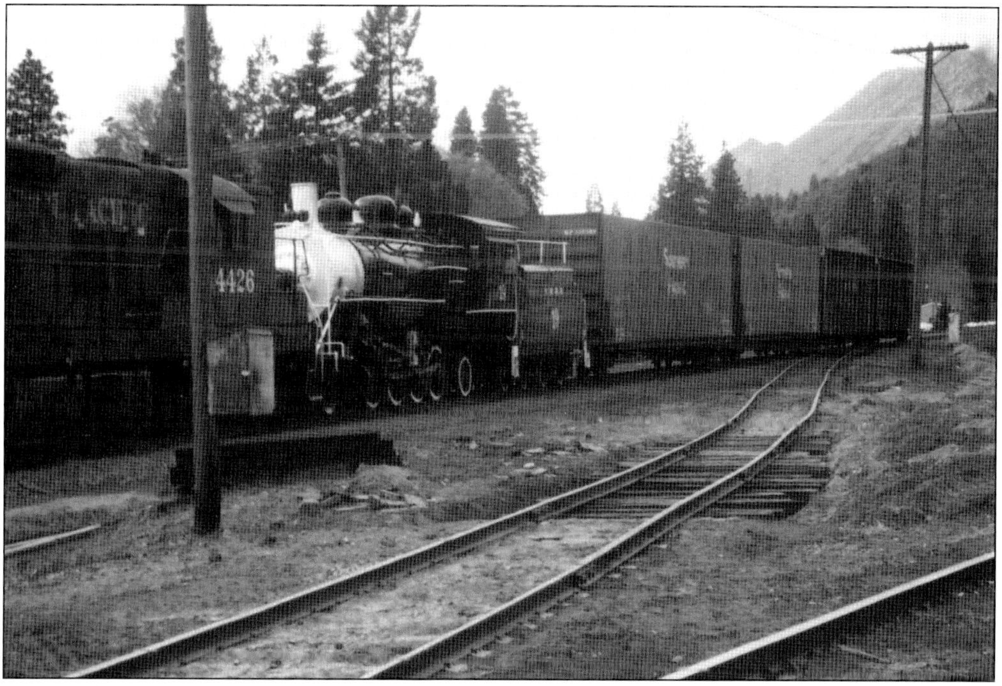

On April 30 and May 1, 1994, No. 19 again ventured to McCloud for two special excursions to Lookout and Burney, California. The photograph here shows No. 19 arriving in Mount Shasta City as part of the Southern Pacific Montague local.

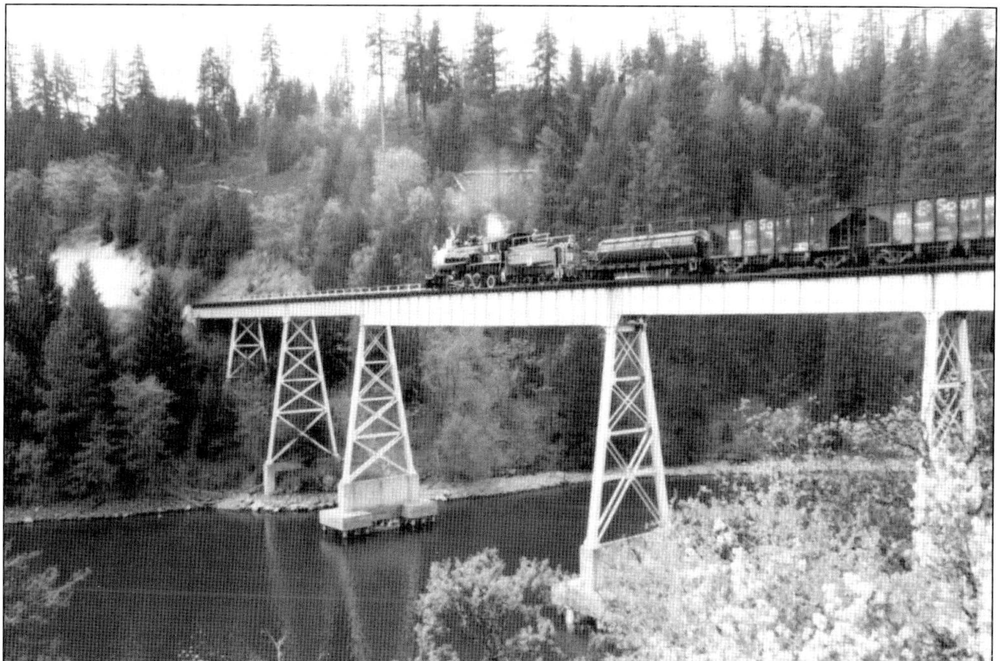

The next day, Sunday, May 1, 1994, No. 19 and her train ventured south of Bartle to the town of Burney, California. The train is shown here, crossing the spectacular bridge over Lake Britton near Burney.